Named in remembrance of

the onetime *Antioch Review* editor

and longtime Bay Area resident,

the Lawrence Grauman, Jr. Fund

supports books that address

a wide range of human rights,

free speech, and social justice issues.

The publisher and the University of California Press Foundation gratefully acknowledge the generous support of the Lawrence Grauman, Jr. Fund.

Accidental Sisters

ACCIDENTAL
SISTERS

Refugee Women Struggling Together
for a New American Dream

KIMBERLY MEYER

with ALIA ALTIKRITY

AND THE SISTERHOOD:
Elikya, Mendy, Mina, Sara, and Zara

UNIVERSITY OF CALIFORNIA PRESS

University of California Press
Oakland, California

© 2024 by Kimberly Meyer

Library of Congress Cataloging-in-Publication Data

Names: Meyer, Kimberly, author. | Altikrity, Alia, author.
Title: Accidental sisters : refugee women struggling together for a
    new American dream / Kimberly Meyer with Alia Altikrity and the
    sisterhood, Elikya, Mendy, Mina, Sara, and Zara.
Description: Oakland, California : University of California Press,
    [2024] | Includes bibliographical references and index.
Identifiers: LCCN 2023029704 (print) | LCCN 2023029705 (ebook) |
    ISBN 9780520384675 (cloth) | ISBN 9780520384682 (ebook)
Subjects: LCSH: Women refugees—Social aspects—Texas—Houston—
    21st century. | Women refugees—Texas—Houston—Case studies.
Classification: LCC JV6346 .M48 2024 (print) | LCC JV6346 (ebook) |
    DDC 305.9/069140976414110905—dc23/eng/20230829
LC record available at https://lccn.loc.gov/2023029704
LC ebook record available at https://lccn.loc.gov/2023029705

Manufactured in the United States of America

33 32 31 30 29 28 27 26 25 24
10 9 8 7 6 5 4 3 2 1

for GWEN, my beloved sister, who stood beside me
when I was most alone

and for my brother PAUL, *my heart, my eyes*

But let us, you and I,
sit in my cottage over food and wine,
and take some joy in hearing how much pain
we each have suffered. After many years
of agony and absence from one's home,
a person can begin enjoying grief.
I will tell you my story as you ask.

HOMER, *The Odyssey* (translated by Emily Wilson)

Contents

III · Home

Photos follow page 279

Foreword

US REPRESENTATIVE ILHAN OMAR

My father, a refugee from Somalia who came to this country as a single parent of three in 1995, used to say, "It's hard to hate up close." He had fled his country because of hatred that led to a civil war. And as an immigrant to this country—and as a black man and a Muslim—he could see another kind of hatred and injustice here. But in our immigrant household, there was also a hopeful belief in the fundamental right to participate in the American democratic process, to work to create a more perfect union. So reading *Accidental Sisters: Refugee Women Struggling Together for a New American Dream* resonated with me.

This book gives us, *up close,* some of those human stories of struggle and hope, through the journeys of six women, almost all Muslim, all black and brown, all single mother refugees, several from so-called shithole countries—the multiply marginalized. But one marginalized voice represents many marginalized voices. When one of us speaks, all of us are speaking. It's important that this country hears them.

I know these stories. I know the tragedy of waking up one day to find that the kids you played with in the streets are now carrying guns. Of living in a stable country where everyone is family one day, and the next, some members no longer have a right to exist and nothing makes sense anymore. Of leaving that country and crossing a border and entering a refugee camp. Of losing years of education, and seeing the helplessness of adults as they considered that the children they had imagined bright futures for now had nothing.

I also know what it means to get that golden ticket of opportunity: an offer of permanent resettlement in the United States. In the refugee camp in Kenya, where my extended family had escaped the civil war in Somalia, my grandfather told us, "The United States is different. Only in America can you ultimately become an American. Everywhere else we will always feel like a guest." But, as with the women in this book, our arrival in this promised utopia was disorienting. We didn't get certain basic information. We had no church or mosque or any other kind of community to help us with the minimum we needed to know as we transitioned to our new life.

When we talk about immigration policy, it's important to think about the people behind the policy, because policy choices have real consequences, and we are under a moral imperative, at this moment in our country's history—after the gutting of the refugee program and the attempt to dismantle DACA under the Trump administration, and after decades of inaction on immigration overall—to make it right, to reimagine a more humane system. It's important for us to recognize the human faces, the human lives, the human stories, the human struggles, the human hope that is rooted in the policies we're debating.

Like the women whose journeys are documented here, I also have my own sisters in the struggle, women in Congress and across the country whose values are deeply rooted in the immigrant story. We know that our humanity is tied to one another, and that we need policies that extend humanity and compassion to immigrants and newly arrived refugees. Those policies begin by understanding their stories. This book is a starting place for that understanding.

Cast of Characters

In order of appearance

ALIA   Originally from Baghdad, Iraq, Alia, age 49 at the time of these stories, fled to Amman, Jordan, in 2004 with her three children after the death of her husband, a lieutenant colonel in the Iraqi Air Force, and was resettled in Houston in 2008. Alia eventually helped found Amaanah Refugee Services' Transformed Program and is the case manager for the five other women who appear in *Accidental Sisters* (and many others who do not).

MINA   Also born in Baghdad, Iraq, Mina, age 38, escaped to Kirakkale, Turkey, with her daughter, after her husband, who had worked in Baghdad's Green Zone for the Americans, disappeared while going out for groceries. They lived in Turkey for four years before being resettled in Houston in December 2016.

MENDY   With roots in the Nuba Mountains of Sudan, Mendy, age 46, was tortured by what appeared to be the military police of her country and, after the disappearance of her husband, left home for Zarqa, Jordan, with her two children, where they lived until they were resettled in Houston in August 2016.

SARA Born in Damascus, Syria, Sara, age 29, was smuggled out of Syria and into Jordan in 2013 with her two children after her husband was wounded in the fighting in Darayya, Syria. After his death, she lived in an apartment complex for the widows of martyrs in Amman, Jordan, and was eventually resettled in Houston with her children in April 2017.

ELIKYA Born in Bukavu in the Democratic Republic of the Congo, where her husband served in the military and was murdered by rebels, Elikya, age 52, was resettled in Houston in July 2015 from a refugee camp in Burundi, along with six children and three grandchildren.

ZARA Leaving her birthplace of Hama, Syria, Zara, age 36, entered Jordan in 2012, together with her husband and their three daughters, and lived there until August 2016, when the family, including a son born in Zarqa, Jordan, was permanently resettled to Houston. After years of domestic violence, Zara filed for divorce from her husband and is raising her children on her own.

.   .   .

A note on names and translations: To protect the privacy and security of the women of *Accidental Sisters,* we have changed their names and the names of some of the other characters in this book. The women all chose these names for themselves. Their words as I received them through interpreters have, in places, been lightly edited for clarity.

Prelude

I. An Ending

That morning, she prayed alone in the safety of the dark while the children slept, a moment of stillness. Then the fear came rushing back in. As the sun pierced the eastern horizon, she drank her tea, but when her brother arrived, he told her, "Leave it. Leave everything." So she put the cup in the sink, as if she would wash it later. The driver her brother had hired was silent as they loaded into the black SUV, Alia and her brother along with his wife and all the kids and the babies, and they passed stealthily out of the Mansour neighborhood, where Alia lived among all her husband's brothers and their wives, past the embassies and pastry stores and designer boutiques, past the elite Iraqi Hunting Club, and through the streets of Baghdad, hoping the militia that had killed her husband was not following. In her mind, over and over, Alia begged God to protect them. "I need to get to Jordan with my family—to not lose anyone more," she thought as they merged onto the highway. "I just want to be safe with my kids."

They drove west, passing through Abu Ghraib, more or less a suburb now of Baghdad. They skirted Fallujah. They followed the bends of the Euphrates River to Ramadi, then out into the dry desert hills of Al Anbar province.

All along the way they could hear the shriek of incoming artillery, the reverberations of tank rounds, so near, though Alia could never tell from which direction the danger was coming. She nervously unwrapped and rewrapped her silk headscarf. She twisted the diamond-encrusted band around her finger. She'd worn as much jewelry as she could—several necklaces, a watch, rings. But she'd left everything else at home, even the family photos. Especially the family photos, and the photos of her husband in uniform. Those might give them away, might signal to the border guards that they were leaving for good. All she'd packed was a handbag with snacks for the kids and some diapers for the baby, who was nine months old. "Be careful! Be careful!" she heard her brother say to the driver. And the driver told him, "Don't worry, I made a deal. They will not shoot us." But this calmed no one. "Read the Qur'an! Read from the Qur'an!" the driver told them. "We will be safe!" Military vehicles prowled the roads, lined with cars, incinerated and on fire. Did the Humvees and tanks belong to the Americans, or insurgents?

In one bombed-out car they passed, Alia imagined the family that might have been trapped inside. But she tried not to let the children see her fear. They had lived through their father's brutal death the fall before, after the American invasion, when he'd been assassinated in their car as Alia, pregnant, sat beside him. All Alia could remember were the barren, rolling hills on the road to Sulaymaniyah and a truck hurtling toward them. It was late November 2003, the second day of Eid at the end of Ramadan.

Now, not quite two years later, as Alia sped toward Jordan, she could see groups of men running along the side of the road with covered faces, only their eyes showing through the scarves they'd wrapped around their heads. But Alia had no idea if they were rebel fighters or kidnappers, Al Qaeda jihadists or Shia militants bent on slaughtering Sunnis like her. "Iraq is not anymore Iraq," she thought, looking out the window. And she knew that those men with covered faces, running, could turn on them at any moment and kill her kids in front of her.

There were so many reasons she had to leave, but the brutal murder of her sons and daughter before her eyes was Alia's deepest fear. In the haze of her grief after her husband's assassination, and in the months after the birth of their youngest, the cooks and gardeners and housecleaners and nannies had drifted away—afraid, Alia imagined, to be associated now with her family, marked as they were. Neighbors and shopkeepers were warning Alia, when her older son went out into the streets, to keep him safe inside.

Alia understood the endless logic of vengeance: her husband, a lieutenant colonel in the air force, who had fought against Iran, had been killed by Iranian militia in retribution. His son would surely one day avenge himself on those who had killed his father. So the son must be killed before he grew old enough to take his revenge. But Alia also understood another kind of logic: "They will come to kill my kids in front of me. Then after that, I will kill myself." Of this she was sure. She couldn't sleep. She couldn't think straight. She cried all the time. Once, she crawled under the dining room table with her children when she heard the bombing in the city, as if this would protect them. When her brother saw that, he knew he had to get her out of Iraq. "We will leave for a few months," he said. When things calmed down, he assured her, they'd return.

It was night by the time they reached the long line of cars at the Turaibil border crossing. In the harsh neon light from the station office, Alia could see those who were being turned back, sobbing. She was terrified the Jordanians would reject her, too. But while Alia knew that safety lay on the other side of that neon light, beyond the murderous confusion of the country that was her home, she still dreaded crossing over. She would be cutting herself off from her history, from her family, their roots in that ancient land, and entering into a place where she knew no one.

Her brother went through first, with his family. "This is my sister," she heard him tell the border guard after he'd let them pass. Then the officer turned to Alia. "Yes, sister. You can come. Tell me your name," he said, motioning to her. She gave him her father's name, a Sunni name, just as her brother had done. But on her ID was her husband's name, because she was a married woman. And her husband's name was also on the IDs of their children. Would the officer recognize him—the eminent pilot, who had once even trained members of the Jordanian royal family? Would that help them? Would he know that her husband had been on an Iranian hit list? Would that hurt them?

"Where is your husband?" he asked Alia, watching her closely. Alia looked around. In this liminal space between peril and protection, she was scared to say the truth. "They killed my husband," she said. "I'm a widow now." The officer, understanding, as he scanned her documents, who she was, came round from behind his desk to where Alia and the kids were standing. "We are with you!" he told her. "Don't feel alone. Come inside."

She had a baby and a handbag in one arm. Her daughter and son stood beside her. They were, she knew now, safe at last. They would be in the capital of Amman within hours.

II. A Field Guide to Resettlement

I once drove east out of Amman into the desert that Alia passed over traveling west from Iraq. It was the summer of 2018. Jordan, which has taken in wave after wave of refugees fleeing nearby conflicts over the decades—Palestinians, Lebanese, Yemenis, Sudanese, Somalis, Iraqis, Libyans—was then grappling with an influx of 1.5 million Syrians.

By that point, I had been immersed in the world of refugee resettlement in my home city of Houston for a couple of years, writing about refugees from Iraq and Syria and Congo, who had been resettled there. The more time that I spent in their homes, understanding the idiosyncrasies but also the commonalities in their journeys out of their homelands and into lands of displacement, then through the process of resettlement in America, the more urgently I wanted to document these encounters, in part as an antidote to all the misinformation obscuring the human beings at the heart of the world's current mass migrations.

That was the summer of family separations along the US-Mexico border, and at night in my hotel room in the capital of Jordan I would scroll through the news from home, the Trump administration's depredations so new and so grotesque that they still registered as shocking. For a while now, they had been trying to shut down the border by claiming that terrorists were streaming into the country through Mexico. Then, two days before my drive across the Jordanian desert, the Supreme Court upheld the Muslim ban, which barred all Syrian refugees from resettling in the US indefinitely and prohibited foreign nationals from seven other predominantly Muslim countries from entering. Because under US law refugees have the right to petition, through several family reunification programs, to bring immediate family members here, the Muslim ban became another de facto form of family separation, given that many of those banned were the mothers and fathers, the husbands and wives, the unmarried children under the age of 21 of refugees who had previously been resettled.

I had come to Jordan to do research and conduct interviews to help me understand some of the context for what would become this book. But I now realize that the book had really been born well before all of that, on an earlier trip to the Middle East back in 2015. I was there during Ramadan, and had been invited to an iftar dinner breaking the day's fast in Beit Safafa, a Palestinian neighborhood within Jerusalem. Donald Trump had just declared his candidacy, promising to Make America Great Again by building a wall along the border with Mexico, and my Palestinian hosts, living in a city of walls that separated them from family, from land, from livelihoods, were worried what someone like him meant for people like them. After consuming platters of spiced rice and roasted meats and stuffed vegetables, after kibbe and tabbouleh and fresh chopped salads, we had settled comfortably into folding chairs beneath a grape arbor, drinking tea and eating kanafeh as the darkness deepened. The patriarch, vigorously smoking a cigarette, was wondering bitterly if any kind of peace settlement with Israel would be possible with Trump as president. But I knew how preposterous his anxiety was. "Don't worry," I told my naïve host, who clearly knew nothing about the American populace. "Trump is a *joke*. He will never be elected."

Back home in Houston that fall of 2015, I saw images on my screen of the unending waves of Syrian refugees washing up on the shores of Greece in rubber boats, drowning as they tried to reach dry land, trudging across Europe on foot, winding ropes of human desperation. Inspired by my recent Middle East travels, I had started taking Arabic classes, and perhaps because of that, my antennae were more finely tuned to the news that some of those Syrians had begun arriving in Houston, an epicenter of refugee resettlement in the US.

Growing up here, I had unconsciously witnessed Houston transforming itself from a majority-white city of big oil and urban cowboys to one that is now majority minority. According to Stephen Klineberg, a demographics expert and founding director of the Kinder Institute for Urban Research at Rice University, which has been charting this transformation since 1982, Houston is by some measures the most ethnically and culturally diverse metro area in the country, surpassing even New York. We've had a sizable and influential African American population since Emancipation, when former slaves migrated here from the surrounding countryside and founded "freedom colonies." In those same years, waves of Germans and Czechs disembarked, sea-weary, at the port of Galveston and moved inland to Houston or fanned out further across the state.

Long before that, Texas had been part of Mexico, and over the years, Mexican migrants and others from the Northern Triangle of Central America—El Salvador, Honduras, Guatemala—as well as from Colombia and Venezuela in South America crossed that shifting southern border, with and without papers. Houston is now approaching 50 percent Latino.

In the twentieth century, the city became a migration hub for families from China, Korea, Taiwan, the Philippines, India, Pakistan, Nigeria. And all of these cultures remade Houston and helped it to reimagine itself.

Klineberg, in his 2020 book *Prophetic City: Houston on the Cusp of a Changing America,* argues that Houston is at the vanguard of rapid demographic and economic changes that are redefining all of American society. "No city has been transformed more by immigration than Houston," he pointed out during a 2019 lecture I attended. Though just under a quarter of the population, immigrants make up 30 percent of the workforce, often working very cheaply as housecleaners, cooks, janitors, cashiers, ground maintenance workers, carpenters, and construction laborers. But they also make up about 35 percent of STEM (science, technology, engineering, and math) workers. Immigrants contribute over 26 percent to the city's GDP, and their earnings add $3.5 billion to state and local taxes— not to mention $9.2 billion to federal taxes. These economic numbers and the immigrant share of the population are only projected to increase in the coming decades, and Houstonians, Klineberg's data shows, welcome that, along with the more intangible cultural gifts that immigrants carry with them from their homelands— particularly, although I may be speaking personally here, their food.

Among its various immigrant groups, Houston's refugee community is small. Refugees are a specific sort of immigrant: they have had to document to the United Nations High Commission for Refugees

(UNHCR) that they fled their home country because of war, violence, or persecution and are now unable to return out of fear of human rights violations. To be a refugee is a legal status, affording rights to international protection. In 2016, around the time the women in this book arrived, a quarter of Houston's population of 6.8 million were foreign-born; yet only 5 percent came here as refugees, through a formal program overseen by the Office of Refugee Resettlement (ORR) within the US Department of Health and Human Services.

Still, an outsize part of Houston's shifting sense of its own identity has stemmed from its role in resettling refugees—the Vietnamese after the war in Southeast Asia, Jews seeking asylum from persecution in the Soviet Union, Bosnians, Somalis, Eritreans, Ethiopians, Rwandans, Iraqis, Afghans, Sudanese, Burmese, Cubans, Congolese, Syrians. In the last decade or so, Texas has resettled more refugees than any other state in the US, and Houston has resettled more refugees than any other city in the state. The city takes great pride in this.

And yet, when we widen our lens to consider the international refugee crisis, the role Houston plays—and indeed, the role of the US as a whole—is miniscule. Of the roughly 103 million human beings who, as of mid-2022, have been forcibly displaced worldwide, only about 1 percent will ever be permanently resettled in another country. Of the rest, 53.2 million are internally displaced within their own countries, 32.5 million have been granted UN refugee status and the legal protections that come with it, and 4.9 million are still in the process of seeking asylum. Palestinians and some Venezuelans who hold more particular forms of asylee and refugee status make up the other nearly 10 million. Seventy percent of all refugees are women and children. The technical distinction between these refugees and asylum seekers (like those from, say, Guatemala, Honduras, and El Salvador) comes down, in part, to how a person enters the United

States. Asylum seekers arrive at a port of entry or cross our border and ask for asylum once they are on American soil. Refugees, having fled their home countries, ask for asylum from the UN while still outside the US.

But increasingly, it seems to me, this is a distinction without a difference. And with climate change, the numbers of the displaced will only grow. They are already growing. Facing impossible choices, fathers and mothers, sons and daughters, brothers and sisters wrench themselves from their homes and homelands because they will not survive if they stay. One in every 88 human beings on the face of the earth has been forced to flee their home.

The statistics are incomprehensible and overwhelming. Let's narrow the lens back down again. In 2016, the year most of the women in this book arrived, Houston resettled 9,573 refugees. They came from forty-nine countries, including Afghanistan, Bhutan, Burma, Congo, Cuba, Ethiopia, Iraq, Somalia, Sudan, and Syria. I was curious to understand more about my city's role in the nation's resettling of refugees through that formal UN program, administered here by the Office of Refugee Resettlement. So in early 2016, I began meeting with Syrians, recording what they told me.

During these early visits, it was usually the men who did the talking. They told me stories whose point was often their disbelief at what had happened to them, their desire to maintain their dignity when all the former markers of status had evaporated, their struggles to provide for their families in this country that asked so much of them so soon after their arrival. The stories of these fathers moved me.

From time to time, though, I'd find myself alone with the wife and a translator, and we'd get to talking. I started to catch glints, in their stray remarks and fleeting memories, of a world of women with growing children and backyard gardens. Women who cooked dinner and folded laundry and drank tea sitting on floor mats on balconies, or in living rooms ensconced on formal, overstuffed couches with their mothers and sisters and friends. Women whose dreams for their own lives had dissolved in the upheaval that forced them to leave their countries. Women who suffered from a profound, unbearable loneliness in the isolation that greeted them here.

These women and men, refugees from Syria, were part of a vast human story of our day, and it seemed crucial to document everything they said.

But as Trump was crowned the Republican nominee and as the rhetoric of his campaign became more virulent, I began to see my documentary work as a small act of resistance as well—handing the mic over to the human beings he was dehumanizing so they could speak on their own behalf. *In the end,* I thought to myself optimistically, *we shall overcome.*

Then came election night 2016. I was visiting the apartment of the Horo family, Kurds from Aleppo. Mohammed, the father, had been working out an arrangement of our national anthem for the buzuq, a long-necked lutelike folk instrument from the Levant that he had carried here with him from Turkey, to which they'd fled after their home had been bombed by the Syrian government. He was training himself by watching YouTube videos on his cellphone. His goal was to have his five children sing while he played.

Leaving the Horo apartment that night, I felt flush with a buzzy energy approaching joy. Persecuted Kurds from Syria who had found refuge in Houston, Texas, were strumming "The Star-Spangled Banner" on an ancient instrument, precursor to Willie Nelson's guitar, and Hillary Clinton was about to become the first woman president. I loved my country, where anything was possible, and I loved my city, this place of optimism and incongruity. As I walked through the apartment complex to my car, practicing my beginning Arabic with a group of wiry boys kicking a soccer ball across the asphalt, I checked my phone. "You watching this?" a friend had texted, meaning the election returns. "Not good."

. . .

This book is about the sisterhoods that save us: the networks of support that women create, roots beneath the soil's surface, to help nourish and strengthen each other when a harsh wind blows. It's about those harsh winds, too—war, persecution, displacement, as well as the struggle to make a new home in a new land—and the way that all these traumas affect women, and mothers in particular. It documents the friendships that emerge among accidental sisters, thrown together by chance after upheaval in their homelands; informal attachments that give them the resources, psychic and actual, to survive when they are cut off from their families and from formal sources of help. And it suggests that this kind of love, which we can all extend to our neighbors, to the widows and orphans, to the strangers among us, is central to the hopeful grassroots work of building—or rebuilding—our communities and our democracy in the face of overwhelming systemic forces that might seem beyond our control.

This regenerative love is also the hard-won philosophy of Alia Altikrity, who in 2017 was living in Houston, where I first met her at that year's graduation ceremony for Amaanah Refugee Services' Transformed Program. The Transformed Program pulled together a cohort of roughly thirty single mother refugees each year—some of the most vulnerable human beings on earth. These were women who had so far been unable to demonstrate "self-sufficiency," as defined and required by the US refugee resettlement program. Amaanah is a post-resettlement organization that stepped in, often at the request of local resettlement agencies when the federal aid from the formal US refugee resettlement program had ended, and tried to co-create a personalized plan for these single mothers that would put them, by year's end, on a path to a more sustainable life in this country.

I had heard that Alia, one of the founders of the program and a case manager in it, had herself been a single mother refugee from Iraq, who had sought asylum in Jordan, and that Amaanah helped her when she first arrived in America, about ten years before. That December night of the 2017 Transformed Program graduation, I watched as Alia moved from table to table, hugging the women from Congo in their hallucinatory wax-cloth patterned dresses and head wraps, the women from Sudan in their vibrant, draped thoubs, the Eritrean women with intricately braided hair, the women from Syria and Iraq and Afghanistan, some modestly dressed in abayas and hijabs, some in exuberant party dresses. They all responded to Alia's kindness with gratitude and affection. They called each other *sister.*

By then, the #MeToo movement had begun—a worldwide channeling of female solidarity. In a month, Donald Trump would be inaugurated president, and a few days later he would institute his Muslim ban, cutting off the possibility that many of the women here would be reunited with their family members, an act that would be upheld by the Supreme Court during the time I was in Jordan. But for now, this sisterhood seemed to buoy the refugee mothers, far from actual family, laboring to move beyond the loss they'd endured. I felt a resilience pulsing through the room. I thought how this sisterhood might be the most primal form of resistance: something life-affirming and connective that pushed back against the annihilating forces arrayed against them. *Nolite te bastardes carborundorum.*

When I introduced myself to Alia and told her that I had been writing about refugee families for a while now, and that I had grown particularly interested in hearing more stories from women, she nodded and smiled and said, "You have come to the right place." Later, when we met for coffee and she told me that this had been a dream of hers for many years—to tell her story and the stories of other refugee women—she seemed to be ushering me across an invisible border.

. . .

Because men have always fought wars, there have always been war widows and orphans and refugees. They are already on the scene in Homer's *Iliad* and *Odyssey,* and in the later Greek tragedies based on those myths, some of the most ancient literature of the Western world—Trojan women and their children herded onto the shore outside the walls of the burning city, lingering in haphazard camps to be hauled in ships to Greece as slaves. But because the journeys of the war widows and orphans who appear in this book began when they claimed asylum with the office of the United Nations High Commissioner for Refugees, let's start there.

The UNHCR was created in 1950 during the aftermath of WWII to aid the millions of Europeans uprooted from their homes and homelands. The 1951 Convention Relating to the Status of Refugees defined the term *refugee* as anyone who, owing to a well-founded fear of being persecuted for reasons of race, religion, nationality, membership in a particular social group, or a political opinion, has been forced to cross an international border and is unable to return home. The Refugee Convention also outlined the rights of refugees, and the responsibilities of nations that accept them.

The United States, grappling with that same postwar crisis, had already passed the 1948 Displaced Persons Act, which admitted just over 200,000 European refugees over the course of two years. And for roughly the next thirty years, the US dealt with various international refugee crises—the Hungarian Uprising in 1956, the Cuban Revolution in 1959, the fall of Saigon in 1975—on an ad hoc basis that led to an inconsistent patchwork of refugee resettlement programs here.

The passage of the Refugee Act of 1980 standardized this system. Its big-hearted goals, laid out in Title I of the act, were to offer humanitarian assistance for the care of refugees where they have claimed asylum outside the borders of their home countries, and to promote opportunities for their resettlement in a third country or else voluntary repatriation to their homeland. For those refugees "of special humanitarian concern" to the United States, the act offered aid for transportation to the US and provisions for transitional assistance once here. The objective of these permanent and systematic procedures, the act states, was "effective resettlement and absorption of those refugees who are admitted."

Besides laying out these intentions and formally adopting the UNHCR's definition of a refugee, the 1980 Refugee Act created the Office of Refugee Resettlement (ORR) within the Department of Health and Human Services to carry out its objectives, delineated the roles and responsibilities of the various federal agencies involved, and established the process for determining a yearly refugee admissions ceiling through consultations between Congress and the president.

This act, introduced in the Senate by Edward Kennedy and by Elizabeth Holman and Peter Rodino in the House of Representatives, passed easily—unanimously in the Senate, in fact, and nearly so in the House. To put this in perspective, given the politics of our own era: even Strom Thurmond, white supremacist and staunch opponent of civil rights, voted for the act.

Writing about the Refugee Act's legislative history a year after its passage in the *International Migration Review,* Senator Kennedy acknowledged that there had been some concern over the potential cost of resettling refugees, but statistics showed that, within a few years, the vast majority were earning a living and paying federal income taxes in their local communities. This convinced Congress to move forward. "Of course," he went on, it is impossible to put a dollar value on saving the life of a refugee. The humanitarian concern for refugees goes beyond economic statistics or cost-benefit ratios. Those figures are impressive for most refugee groups. But, far more important, refugees and all migrants bring other benefits to the United States—richness in culture and diversity, new economic vitality, and other themes as old as the country's history. America's immigrant heritage, more than any other factor, was responsible for successful Congressional action on the refugee bill.

Still, almost immediately, as Yan Digilov and Yehuda Sharim document in "Refugee Realities: Between National Challenges and Local Responsibilities in Houston, TX," a report published by Rice University's Kinder Institute for Urban Research in 2018, the year of the events of this book, "the early architects of federal resettlement maintained a central focus on preventing refugees from becoming dependent on public welfare. While this concern was unsupported by the data, attempts to track the outcomes of resettlement revolved entirely on measuring the rate of dependency for each nationality being welcomed." Various benefits established by the resettlement program were quickly whittled away: a 60-day exemption from work registration requirements was eliminated in 1982, and that same year, the period for which refugees received certain forms of financial support from the ORR—Refugee Cash Assistance and Refugee Medical Assistance—was reduced from 36 months to 18 months. By 1992, this period was further reduced to eight months. And in any event, funding levels for these and other resettlement benefits have, over the decades, "failed to keep pace with the needs of refugees and local communities," as "Unfulfilled Promises, Future Possibilities: The Refugee Resettlement System in the United States," a 2014 report by Anastasia Brown and Todd Scribner in the *Journal on Migration and Human Security*, makes clear.

The antidote to "dependency," according to the federal government that funds the resettlement program, seems to be "self-sufficiency," defined entirely in economic terms—*Do you have a job? Can you pay your rent and bills?*—which refugees must achieve within four to six months of arrival here. Resettlement agencies officially support their clients for up to five years with social services, but the initial funding refugees receive, by and large, ends very quickly. This requirement to be self-sufficient, then, places an intense pressure on refugees to find work immediately—or, put another way, on resettlement case managers to make sure that happens, often by coordinating with large employers, who, incidentally, benefit from hiring from a pool of workers who don't speak the language or know the laws that govern their employment. The pressure to place refugees in jobs right away gets magnified in states like Texas, where an increasingly conservative state government has profoundly limited funding for social services.

The ORR does operate a Preferred Communities Program, which serves especially vulnerable refugees—those with physical disabilities or medical conditions, survivors of torture, refugees experiencing emotional trauma, women at risk, the elderly, youth without parents, LGBTQ refugees—with the help of intensive case management services "for a fixed term," as their guidelines state, "to overcome the barriers they might face on the path to integration and self-sufficiency." The Preferred Communities Program defines self-sufficiency more broadly than mere economic self-sufficiency. Clients work with their case managers to map out a service plan, and are deemed self-sufficient when they are stable in those areas affected by their vulnerability and living independently outside of the refugee agency's services—through the refugee's own individual capacity, through family support, or through whatever community support services they require and can access.

By and large, though, refugees are governed by the goal of *economic* self-sufficiency and must achieve it without individualized help. What they find when they get to America, then—as I try to show throughout this book—are low-wage jobs (without health or dental insurance), which prevent these newcomers from taking advantage of some of the benefits of the national refugee resettlement program that are their due: learning English, taking driving classes, completing recertification programs for training and degrees they already have, much less gaining new technical skills that could help them find better work. Also almost impossible: seeking mental health resources, or participating in any kind of sustained cultural orientation that could ease the transition from displaced refugee to permanent resident and, eventually, American citizen. For the single mothers of *Accidental Sisters,* who have no support system, no reliable childcare, no other breadwinner to help, their position is even more precarious.

As a friend of mine who came to the United States as a refugee from Bosnia in 1992, and who worked as a case manager himself in refugee resettlement in Houston for many years, says of the requirement for rapid employment, it makes refugees members of the working poor—"at the very best. At worst, you're homeless. The window of opportunity for people to get *self-sufficient,* whatever that means, is six months. That's craziness. That's pure craziness. The pressure on people to take the first job is immense. And then you get buried in that job and you're continuing to be in survival mode, which is not much different from what you were prior to coming here." So really, he says, as a refugee you have two consecutive traumas: "The trauma of whatever you experienced back home, and the trauma of resettlement itself." To be engaged as a case manager in that work of trying to move refugees from "dependency" to "self-sufficiency" before their meager resettlement funds had been exhausted was, he remembers, "a soul-crushing enterprise."

. • .

Out of the time I spent with the refugee women who make up the accidental sisters of this book, and through conversations over the years with other refugee families and those working formally and informally in refugee resettlement in Houston, certain insights emerged that inform the underlying themes of this book.

First, I explore the idea of sisterhood as a creative and nourishing force running beneath and sometimes quietly resisting certain systems of power. It replaces, out of necessity, essential familial relationships the women once relied upon for safety and security in their home countries, and gives them common ground in an unfamiliar geography. This sisterhood—between Alia and each of the other women, between those other women and the friends they met while displaced and on whom they still rely—fosters a sense of belonging that combats the often crippling isolation and despair of being a refugee, torn from the culture of one's homeland and from one's community. It offers emotional shelter from the domestic violence under which many of these women suffer, or the memories that haunt them when they have no access to mental health resources. It tenders mutual aid that can blunt their poverty. Founded on shared stories and shared understanding, this sisterhood empowers these women to face the external world, sometimes patriarchal, sometimes genocidal, sometimes just grindingly hard.

Second, I examine the refugee resettlement program, both the crucial safe harbor that this system offers and the limitations it imposes. While the requirement for rapid employment and economic self-sufficiency can, in theory, lead to integration—supporting oneself, working among others, paying taxes that aid the commonweal—in practice it often makes meaningful integration into this new home very difficult, sometimes helplessly so. As we rebuild the US refugee resettlement program (which was effectively ended under the Trump administration), this book urges that we reexamine this central tenet of resettlement.

Self-sufficiency is an ideal enforced by our refugee resettlement program, but it's also enshrined in the American mythos, and in the end, *Accidental Sisters* is also a meditation on this delusion embedded deep within the American Dream. Our heroes so often, like Huckleberry Finn, want to *light out for the Territory ahead of the rest.* They crave independence, freedom, the open road. Self-reliance, the authority of the individual, is held up as an unquestioned good, in opposition to "sivilization," which stands for the conformity of little minds, and which must be escaped at all costs. In Texas, perhaps more destructively than anywhere else in the country, this mythology has become entrenched in public policy around social services—and just about everything else. The opening voiceover of the Coen brothers' film *Blood Simple* captures the response here to "complainers"—those in need of help in a world of uncertainty. In communist Russia, the voice says, everyone takes care of everyone else. "But what I know is Texas . . . ," he concludes. "And down here . . . you're on your own."

That American myth of the solitary hero tramping through the wilderness has been written *about* white men *by* white men. We need a new story.

I increasingly saw the sisterhood between Alia and the other women as that new story, an alternative American Dream, one grounded not in self-sufficiency but in the way we accompany one another. Alia loves this country because people in it extended a hand to her when she could not find a way to stand on her own. They pulled her in and made her feel that she belonged. This sense of belonging that Alia instills now in other single mother refugees, and they in their children, gives newcomers hope and offers them a reason to participate in the life of their community. It therefore nourishes our democracy.

I once interviewed Andrea Meza, an attorney and the director of family detention with RAICES (the Refugee and Immigrant Center for Education and Legal Services), when the organization was awarded *Glamour*'s Women of the Year Award for their work at the border during the Trump administration's family separations. She told me that she often wonders, as she listens to her clients' stories, what would happen if the system were flipped and black and brown women, women who have experienced the worst, who have put their lives on the line for their families, could be the decision makers for once; if the powerful wisdom of the marginalized, who understand that life is about human connection and sacrifice and solidarity and compassion, could trickle down. She sees it happening in San Antonio, where she lives, but it's happening everywhere, she senses. "It's just going to elevate everybody," she told me. "I really believe that that's the key to a better future for all of us."

This new story need not be only for immigrants and refugees, though. Indeed, it cannot be. Many citizens feel a similar diminishment of their prospects, a sense that the American Dream has become a hopeless illusion. For some of them, Donald Trump, joined by those on the far right who have gained positions of power, offers an America that they'll make great again together and where they could belong. But the resentments, grievances, and lies upon which that vision was built have led to an unraveling of our democracy—or to a hastening of a process that had already begun. I don't know how to fix that systemic problem. But I believe that an answer has something to do with each of us making our small spheres more like the sisterhoods of the women with whom I spent the year documented here.

. . .

Alia's journey—from her mother country of Iraq, to Jordan where she fled as a refugee, to her early trials in America, through her experiences helping other refugee women find a home here—forms the framing story for *Accidental Sisters*. Alia is my guide and co-investigator, as we travel into the worlds of five of the single mothers she served during the Transformed Program of 2018, that central year of the Trump administration: Mina, 38 at the time of the events of this book, from Baghdad like Alia, who traveled to Turkey with her young daughter after her husband disappeared, where she suffered through a suicidal depression waiting to be resettled; Mendy, 46, from the Nuba Mountains of Sudan, a computer technician and mother of two, kidnapped and tortured and accused of supporting the opposition to then-president Omar al-Bashir's regime, who escaped to Jordan before eventually arriving in Houston; Sara, 30, from Damascus, Syria, whose husband was mortally wounded fighting in the civil war, and who found uncertain refuge in Jordan under the authoritarian regime of a petty religious tyrant; Zara, 35, from Hama, Syria, who arrived in the United States with her four children, married to a man who abused her for years and longing for the friend, her soulmate, whom she'd left behind in Jordan; and Elikya, 52, from the Democratic Republic of the Congo, married, like Alia, to a high-ranking military official brutally murdered beside her, who managed to collect her scattered children and some grandchildren and make it out of her shattered country, first to a refugee camp in Burundi, then to Houston.

Mina, Mendy, Sara, Zara, Elikya. I followed other women that year, Transformed mothers who had different case managers and whose stories were just as compelling. But in the end, I wanted to share what I saw growing between refugee women when they told their stories to one another. So into the frame story of Alia's journey are woven the stories of these five women, as revealed, little by little, to her.

Structurally, *Accidental Sisters* is always moving on two tracks: forging ahead through the Transformed Program with Alia and the five women, beginning in the spring of 2018 and ending in the spring of 2019; and circling back through their past lives and their arrival here.

The focus in Part I, "Mother Countries," is on the lives these women lived in their homelands, and their necessary departures in order to save themselves and their children.

The title of Part II, "Between the Ground and Sky," comes from a phrase of Alia's and describes the limbo of displacement the women experienced once they crossed a border into an unknown country to become a refugee, and then began the uncertain wait for permanent resettlement in yet another land.

Part III, "Home," charts their arrival in America and the transformations, both forced and embraced, that follow.

This sisterhood of refugee women are Muslims or women of color or both. They all arrived in Houston just prior to or during the 2016 presidential campaign, marked by Donald Trump's dehumanizing rhetoric aimed at refugees and immigrants and by his degradation of women. They were all trying to build new lives for themselves at a time when US policy under the Trump administration was intent on keeping them out and shutting them up.

Alia and these sisters are not voiceless, though, and I am not a voice for them. Still, women in their positions are rarely heard from, in part because of language barriers and cultural prohibitions. If we hear their stories, they are more commonly told by their grown children, who have had to act as their mothers' translators since they were young. As single mothers without husbands to attend to or to constrain them, these women were perhaps uniquely freed to speak openly about their experiences. This book is based on countless interviews with Alia and on the intimate oral histories these women shared with us (and at times, with me and other translators, themselves all women, all immigrants). Week after week, month after month, they recalled with us the places they came from, the complex reasons they were forced to leave, their brokenness and their resilience in the face of such loss. They had plenty to say, they wanted their stories to be known, and, with their permission, I recorded everything. Then, aided by a collective of students from the University of Houston, most of whom are the children of immigrants themselves, we transcribed those recordings.

The women whose stories are documented here are unique human beings who come from specific places. What they have undergone is singular, not representative. *Accidental Sisters* makes no claims to be telling the story of *the* refugee experience, or *the* single mother refugee experience, or *the* single mother refugee experience in Houston. And of course, even these individual stories of Alia, Mina, Mendy, Sara, Zara, and Elikya, as I recount them, are incomplete. What did I not think to ask them? What did they no longer remember? What did they want to forget?

But while I am not trying to write a history of the refugee crisis circa 2018, I have still tried to absorb the techniques of Svetlana Alexievich, author of *Voices from Chernobyl: The Oral History of a Nuclear Disaster,* among other books, and winner of the 2015 Nobel Prize for Literature. In the "monologues" she crafts from the oral histories of catastrophes that she gathers from people she visits again and again, she trusts in the voices of her subjects, who are usually those without power. Often her focus is on women. "Women tell things in more interesting ways," she said in a 2015 *New Yorker* profile of her. "They live with more feeling. They observe themselves and their lives." In *Voices from Chernobyl,* Alexievich gets her subjects to descend deep into themselves, and their stories merge into a kind of tragic chorus. Alexievich has, said Sara Danius, permanent secretary of the Swedish Academy, in announcing the Nobel Prize, invented a new literary genre—"a history of emotions—a history of the soul."

My conversations with these women often felt like a descent into something dark, but also sacred. They reminded me of the ancient Greek tragedies and epic poems that I taught for many years at the University of Houston. What emerged from them, namely, were not simplistic stories of immigrant successes that I could reflexively deploy against the false narratives of immigrants who steal jobs and are murderers and thieves. Rather, these conversations forced me to ask complex questions about our shared human condition—questions without easy answers: What does it mean to be an exile? Who are you when everything that shaped you has been stripped away? What is freedom? How do you live with dignity in a system that oppresses you? Can you make a home in a place that is not your homeland?

And there were questions, too, that I began to ask of my own country: Who are we as a people? What do we owe those who suffer because of our history or because of our actions abroad? How should we welcome the stranger, and for how long must our obligation to them last? What light does their perspective shed on our traditions and beliefs? What can we learn from what they've carried with them? How can we form a more perfect union with their help?

III. The Beginning

On the flight to America, Alia watched as Jordan receded behind them, and beyond that, Iraq, her only country. As Europe came into view, then likewise faded, as the flat metallic waters of the Atlantic stretched beneath them, she tried not to let her kids see her cry. She carried almost no money with her—the jewelry she wore when they left Iraq had been sold off. She only knew a word or two of English. She had no profession, no skills. And when they landed, there would be no one waiting for them. It was August 2008.

In the nights before they left, she had lain awake, asking her mother, her father, her husband—all those who had passed away—*Please, show me my way! Is this right? Will I lose my kids in America?* She didn't want anyone to find blame with her—she didn't want to blame herself—if she was making the wrong decision. But what else could she do? She couldn't continue in Jordan. She couldn't go back to Iraq.

One night she had a dream. "Go," her husband was telling her. "You will live a nice life. And I will be with you. You're not alone." But now, over the infinity of the Atlantic, that's not how she felt. She asked God for someone in America who could guide her.

At the airport in Houston Alia clung to her children and to the white plastic bag with the royal blue International Office of Migration logo that their representative handed her before she boarded the airplane in Jordan. Alia's name and United Nations refugee case number were scrawled in black marker across the top. That bag had the answers in it, the papers that explained who she was. She was afraid that if she lost it, she and the children might never be found. She carried it against her chest like a shield.

A caseworker from the resettlement agency picked them up, and drove them through the strange city with its highways of endless lanes, with its houses made of wood instead of the cement and brick and stone of Baghdad. Alia could not read the signs. Her caseworker spoke to her in English, which she could not speak. And as they drove, someone called him—perhaps his wife. He replied in Farsi, the language of Iran, the country that had sent a militia to kill her husband. She could not have imagined, back then, that his enemy, like hers, might have been that same government. They sat in silence, Alia in the front seat with the caseworker, her kids in back. She tried to appear strong, smart, familiar with everything. She tried to look as if she understood what was happening, as if she was not terrified. But inside, she was filled with questions: *Will he kidnap me? Will he steal my children? Will he kill me?* And she answered herself: *No, he can't. This is America!*

In the parking lot of the apartment complex on Fondren Road, in the waning light of that August evening, the humidity pressed in around them. The faces of the people, to Alia's eye, then, seemed harsh and poor and threatening. Inside, although it was clean enough, the dark, cramped apartment appalled Alia. Her caseworker opened the refrigerator and the cabinets, showing her the basics they'd provided. He told her not to answer the door to anyone until he returned the following day.

After her caseworker left, Alia propped herself against a wall of the living room with its single small window. She held Mustafa, the youngest, to her chest as he slept, while her daughter, Haneen, lay her head on Alia's shoulder, and her son Habib leaned against her on the other side. In Iraq, she had lived in a palatial house with crystal chandeliers and floor-to-ceiling windows among the Baghdad elite. She had cooks and chauffeurs, nannies and housekeepers and gardeners. No one would dream of bothering them, because they were part of the Iraqi power structure. She was *something* there.

Sitting on the floor with her children around her, she saw that she was now nothing, in this place that she did not understand. And in her heart, she asked herself another question: *Did I make a mistake in coming here?*

I *Mother Countries*

"Did you lose your husband? Did you lose your children?
Why are you crying?"

"We lost our country. We lost our homeland.
We lost everything."

1 A Handbook for Forgetting

That first February morning, I drove with Alia as she threaded her red VW Jetta through southwest Houston, past halal markets and Afghan restaurants, Arabic bakeries and Korean barbeque joints, taquerias, panaderias, and carnicerias, Ethiopian and Rwandan and Nigerian groceries. We hopped on Fondren Road, crossing Bellaire Boulevard whose signs, a little further down, are all in Vietnamese. Behind the strip malls, apartment buildings, and gas stations lining the main thoroughfares were neighborhoods of ranch houses and wide lawns and cul-de-sac streets with names like Hiawatha, Osage, Moonmist. We turned onto Harwin Drive. To the east was the Mahatma Gandhi District, but we headed west past wholesale warehouses offering Virgin of Guadalupe blankets, imitation Persian rugs, hookah tobacco. One sign advertised "Middle Eastern Dress, Mexican Dress, African Dress, Party Dress," and another, "Quinceañera and Prom Gowns." Gold-plated elephants, Chinese stone lions, winged angels, and replica Greek goddesses stood guard over the parking lot of a floral design studio. A shopping center, its name written in Chinese characters, boldly listed its inventory in English: "Caps and Hats, Beauty Supplies, Tennis Shoes, T-Shirts, Hosiery, Human Hair." I felt like I was driving through some delirious Walt Whitman litany, updated for the twenty-first century.

As we drove, Alia gave me a quick rundown of the women she was assessing now for placement in the Transformed Program's 2018 cohort. All single mothers, all refugees, they had been referred to Amaanah by various resettlement agencies around the city, or had heard of the program from friends when they found themselves in varying states of desperation, beyond the roughly six-month limit of federal financial assistance given to refugees upon arrival. Name a contemporary conflict, and most likely there was a woman from that place on Alia's list: Afghanistan, Burma, Congo, Eritrea, Iraq, Sudan, Syria. "Different countries," Alia said as we turned into an apartment complex, "but you see, Kim? In the end, it's all the same reason they are here: war."

. • .

"I will tell my story also," Alia reassures Mina in her bedazzled jeans and camo t-shirt with red sergeant stripes, her long, auburn hair hanging down her back like a cape. They are sitting together on one half of a dark leather sectional, Mina's knees pressing together, her hands clasped in her lap. Alia needs to collect the basic outlines of Mina's story. Outside, it is already spring, cool and clear, the fuchsia crape myrtles breaking into bloom. Something about Alia's encouragement seems to have the same effect on Mina, who, almost imperceptibly, seems to be unfolding herself. She hesitates, and then laughs.

On the coffee table, Mina has laid out a tray of tea and sugar and sweets. Tacked to the dingy taupe wall above her head is a collage of photos: Mina as a college student, her long hair pulled to one side, her eyes darkened with kohl. Mina in a mint green silk headscarf, chicly draped, with her daughter, Tia, four or five years old, in poufy white tulle against a hazy pink background. An even younger Tia beside Mina's mother, who wears a black abaya and veil. Tia, eight or nine now, her dark hair also pulled to one side, hanging down past her waist—an echo of her mother. Among the pictures dangles an amulet of round cobalt glass painted with concentric circles of white and pale blue and black: a charm against misfortune's evil eye.

The first question on the assessment form: *Can you describe your life in your home country?* Alia asks the question in Arabic. Mina responds, Alia interprets for me. "I was in Iraq," Mina begins. Once upon a time.

This would have been ten years after the American invasion. The year 2013. Mina was feeling, she tells Alia, deeply uneasy. She and her husband ran a small shop selling agricultural supplies in Baghdad when they started getting threatening phone calls and texts. Tia was five.

As Alia translates, I notice her pronouns shapeshifting. At times, she speaks in the first person, channeling Mina's story as if it is her own. At other times Alia is outside the story, watching it in third person. This seems to me like a parable for something. "And her husband told her this secret," Alia says in English as Mina's Arabic runs underneath. "He told her that some people, maybe they will harm him. And he told me what I should do. He told me to not stay here if anything bad happens to him, but to take his daughter and leave immediately."

"Yes, yes," Mina nods in English, following along as best she can with Alia's translation of her story.

"And he told her," Alia repeats, in the first person this time, "'If anything happens to me, don't stay here. Take my daughter and leave Iraq.'"

. . .

When the Americans had invaded back in 2003, Mina, unmarried then, was in her final year at the university in Abu Ghraib studying agricultural engineering. For months, classes were canceled. Eventually, after Saddam Hussein fled and the government dissolved, classes resumed. But now American tanks swarmed the roads through the city toward the prison, which was their base. Mina and another student paid for a driver to take them to the university three days a week. The ride was harrowing, but they were so close to graduating and they just wanted to finish.

Mina remembers the news reports that came out from the prison in Abu Ghraib about the torture, the sodomy, the rape. And she remembers the photos—grinning soldiers beside naked Iraqi prisoners giving the thumbs-up sign; naked prisoners covered in feces; naked prisoners forced into a pyramid formation; prisoners in orange jumpsuits, cuffed and kneeling, dogs lunging at them; a hooded prisoner draped in a fringed blanket, his arms held out as if in crucifixion. Abu Ghraib seemed to tear a veil away from the eyes of the Iraqi people. They had thought, Mina recalls, that the Americans were coming to help them. But after Abu Ghraib, something changed. And as the fledgling Iraqi government was forming, the Iraqi people no longer wanted the American army patrolling their country. "We wanted them to leave," Mina says.

Mina remembers the insurgency attacks on the Americans that began then—the IEDs, the roadside bombs. And how the Americans started getting jittery. Like they didn't know who to trust any more.

The chaos that the invasion spawned kept widening out. And the divide between Sunni and Shia, which before the war was hardly a thing, now fed that destruction. During Ramadan in 2006, as her family was waiting to break their fast at sunset, their home in Baghdad's Al Saydiya neighborhood was hit by a couple of mortars, filling the rooms with black smoke, shattering windows. Her family were Sunni. The attack, Mina thinks, was Shia. But she doesn't know for sure.

Mina knows that Saddam Hussein hauled the country into war after war. She was born in 1980, the year that Iraq invaded Iran. That

conflict lasted her whole childhood. Then in 1990 Iraq invaded Kuwait, and the Gulf War followed. But in the Baghdad where she lived,
life was mostly safe and stable. Saddam's authoritarian regime kept
all of the different factions in balance—not just Sunni and Shia, but
also Arab, Kurd, Christian.

After the Americans arrived in April 2003, Saddam fled, and no
one felt safe out in the streets. Crime was rampant. Kidnappings
grew common, and brutal murders were committed indiscrimi-
nately. Everyone seemed to be on edge, waiting. In the morning
when they left for work, they wondered if this would be the day
they'd be kidnapped or killed. Running errands, they would tell their
families, "Maybe I will not come back." Everyone was like that, remembers Mina.

Alia remembers that time, too, before she left. In the lawless
landscape, pilots like her husband, Osama, who had fought in the
war with Iran, started turning up dead. At first, no one saw the pat-
tern. But one by one, people she and her husband knew were killed—
engineers, government officials. And eventually they understood:
the killings were systematic. Members of the air force were being
kidnapped, by the Badr Brigade most likely—Shia Islamist death
squads trained and financed by Iran to exact revenge for the sorties
they'd flown during the Iran-Iraq War. Sometimes they'd be killed in
their own homes. Others would just disappear, their mutilated bodies dumped days later.

By October 2003, six months after the invasion, Alia was pregnant with the baby she'd wanted for reasons she couldn't explain.
Haneen, her daughter, was thirteen, and her son, Habib, almost
eleven. Osama had always shielded her from what they both imagined she could not handle. She loved clothes and jewelry, trips to the
salon, tennis lessons and aerobics classes at the Iraqi Hunting Club.
She hadn't really ever paid attention to politics. But she was scared
now. And Alia's fear, and the new baby on the way, along with the

mounting death toll, must have been weighing on her husband's mind, too. He started talking about finding someplace outside of Baghdad where they'd be safe. At first, this didn't register with Alia. But slowly his worry came into focus, and Alia remembers turning her face to his. "Why are you talking like that?" she asked.

"I feel it is not safe anymore, Alia. It's not the same as before," he replied. The Badr Brigade had killed two of his cousins, also pilots. "They will kill me, Alia. They will kill all of us."

And then they shot Osama's best friend, Hussein Ali Marhoon, in his driveway. After that her husband told Alia, "It is my turn."

All of the nearly thirty pilots from Osama's flight school class would soon be assassinated. That's probably why, in the midst of the killings, Alia and Osama had driven up to Sulaymaniyah in the north, in Kurdistan—an autonomous region not controlled by the disintegrating Iraqi government. It was Eid, late November. Most likely, her husband was looking for a place for them to live. But whatever his plans were, he didn't share the details with Alia. Even then, he was trying to shield her. Only once had he asked her, "When something happens to me, Alia, what will you do?" It was that *when* that Alia would later remember. Then he'd answered for her: "Protect my kids and yourself."

A year before, life had been as it had always been in Baghdad. Their house in Mansour sat on a street owned by her father-in-law, who had built houses for all his sons and daughters there. Every afternoon, Alia and her sisters-in-law and their collective children would gather at the home of the eldest brother. The boys would run around the backyard, kicking the soccer ball, while the girls played with their Barbies or drew hopscotch boards with chalk on the driveway. When the boys, scuffling with each other, came complaining to the mothers sitting together at the long outdoor table, the mothers would shoo them away. Then they'd go back to talking and laughing. The men, as they came home from work, would join the women.

There was always kleicha, the date-filled pastry flavored with carda-mom and rose water, along with tea served in small clear glass cups. And, as evening came on, watermelon slices piled onto a massive platter by the cook. Then they would all say goodbye and each small family would wander off to their own homes for dinner.

When the war started, they moved the afternoon ritual inside. That was the beginning, the first concession that something funda-mental was changing. Eventually, the gatherings had to stop entirely: it felt too dangerous to move between houses with the bombings, the shootings. Still, it seemed unfathomable that all this would end for-ever, or that Alia and Osama should ever have to leave. This was the place where they'd been born, where they'd grown up, where they'd had children. This was the place where they'd expected to be buried. It had been that way in their families generation upon gen-eration.

But then everything had been overturned so suddenly, from the safest life to the most unstable. Now, people they knew were being brutally murdered, and strangers roamed the streets. They needed to leave, and to leave behind everything—to protect those who were still in this life.

Alia thinks sometimes of the dream she had a few days before Osama died—a dream that was like the truth coming toward her. In it, she is in the cabin of a Ferris wheel, the one she used to see as she drove through Baghdad on her way to her grandfather's house. The wheel is slowly lifting her as the cabin sways. She is alone. Her hus-band is not beside her. And then, as she reaches the top, something suddenly goes sickeningly wrong. The gears that had kept everything relentlessly turning have busted, a cord has been severed, and she is falling from that great height, falling so fast that she gasps for breath.

But when she awoke, she looked around, and there, as always, was Osama. "Alhamdulillah," she said to herself. "Thank God it was just a dream."

Two or three days later, they killed him in their car, Ghadah beside him, in a staged accident on the road outside of Sulaymaniyah.

It would take years before she understood the full truth of what she was being shown that night. There was still so far to fall, so many things she would have to lose.

. . .

If anything happens to me, don't stay here. Take my daughter and leave Iraq. That's what Mina's husband had told her. *When something happens to me, what will you do?* Alia's husband had asked her. *Protect my kids and yourself,* he'd said.

We're sitting around the coffee table in Mina's small living room, far from Baghdad. But as we pour tea into china cups and stir in the sugar, our spoons clattering, the question from the checklist still remains unanswered: *Can you describe your life in your home country?*

Mina's husband had worked security for the Americans in the Green Zone, but he had left that work behind when he and Mina married in 2007. There were so many militia roaming Iraq with so many agendas that maybe his past work was the problem. But it could also have been that, when he married Mina, he left Shia Islam and became Sunni, like his wife. He and Mina had opened their store in their largely Shiite neighborhood, and Mina would help the customers who came in. They made a good living. Still, she could see in the eyes of the people around them, and in the eyes of his uncles and brothers especially, that they did not accept the situation—his renouncing Shi'ism after he married her.

By the time he disappeared in August 2013, Mina had been receiving threatening messages on her phone from a number she didn't recognize for months: "We will take revenge on you." "Our flesh is bitter"—meaning, *We are a hard people, merciless.* "We will never leave you in peace." He'd been kidnapped once before by some militia. They beat him and asked him questions and then left him. But this time, he went grocery shopping and never came back.

"After that," Mina tells Alia, "I traveled to Turkey because I remembered that he told me not to stay if anything happened to him, to take care of our daughter, Tia, because he loved her a lot."

Mina still has the number of the phone that sent the messages. She doesn't know why. And copies of the police report she made, even if there would never again be any use for it.

But the mention of Turkey today seems to have opened up something in Mina, and Alia translates: "She wants to talk."

"I was living in Turkey, in Kırıkkale," Mina begins. She had applied for asylum when she arrived and been granted refugee status by the UN. "We lived in an apartment. I brought money with me, but in the end it was gone. I started working. I didn't have a car. I would take Tia to school, then go to work. I worked in a restaurant and I worked in a salon. I did many things. But it was not enough. And they were not fair with me because I was not a Turk and I didn't have a job permit."

"You have come to the right place," Alia pauses translating to tell her, maybe because here, refugees have the right to work as soon as they arrive.

"My dream was to reach America. My dream was to come here," continues Mina. "But the processing for refugees, it takes so long. I wrote a report to the UN—*Please come to visit me, come see my situation. I'm waiting, and you won't say if you will accept me or not.* I was in the middle of the way. I wanted to know where I was." At the memory of this time, Mina's voice breaks. She bends over into herself and holds her head in her hands, weeping, her long hair cascading over her knees.

"Sometimes we need to cry and we need to talk," Alia soothes Mina as Mina heaves. Alia pauses to make space for the keening. "I know," Alia says. And now she, too, is crying. Her mascara begins to smear and she wipes the corners of her eyes with the side of her hand. "I understand," she says again, letting Mina's spasms of grief rise and subside like waves. "But you are lucky now," Alia tells Mina, almost pleading, when she herself can speak again. "You reached your dream: America. You are here. You are *here*," Alia insists. "You are here."

Something in what Alia is saying has begun to pull Mina out of the quicksand in which she'd been sinking. "You are lucky," Alia repeats. "Tia is with you."

"Yes," says Mina.

"And you are here," Alia reminds her.

"Yes," says Mina. A kind of call and response.

"And you are strong!" Alia goes on.

"Yeah."

"You are strong!"

"Yeah."

"You did what you wanted."

"Yes."

"But we need to cry sometimes."

Now Alia leads Mina back to the story. "You told them, 'I want to know where I am in the process . . .'"

And Mina picks up the trail and goes on. "I told them, 'I'm waiting a long time. I will kill myself. But take care for my daughter because really I feel tired.' So after that they started to help me. 'Don't cry,' they told me. 'Don't do anything to hurt yourself. We will help you.'" After almost three and a half years in Turkey, she and Tia were approved for resettlement in the United States.

Alia and Mina are both sniffling now between sentences. Their mascara has run down their cheeks and dried. "Inside, my heart is broken from all those years in Turkey," Mina tells Alia. "And I feel it right now more than before because I remember what happened to me there. It broke everything inside." Mina confesses that, in fact, she had been sent home several times from her job in housekeeping at one of the city's swank hotels when she could not stop crying. But then Mina says in English, quietly yet with conviction, "I love America."

And it is as if Alia has suddenly been plugged into an electrical outlet. "You love it? You see! Also me!"

"I love America!" Mina goes on then, in Arabic, while Alia translates into a joyous, triumphant English, "It is a dream of all the people to reach America, but I *did*."

Alia turns to look directly at Mina now. "So this is what I want from you," she commands. "Sometimes, cry. And between me and you," she says, "I need sometimes to cry. *But!* Keep reminding yourself: You are strong. You reached your goal."

"Yes," says Mina.

"You got through the processing and paperwork. You are in the country of freedom. Here, women are respected. In our country, the woman can't work outside the home. Men bother her. Here no one can bother you."

"Yes," says Mina.

"You are amazing. You came to the country that is the dream of all people. You did something that not even many men could do."

Mina has grown quiet now. She seems to be taking in Alia's words like a wilted plant drinking in the rain. "I'm happy I will be in this program," she says. "I feel right now I have some people around me. This is the important thing: I don't feel alone anymore here. I have family around me because you are with me. I don't feel homesick anymore."

I am a little taken aback: is Mina's instant attachment to Alia a sign of her desperation? Or is this conception of family somehow rooted in Iraqi culture? Or is it something else?

"Sure," Alia nods and smiles and reaches out toward Mina.

"*Habibiti*," Mina says in reply. *My love, my dear one.* Her smile illuminates her face.

Alia tells her, "Really, I'm a sister for you here." Whatever is happening, it seems genuine.

Alia continues now with the assessment form: *If you are accepted into this program, what do you hope to achieve?* Mina grows somber again, momentarily. "I want to skip the saddest story for me," she says quietly. "I want to forget the things that make me tired and sad. And I want to feel some people are behind me to help me when I have an issue or problem." Then she brightens again, "And I want to continue my studies. I want to learn English."

"Ohhhhh," Alia nods with approval.

"This is the important thing for me: to learn English."

Mina gets up and goes to the kitchen to make coffee. As she starts some water in the kettle on the stove, she calls out over her shoulder to Alia, "I'm sorry I made you cry." But Alia says, "No, no! I'm thankful for you! I don't want to forget my background." But there's more to it for Alia than that. She turns to me and explains how women like Mina keep her focused on her purpose, her life's work—"to keep helping these people. To keep saying to Trump: Let them come here—refugees—because they really need help."

As Mina continues to rattle around in the kitchen, Alia notes that Mina still sometimes feels that she wants to kill herself. "But she said, 'You give me power,'" Alia tells me. "They need that. They need psychiatric help. You know, because they come to the point where they feel life is not good with them. Why is she in this situation? It is not fair in the life."

This reminds me of something Alia had said earlier, when we were driving and she was talking about war—the catastrophe that unites all of her clients and has brought them here. Sometimes, she told me, she wishes she could ask people, "Why are you fighting? We are all human. We are all going in the same circle."

As Alia fills out her paperwork, I get up and wander over to the dining nook, the narrow table covered with a white damask tablecloth, which in turn is covered by clear plastic sheeting. Taped to the wall is Mina's diploma from the University of Baghdad College of Agriculture in Abu Ghraib. Next to that hangs a mirror, embossed in gold with Arabic calligraphy. I am trying to make out the words when Mina steps out from the kitchen and stands beside me. She points out her name embedded in the swirl of characters on the mirror. Then, tracing her finger around the outline of the shape the letters have made, she says, "Iraq." And suddenly I see it: the map of her homeland.

When my husband and I married in 1995, he was serving in the army, stationed at Fort Sill in Oklahoma. Fort Sill had originally been a frontier fort, established to protect settlements of those pioneers from indigenous tribes in the border-states of Kansas and Texas. The settlers needed protection, of course, because they were trying to colonize native land that did not belong to them. Later, Geronimo and nearly 350 other Chiricahua Apache were brought to Fort Sill as prisoners of war. Geronimo died and is buried in the Apache cemetery there.

After my husband left the army, we moved to Houston, where our families live. I was pregnant with our third child. With the terrorist attacks of September 11, I remember the flags that went up on the porches all through our neighborhood, and the way it felt, for this brief window, like we were a united nation, embraced by the world. I remember, in the *New York Times*, the portraits of the victims published every day for months. And then I remember the unraveling: the hateful rhetoric around Muslims, the declaration of war on Iraq, a country that had nothing to do with the 9/11 attacks. I remember my husband and I standing in the living room of our house, dumbfounded, as NPR reported news of the impending war.

We took our daughters to a protest near downtown at a park along Buffalo Bayou, named for those magnificent creatures who once roamed the tall grass prairie stretching west. I don't remember exactly what I was protesting. The stupidity of the invasion, perhaps. The lies on which it was all built. The inevitable coming slaughter. I do remember the rolling list of names of the dead American soldiers at the ends of the newscasts at night. And how it was much more difficult to find reports of Iraqi civilian casualties. But there was not yet, for us, a face to the catastrophe.

Alia has come over to join me and Mina now before the mirror with the gold calligraphic lettering of Mina's name in the shape of Iraq. We stand together, looking at that map of their mother country, our faces all reflected in it.

2   *Like a Woman Drowning*

For her daughter's birthday, Mendy took the bus to the flea market on Hillcroft, with its cheap electronics and piñatas and paraffin candles in glass jars with images of the Virgin Mary, its jewelry stands with layaway plans, its rows of cowboy boots and cowboy hats, its stacks of velour plush blankets decorated with lions and roses, its action figure backpacks and baby dolls in baby strollers and soccer jerseys and little girls' candy-colored, tulle-lined dresses, its food stalls selling elote and papusas, sliced coconut and jicama and mango with chile powder, and all manner of aguas frescas, its tattoo stand, its palm reading station, its miniature horses with unicorn horns—all of it the longing for a homeland made manifest—and she bought two parakeets, one blue and one yellow. Sometimes Mendy lets the parakeets out of their cage, to give them their freedom, she says. In Arabic, the word for cage is the same as the word for the ribs that enclose the beating heart. Maybe the birds in the cage are a metaphor for Mendy's heart. Maybe the freed birds are the metaphor. It's too soon to tell.

This clear February morning, the parakeets are chirping and chatting, oblivious of Mendy, who lies on the couch, her right foot propped up and bandaged from a recent surgery. Her daughter, Shahad, ten, and her son, Mohamad, eight, are at school. Mendy is scrolling through WhatsApp messages from her Sudanese friends, those back home and others scattered like seeds abroad. Beneath her eyes curve ashen half moons, and her black face is framed by the white head wrap covering her hair, which is in turn covered by a peony pink hijab. When Mendy hears the knock on the door, her slack face becomes radiant.

Alia has come to conduct the Transformed Program's initial assessment, as she had done with Mina a couple of days before, and I am trailing along again. The small landing outside Mendy's apartment is cluttered with flip-flops and sneakers, and as we take off our shoes and enter, Alia insists on leaving the front door open, as she does at all of the apartments of all of the women she works with. She thinks of the fresh air and sunlight as a tonic to the cloistered darkness, the fearfulness in which her clients too often live.

I get the feeling that Alia is a tonic, too, in gold-rimmed aviator sunglasses this sunny day, and sheer mauve head scarf and manicured blush-colored nails, traces of the luxurious life she once lived. She and Mendy exchange kisses on the cheeks and greetings in Arabic, small poems.

"*As-salaam alaikum,*" says Alia, smiling. *Peace be upon you.*

"*Wa alaikum as-salaam,*" Mendy replies, smiling back. *And upon you, peace.*

"Tell me, *habibiti,* how much do you pay for rent here?" Alia asks after settling onto the love seat beneath the sheer zebra-print curtains and explaining how the Transformed Program works. And as the parakeets prattle in their cage, Mendy answers Alia's questions. Mendy pays $580 in rent for this one-bedroom apartment, she says, plus $40-$50 for electricity, $35 for water, $15 for internet, and $25 for her cell phone. Yes, she receives food stamps—$370—but usually that's not enough to get her and her kids through the month, so she spends maybe another $100 or so for groceries. She has been working in housekeeping at the Crown Plaza Hotel near downtown making $8 an hour, and she's usually scheduled about thirty hours a week. Like Mina, like everyone with whom Alia works, no one is given full-time work, so the companies don't have to pay benefits.

Mendy also has no car. She tells Alia that she wants to be able to take her children to the park. She wants to take them shopping. But without a car in this sprawling city, and now with her bandaged foot, that's a problem. And anyway, she doesn't even really know where to go. She takes the bus to work—about an hour, even though it's less than ten miles away. The surgery has made it painful to stand. "But I work," she tells Alia, holding her bandaged foot, more subdued now. "What I can do?"

As Alia continues to collect and record facts, Mendy gets up and limps to the kitchen a few paces from the couch to make tea—black with dried sage and sugar in the Sudanese tradition. When she limps back, she places the tea tray on the side table between couch and love seat and pours a small clear glass for each of us, smiling, then settles back into the pillows. Alia unwraps her scarf and drapes it around her shoulders, revealing her coppery hair, pulled back into a low bun, the subtle layers, slightly flattened from her scarf, framing her round face. As we drink, Mendy laughs, and her laughter is joyous and infectious. Underneath that sound, though, courses something else—a relief, perhaps, to be rid momentarily of the loneliness that traps her. In her laughter one can sense the self Mendy could be, unburdened by what she has lost.

Mendy's apartment on Fondren Road is just down the street from Alia's first apartment, where she and her three children were initially resettled in August 2008—where, after the caseworker had left, they'd all sat on the living room carpet as the evening passed and the night took over and the squares of the small window darkened. Later, she had settled the older children in one room, and then curled up with Mustafa in his twin bed in the room they would share. Looking at him, so small and vulnerable, Alia knew that her children believed she could protect them. But she herself felt so weak.

At the resettlement agency the following day, the director went through Alia's welcome package with her—the lump sum she'd be given, as well as the monthly rental assistance she could expect for the next four months, the immunizations that would be required in the coming days, the necessity for getting her and the children registered with Social Security, which would allow for Medicaid and food stamp benefits. But then Alia had asked the woman in the best English she could muster, "May I go back to Jordan?"

"Why, though?" the woman had asked, shocked. "You're here!"

Alia had persisted. "Is it possible, please?"

But of course, it was not possible. The plane tickets that had carried her and the children to Houston had been secured by the International Office of Migration through an interest-free loan, which Alia would have to repay, and they were only one-way.

For weeks, Alia kept their suitcases by the living room door, unable to bring herself to unpack. At night, she would pull out pajamas. In the morning, she would repack them and choose clothes for the day, saying to herself, "I am only temporary here."

And she did not feel entirely safe. One night soon after they arrived, her neighbor, fighting with his wife or his girlfriend, Alia wasn't sure which, punched a hole in the wall between their apartments. Doing her laundry in the apartment complex machines, she felt watched in her headscarf. "Where are you from? What is your name?" people would ask her. "I'm not speak English," she would reply, and hurry back to the bare apartment.

And then there was the other family in the complex that her caseworker introduced her to—Iraqis, he had said. They spoke Arabic, which he did not. But when she met them, she could tell they came from the south, from an area that had been persecuted by Saddam. Though they were refugees from Iraq like Alia, they had seemed as suspicious of her as she was of them. Still, Alia knew no one else that she could ask about navigating the city. Where should she shop for groceries? How did she catch a bus? She relied on the family, though she could not trust them.

And there was another threat, too, more existential. In those first few days after their arrival, when Alia went to the local elementary school with her caseworker to register her kids, although the women at the front desk were all very kind, Alia was alarmed—at the tattoos, at the revealing clothes, at the girls in the halls who were clearly pregnant. And underneath pulsed an attitude, a spirit, harder to define. In Iraq, when Alia was a student, she would cast her eyes to the floor when she spoke with a teacher, in a sign of respect. But here, she noticed, when students interacted with teachers and administrators, they would look them in the eyes and speak casually, familiarly, or even joke around. This freedom unnerved Alia. And it confused her. "Am I right?" she asked herself. "Or wrong?" And then another question: "Will I lose my children here?"

Now with Mendy and the chattering parakeets, down the street from the site of those memories, Alia picks up her glass of tea with sage and sugar and takes a sip, then says, gently but firmly, "Tell me, Mendy, you are a single mom here. Where is your husband? What happened to him?" Mendy stares out the open door for a moment, a scrim falling over the light of her eyes. The sound of neighbors calling out to each other in Spanish and Dari, Vietnamese and Swahili, fills the emptiness. "I don't know till now," she replies.

.   .   .

Mendy's earliest memories are of climbing the green slopes of the Nuba Mountains, the shepherds herding cows and sheep, the terraced fields, the round homes built from mud bricks, their conical roofs thatched with straw, the windows and doors covered by curtains instead of glass. Then as now, no paved roads led through the mountains, and the villages within them were threaded together only by footpaths. They say that there are ninety-nine mountains, and on each one is spoken a different local language. The Nuba people have lived in these mountains for thousands of years.

Mendy's father and grandfather and great-grandfather, all of her ancestry, are Baggara—ethnically Arab, traditionally nomadic cattle-herders. Over the centuries, the Baggara mixed with the Nuba people. Many now lead a settled existence. Growing up, Mendy's parents spoke only the dialect of Alkadaru, the mountain territory of their clan, and continued to, the two of them together, even after her father took his family away from their ancestral lands to Kadugli, the big city in the region of South Kordofan which encompasses the Nuba Mountains. There his children could get an education and learn Arabic, the official language of Sudan. Though he never went to elementary school, never saw the inside of a classroom, he taught himself Arabic, and some English, the other official language. Although he later became an accountant, throughout much of Mendy's childhood her father drove a tractor in fields where cotton was being grown. And after he finished work in the fields, he would return home and practice writing in Arabic on a chalkboard propped up against the wall—stringing the letters together from right to left like birds on a wire.

When Mendy was still quite young, she asked her father for a desk. None of his children had asked for this before. There were three boys and seven girls, and her father told his daughters not to bother asking to marry until they had a high school diploma. And after high school, he told them, "You go to college or you get married. Make your choice." But he knew Mendy was special. He told her to follow only the people who could advise her, people from whom she could take information into her mind. "Don't be like everyone else," he told her. "Be *additional*."

Mendy studied accounting in Khartoum, the capital city at the confluence of the Blue Nile and the White. In Sudan, in that traditional culture from which Mendy came, it was difficult for women to travel alone to a city, far from their families, to study. But her father told Mendy, "I trust you. Go and get what you need." She loved her dorm room at the university, the spareness of it with its narrow bed and cabinet and desk. She had only a few clothes and a single pair of shoes. She had no television, but her father gave her his own radio, and on it she would listen to the news. When you have lots of clutter around you, your mind is busy with that, Mendy believes. But in her dorm room, with all excess pared away, she could just think, which is what she loved to do.

Mendy was studying accounting, but found herself drawn to the computer classes on campus. Sometimes she would sneak in and listen. She sensed that, while accounting always stayed the same, with computers there would forever be something new, and that to study computers and to work with them, you could always be advancing. Mendy doesn't like anything that stays static. With accounting, she thought, you could not update yourself. But with computers, there would be constant discovery. This yearning within Mendy is part of the reason she now lives in Houston. But in Sudan, in those years, she only knew she was following an inner call, some craving of her mind that was seeking satisfaction.

Mendy had some friends at the university whom she would sometimes meet in the park, where they would sit and talk. One of these friends had a small business in computer programming. "Come see how I do it," he told her. "Everything I will show you." And he did. Mendy told him, "Don't look at me as you do the ladies." She was not married then, and she didn't want him to think about her like that. He respected that.

Mendy had no money and, being from the Nuba Mountains in the south, the Islamic government of the north under Omar al-Bashir refused her scholarships and financial aid. But a friend helped fund her further education, telling her, "Mendy, if you want to be equal to other people, rich people with money, don't think about them. If you have a mind, you will be equal."

By the time she finally married, Mendy was in her thirties, working in a computer maintenance workshop. A cousin of Mendy's had introduced her to a friend of his named Bedawi, who drove a minibus, transporting both people and goods. Unlike Mendy, Bedawi was not a serious person. He was not interested in learning new things, even when Mendy prodded him. But he had a sense of humor, and when their daughter, Shahad, was born in the summer of 2008, his love for her was immense and protective.

Across the Arab world, when a first son arrives, the parents assume an honorific title that incorporates the baby's name: thus *Oum* X, the Mother of X. The same goes for *Abu,* meaning Father. Bedawi became Abu Shahad, though Shahad was a daughter. And even when their son, Mohammad, arrived two years later, Bedawi refused to relinquish his original title to become Abu Mohammed, which would have been the traditional move. He loved his daughter that much.

Mendy and Bedawi were back in Kadugli by then, far south, away from the nation's focal point of Khartoum. Mendy had opened a small store for the repair and maintenance of computers. But the couple was saving money so they could return to the capital and send their children to the better schools that were there.

Since Sudan's independence from Great Britain in 1956, the country had suffered through a series of civil wars fought largely along old and entrenched religious and ethnic lines: the Arab and Islamic north versus the Black African south, where Christians and animists predominated. Ultimately, the south rebelled against the central government of Sudan, and in 2011 it became an independent nation: the Republic of South Sudan. But the Nuba Mountains and its indigenous people, though they had been aligned with the south in their rebellion, remained legally tethered to Omar al-Bashir's Republic of Sudan. And so this region of South Kordofan was, by the time Mendy and Bedawi returned to Kadugli, torn apart by conflict between the Sudan People's Armed Forces of the government and Nuba fighters of the Sudan People's Liberation Movement-North, the SPLM-N. Consequently, South Kordofan and the Nuba Mountains within it became the site of one of the world's worst humanitarian disasters. The government would not allow aid agencies in. This conflict is another source of Mendy's fate, another reason she now lives in Houston.

.   .   .

"You don't know what happened to your husband even now?" Alia asks Mendy as we sit together drinking tea.

And so, reluctantly, Mendy begins. "One day at three o'clock exactly, a man came into my shop wearing a uniform," she says. This was in 2013. Maybe the man was from the Sudanese army. Maybe the opposition, the SPLM-N. She couldn't be sure, but she didn't think much of it. He was having trouble with a computer, so she agreed to go with him to his office. She did that for clients all the time. Once there, she connected a cable and installed some antivirus software. That was it.

But two days later, another man came into her store complaining of computer problems at his office, too. "Come with me," he said, and so she did. There were two men in the front seat of the car and one in the back where she sat. They drove through the city of Kadugli, but then, as the buildings thinned out, Mendy began to ask, "Where is your place? Where are we going?" She was worried about leaving her shop for such a long time. And then there were her children, five-year-old Shahad and three-year-old Mohammad, being cared for by a neighbor. It was getting late in the afternoon and she would be expected home soon. Looking out of the window, she told them, "This area where we are, it's impossible to have any work for me out here." But still they kept driving. And when she asked again, in a panic,

"Where are we going?" one of the men in the front seat said ominously, "We don't have any job for you." And the man beside her took her hands and tied them behind her back. When she started screaming, they gagged and blindfolded her.

When the car finally stopped, they pulled Mendy out and walked her down into a building, then untied her hands and took off her blindfold and the gag. This time Mendy kept her mouth shut. But a voice inside her head was speaking: *God is here and he will take care of everything. Whatever is going to happen is going to happen. God will take care of it. If I die, then I die. God is here.*

In the building was a man in civilian clothes sitting at a table holding a pen. There was no computer, only some tools lying around. Mendy remembers pliers in particular. When she saw the man at the table, she was sure she would be killed. "Do you know why you're here?" he asked.

Mendy refused to answer.

"Do you know why you're here?" he asked again.

"No, I don't," she finally replied.

"Yes, you do know," he insisted. "You are distributing fliers for the opposition faction."

Mendy had no idea what he was talking about. She didn't even understand why there was fighting. She had been away in Khartoum for so long, and back in Kadugli she was so busy with her business and her babies that she had not really been paying attention to the conflict, hadn't really heard much about the atrocities happening in the mountains. But the man with the pen claimed that at her store she was helping the rebels at war with the government—printing material for them, even though she had no printer there.

So again he asked, "You don't know why you're here, you dog?"

It was that *dog*—one of the most demeaning slurs in Arabic culture—which provoked her. "None of this is correct," Mendy insisted. "If you have anything against me, please prove it."

"*You* do not ask *me*," he warned her.

"I'm going to ask you," she told him, "because *you're* the one who brought me here. I didn't come by myself. I don't know you. *You* looked for *me.*"

They threw her into a room with nothing but the floor and walls that shaped it. She kept talking. "Why did you bring me here? Why are you asking me questions? Do you think that you are going to get something out of me?" she asked. "There is nothing to get out. Even if you left me here for a year, nothing is going to come from it. I'm not the person you are describing." Even when they beat her with the metal rod, even as it dug into the flesh of her leg, she wouldn't confess to something she hadn't done. *If I die,* she thought, *I want to die free.* All through the night the questions continued, as did Mendy's resistance, until near sunrise the following day, the time of the call to prayer.

"We can't get anything out of her," Mendy heard her torturers say. And that's when they made her sign the papers. She's not even sure what she signed—there were so many pages and she was exhausted and it was all so confusing. But she remembers the conditions for her release that one of the men read to her. "First, you're not allowed to work anymore. No more shop in Kadugli," he began. "Second, you can't talk to anyone about what has happened here. Third, you cannot leave the area without my permission." Mendy signed. What else could she do?

And then the journey rewound itself—the blindfold over the eyes, the long drive, the fringes of the city. Except that when they stopped the car, shoved her out, they told her, because she didn't know where she was, "Just walk and you will find your way."

South? East? North? West? She had no idea which direction she should go. Under a whitening sky, she just kept walking through the dusty streets, past low buildings the same color as the dust, the color of the straw thatch of the conical roofs of the houses in the mountains. Mendy asked for directions to her own neighborhood. "Oh, sister," the people said, "you have far to walk." The wound in her leg made the going slow and painful.

"Where were you?" Mendy's neighbor asked when Mendy got home at last. But Mendy had been ordered not to tell anyone. She didn't want any more trouble. "Well, your children are with me," the neighbor said when Mendy wouldn't answer.

"Where is the father of my children?" Mendy asked.

"Probably he went to look for you," said the neighbor. "Maybe the hospital, or the police station."

Mendy gathered Shahad and Mohammad to her. That day she slept the sleep of the just, but when she woke in the dark, her husband still had not returned.

"Where were you?" Bedawi's friend Omar asked. It had been his knocking that had woken her. But Mendy still did not dare to talk about what had happened. Then he noticed the blood that had soaked through her pants, and for the first time, Mendy noticed it, too. She lifted the fabric and saw what they had done to her. "What's going on, Mendy?" Omar asked again, this time more gently. He had been standing by the door, and now he came and sat on a chair beside her. "Why didn't you go to the hospital?" When Mendy still didn't answer, he coaxed, "I have been with you since we were children. So we are not only friends—we are like family." Mendy was crying then. She was sure that what had happened to her was now happening to Bedawi. "They took me," she finally told Omar. And then she told him everything.

Through the night they talked, Mendy and Omar. They knew Mendy would now be watched. She couldn't work. She couldn't leave the city. Her leg was mangled and in pain. She had to take care of her children. She had no idea what was happening to her husband, but she was afraid.

"I'm going to take you somewhere safe," Omar told Mendy. His family had a truck for transporting produce. He'd put her and the children in the back with the sorghum and corn and hibiscus and send them to his family in Khartoum ten hours north. On a bus, officials would require her name for the passenger manifest list, in case of an accident, and then she'd surely be found out and sent back to Kadugli, where she'd endanger everyone she knew. The truck was safer. Mendy had no choice. She was like a drowning woman clutching at a straw. She had to go.

In Khartoum, the city at the confluence of the branches of the Nile, Mendy and her children were sequestered in the guest quarters of the home of Omar's family. And for a month she lay low, trying to let her leg heal, trying to keep the children quiet. She would call Omar in Kadugli and ask about her husband, but there had not been any word since the day he disappeared. Mendy was sure that he'd been killed.

"You're not going to stay here," Bedawi's brother, Ali, told her when he came to visit her in Khartoum. "It's not safe for you. You broke the rules of the papers that you signed. You talked about what happened to you. You left Kadugli."

Mendy knew that Ali was right.

"While you were not at fault," he acknowledged, "they took you. And then they took your husband, too. It's been more than a month and we know nothing about him. Your husband got drawn into this because of you. The problem was with you, not with him. It's safer for you to find another country where you can raise your kids." It would also be safer for everyone around them. Ali and Omar thought it would be better to protect Mendy and the children than to lose the whole family. And to protect them, they had to get them out of Sudan. They'd send them to Jordan.

Ali asked her if she had a passport. As Mendy was trying to explain how she stored all of her important documents in her computer shop because the rain couldn't damage them there, and as she was trying to tell him where to find them, and what to do with the equipment that was left, Ali cut her off. "Your store was set on fire," he said. "So all those documents are gone."

Everything Mendy possessed had burned. She was a drowning woman. A drowning woman with two children. Two children and a straw.

.   .   .

"So till this day I still don't know what happened to my husband," Mendy tells Alia in the apartment with the open door in southwest Houston. The morning breeze has stilled. "I wait," she says into that stillness. "What I can do?" She hasn't been able to bring herself to tell the children that their father is probably dead. "After they grow up a little bit, then I will tell them," she says. "Maybe he will come back. I want them to live beautiful days. We are foreigners here. It is harsh for them. I don't want to add another problem. Gradually, they might forget about him. Even if they do not forget, the shock will be less. Let them enjoy their life right now." Sometimes, when the children ask about their father, Mendy calls Ali, the brother who helped save them. They think that he is him, and for the moment they are soothed.

"I see that I am lucky here," Mendy says. Unlike most refugee parents, she has insurance to pay for the surgeries she needs for her leg. It's not like in Khartoum, at the safe house, when she had no money for a doctor to treat her. "But if you are with your family, you do not feel like this," she continues. "It's a different problem, you see? When you have your family?" And Mendy tries to describe how, for the last three days, she has not been able to stand on her feet long enough to cook. "My kids, they have not had anything to eat. I stand up, I sit down, and I lie there. My kids cry. They say, '*Oummy,* my mom, we can call someone in Emergency to come take you!' But I say 'No! No one will take care of *you* if I go to Emergency.'"

"I agree with you one hundred percent," Alia tells Mendy, perhaps remembering that first August night ten years ago, just down the street, when she sat with her children on the carpet on the floor of her apartment, terrified herself, but knowing they believed she would protect them. "Because you are the only one who is responsible for them."

"We lost our family," Mendy says. "No one is with us. They think that I am alone." That fragility that her children sense, Mendy knows, unsettles them.

"You will not be anymore alone here," Alia reassures her, lifting the mauve scarf off her shoulders and onto her head. Alia wraps the ends of her scarf beneath her chin and tosses them behind her, then pulls out her gold-rimmed aviator glasses from her purse. "You will not be anymore alone here, *habibiti*. Tell that to your children, please."

. . .

As lonely as Mendy is, she will be okay because she knows what she wants, Alia says as we walk to her red Jetta in the parking lot, conjunto music cheerily blaring from a passing car radio. "I'm in an emergency situation and I need education," Mendy had replied when Alia asked her what she needed the Transformed Program to help her with. "I want to develop myself—not just housekeeping only." And she'd shown Alia a flier for a computer certification class at Houston Community College, worn soft from folding and unfolding. "I don't want little things," Mendy said.

"We will help you," Alia promised. And then she added, "Anything in the USA is possible."

But as we drive down Fondren Road, Alia is thinking about the husbands whose bodies were never recovered. Mendy's husband, Mina's husband. And she is remembering her own husband, too—

how she'd woken bewildered in the hospital, after the accident on the road in Sulaymaniyah which had taken Osama as she sat beside him in the car, after which she must have blacked out because she remembered nothing; how, after she'd been brought home, her brother had sat with her and said gently, "Alia, I have to tell you something." For days Osama's brothers and father tried to track down his body, while Alia desperately hoped he'd just been kidnapped—she could not believe he was actually dead. They finally paid the bribe to intermediaries of the Badr Brigade, who had assassinated him in revenge for the sorties he flew for Iraq in the war against Iran, and only then had they returned his body to his family. But all the same, his sons were no longer safe in that endless cycle of vengeance.

In Homer's *Iliad,* the great poem of war, Hector, the Trojan warrior, kills Patroclus, blood brother to Achilles, the Greek. In retribution, Achilles kills Hector. And then day after day, he hitches Hector's body to his chariot and drags it around the walls of the city of Troy. But vengeance cannot slake his grief and anger. It makes Achilles inhuman. King Priam, the father of Hector, guided by the gods to end this abomination, travels through the Greek camp at night and into the hut of Achilles to beg for the body of his son and to pay a ransom. It's only when Priam recalls Achilles to the memory of Peleus, his own father, that the fever breaks. Knowing he will never see his father again—or rather, knowing that his father, like Priam kneeling before him, will never see his son again—Achilles weeps, and in weeping, he becomes human. He gives back the body to the father.

I ask Alia if her husband is buried in Baghdad and she says that he is, with his father's family, but that she has never seen his grave. I am surprised by this, and I wonder out loud if this is due to some kind of cultural proscription. "Kim," she replies, casting herself back to that time after his death, "I find there is something strange with me. But I have it and I want to say it to you. I keep myself far from the truth. I don't want to see it with my eyes or to hear it." It is *not* common, she continues: the wife *should* go to the gravesite of her husband. "But I'm very emotional," she remembers of those days after her husband's death, "and I'm sure when I see or I hear, it will stick in my memory more. Is this selfish of me? I don't know."

But unlike Mina and Mendy, she had a body to bury. "You are lucky, Alia," an Iraqi friend had told her when they reconnected in Amman, where they were, by then, both living. "Your husband died quickly. And his family got his body and buried it in the ground. And you are here and your children are safe." *You are lucky* . . . That's what Alia had told Mina as well. Mina, whose husband, like Mendy's, had simply vanished one day. "Imagine," Alia says to me, staring off into the distant past, "in the end he is dead—and we are lucky."

3   *What We Lost*

A man is standing by the sea. A man is standing by the sea and singing near daybreak. The sea is flat and gray, but the sky, torn open in the east by a hazy sun rising behind clouds, is illuminated. Inflatable boats and orange life vests litter the stones on the shore of this nameless island in Greece, somewhere in the Aegean, south of ancient Troy. People mill about, some in neon vests—the authorities. Some are filming the man singing with their cell phones. As he sings, the man lifts his right arm and holds it out, his hand reaching back across the sea that they've sailed, toward Turkey perhaps, or beyond that to Syria. He is singing to the waters. He is wailing. "Be kind to us. It is enough, what has happened," he pleads in Arabic, building this song as he sings to carry what he has seen, drawing out the vowels like a rope cast behind him. "Oh, ocean, do not be deceptive." He has survived the journey across the sea. But many others have perished. And he fears that, in the world beyond the sea, Syria has been abandoned. "The boat holds the children and it's filled with our dreams. Oh ocean, may your waves be merciful. May your waves be a mother to us." On the distant sea, beneath the rising sun, more boats are coming.

We are crowded on Sara's couch, staring at her cell phone, at the video she is playing of the man standing by the sea and singing, dated March 18, 2016—posted almost two years before on YouTube. Young, bearded, wearing a black soccer jacket—the man could have been one of her brothers, who, along with Sara's sister's husband, had also made their way to Turkey and hired a smuggler there to get them from the coast to one of the Greek islands. From Greece, they had walked from border to border with all those other Syrians streaming through Europe to Germany.

Light can be both particle and wave. It can be both the man standing by the sea, solitary, and the slow-moving flow of the collective. Sara is showing us the video from two years before because she is trying to explain what the war has done to her particular family—her parents in Syria, her sister in Jordan, both her brothers in Germany, Sara here. But this is also what the war has done to untold numbers of Syrian families: it has shattered them.

Flipping through her phone, Sara shows Alia a photo, and Alia in turn shows it to me. It's of another bearded man, but this one is lying shirtless on a saffron-colored sheet on top of a makeshift gurney, his head bandaged, his eyes closed. "This is her husband when he was in the hospital, before he died," Alia tells me. "You see, still she keeps the picture all this time? Oh my God."

That would have been in the spring of 2013, by which time the peaceful protests in Syria that had begun two years before in the wake of the revolutions in Tunisia, Egypt, Yemen—a hopeful flowering of the Arab Spring—were being brutally crushed by the Assad government, all that optimistic energy transformed into civil war. The Syrian army was then laying siege in tanks, surrounding opposition neighborhoods, or even whole cities, cutting off access to food, water, medicine, telephones, electricity. When he was injured, Sara had told us, her husband had been trying to get food to his sister, who was living in the Al Kadam neighborhood of Damascus, held by the opposition, during a two-hour ceasefire.

At that time, Sara was living in another one of those neighborhoods—Barzeh al-Balad, in northern Damascus—with her children, her parents, and her brothers and sister in the family apartment. They also couldn't really go out for food and stayed mostly barricaded inside, not knowing what was happening around them. The government's plan seemed to involve starving the neighborhood into submission.

But it had other methods, too. The army would cut the electricity for an area and, in the night, enter with their tanks. When the lights went out, Sara and her neighbors would tell themselves darkly, "Yeah, right now they are going to kill some family." Babies, children—it didn't matter. The army slaughtered a whole family she knew—even their three-month-old. Sara has no idea why. Trying to navigate the new moral order in which everything had been turned upside down, Sara told Adam, her four-year-old son, "If you see the door opening, close your eyes and let them do it."

"It was normal," Sara says now as Alia translates for me. But Alia's voice breaks, and she tells me, confidentially, "In the beginning, I think they don't feel it"—by which she means, right now, the heinousness of a mother having to prepare her tiny boy for his own death at the hands of roving bands of men in camouflage when she may no longer be able to protect him. And the way all of this becomes ordinary. "But after a few years," Alia goes on, "they feel it."

Before Sara's husband was injured, a bus filled with infants and small children—orphans whose families had been killed in the city of Homs—was parked outside a mosque in Al Kadam. The children were being offered up to whoever could take them in. Sara had begged her husband for a baby boy, but he told her, perhaps sensing his own fate moving toward him, "Sara, I think it's enough for you, the burden of our two kids. You'll be raising them alone."

"I want to tell you a secret not even my daughter knows," Alia now says. Before the American invasion of Iraq in the spring of 2003, Alia had been overcome with a desire for another child. Her daughter was twelve, her son was ten, but nevertheless, she'd begged her husband for a baby. "You have a boy and a girl," he reasoned with her. "That's enough." And there were all those nieces and nephews in the houses all around them. But Alia had persisted. That October, half a year into the war, she missed her period. She went to see her cousin's wife, an OB-GYN, who confirmed that Alia was, indeed, very newly pregnant. When Alia went home and told her husband, he began to cry. Alia didn't understand. "You're not happy?" Alia asked him. "I'm worried about you," he told her. "This will be heavy on your shoulders." Like Sara's husband, he seemed to know death was coming for him.

At the hospital where they brought Alia after the accident in which her husband was assassinated, the sonogram showed the baby had survived. But her cousin's wife, thinking of the dead husband, the other two children, the chaos of war, told Alia, "I can help you." In Islam, because it is understood that the soul enters a fetus only after the first three months of gestation, an abortion was still possible, after all. But Alia told her, "No. This is a gift. This is a gift that's coming to me. I swear to God I will not do it. God took my husband, and he left this baby with me."

Before we leave Sara's apartment this spring morning, Sara shows us one more picture on her phone of another bearded man—or rather, goateed. And very handsome. "I have right now a story," she tells us, giggling and gauging how we will take this. The man in the photo is Iraqi, but Sara met him in Amman, Jordan, where she and her children had gone after her husband was shot. Currently this man in the photo is living in Spain. His name is Saam. He is studying political science. He also writes poetry. He has written a poem about Sara, which Sara recites from memory, prefacing her recitation by pointing out the moles on her face and chest to me and Alia. These marks become, in Saam's melodramatic verse, a sign of the beauty with which God created Sara. When his heart is beating, Saam, the lover and hero, declares, one beat is for him and the other for Sara.

Alia can barely contain her delight. "You want to marry again?" Alia asks, admiring the photo. "No, not again," Sara says. But there is mischief in her eyes. "She loves him," Alia says, turning to me. "That's why you see her happy. This is the life. We need love."

. . .

Once, in the lobby of a hotel that now lies in ruins, beside a river whose bridges have been destroyed, in a city where, the Hebrew Bible says, Jonah prophesied God's wrath if there was no repentance, Alia Altikrity fell in love. It was the spring of 1988. Iraqi warplanes had recently dropped mustard-gas bombs on the Iranian border town of Sardasht in the Kurdistan region. Oliver North and John Poindexter had just been indicted in the Iran-Contra affair. Afghanistan was at war with the Soviet Union. And the First Intifada in Palestine had begun.

This is a love story.

Alia had traveled to Mosul, which sits on the western bank of the Tigris River, across from Nineveh to the east, once part of the Assyrian Empire. Mosul was a city, in 1988, of mosques and churches dating back centuries, of museums filled with stone remnants from the ancient world, of sultan's castles gone to seed. Five bridges stitched the east and west banks together.

Alia, a university student, and her friends from the exclusive Iraqi Hunting Club, with its natatorium and tennis courts and banquet halls and gardens, had traveled with their mothers to Mosul on holiday and were staying in the five-star Nineveh Oberoi Hotel, shaped vaguely like a Mesopotamian ziggurat and overlooking the Tigris. Palm trees stood guard over its swimming pool. A Ferris wheel revolved on the grounds. The hotel catered to Baathist government officials, businessmen, dignitaries, military officers—the powerful, the wealthy, the elite.

He was an officer in the air force, staying at the Oberoi on twenty-four-hour R & R from the Iran-Iraq War. Striding through the lobby in his olive green flight suit, Ray-Bans, and Rolex, two friends, fellow officers, by his side, he spotted Alia among the other guests, who were breakfasting, and tried to get her attention. But she wouldn't acknowledge him. So he sweet-talked his way through one of her friends to the revelation of her name and where she was studying. He showed up a couple of weeks later at her university in Baghdad, having done some investigations into her family background. "I want to marry you" was the first thing he told Alia. "I'm not playing around. I'm not joking."

But Alia's mother was having none of it—even though, at first glance, she liked this hotshot young pilot, a first lieutenant in the most powerful air force in the Middle East, a guy with two or three cars, one of them a Mercedes. So when Osama showed up in his slick suit, by appointment, wanting to engage Alia, her only daughter, Alia's mother politely sent him packing.

Alia's father's family were military men from Tikrit, the same city as Saddam Hussein. Her father's father had been a general, even. And Alia's mother's father was military, too. But Alia's mother and most of her mother's relatives had been educated abroad—Egypt, Switzerland, America. Her mother's grandfather wrote books in German and English, as well as Arabic. Alia's mother dyed her hair blond and left it uncovered. She valued her personal freedom. She didn't like the life of a military wife, didn't like worrying when her husband fought in the Yom Kippur War as Arab troops tried to push Israel from the Golan Heights in Syria. And now, with Iraq in the thick of a war with Iran, she didn't want that life for her daughter either. "You are so young, Alia," her mother told her after Osama left. "The life, it is in front of you. I don't want you to be a widow."

But Osama continued to visit Alia at the university. At first, she protested. "Do not come back," she pleaded, afraid of what would happen if her parents found out. "My family will not accept you."

"I will marry you," Osama told her, "even if the whole world does not accept it."

He was older than Alia by seven years, and so handsome. He was educated. He came from a good family. But that wasn't what drew Alia to him. She was like her mother—dyeing her hair, free. She was a little spoiled, by her own admission. But he seemed to accept all of that. So Alia would get her driver, who ferried her back and forth to classes, to delay going home so she could secretly spend more time with Osama. And whenever her driver needed any little thing, he came to Alia, and Alia took care of it, no questions asked. That was the deal.

Osama, lovesick, confessed his heartbreak to his superior officer at Tel Afar Air Base up north near Mosul. Which is how Alia's father received a call requesting an appointment "to talk about Alia." And because this was Saddam Hussein's Iraq, and because this was his air force too, Alia's father could not refuse. "Again we ask if you will give the hand of your daughter to our son," said the officer—*our son,* metaphorically speaking. Alia's father, caught between his wife's wrath and Saddam's military, stalled. "I will talk with my family," he told him. "Give me some time to answer."

This delay meant a further humiliation for Osama. So in an act staged to demonstrate the intensity of his love and his suffering, he downed Percocet until he vomited and had to be taken to the hospital. From his room, Osama's mother called Alia's mother. "Please, I love my son," she beseeched. "He loves Alia, but he will kill himself."

("He didn't really want to kill himself," Alia says conspiratorially to me, suppressing a laugh, when she recounts this story.)

In the end, Alia's mother and father brought Osama flowers in the hospital. And they accepted him. Right around the time they signed the official engagement papers, in the summer of 1988, the war with Iran ended. "Your face is lucky for me," Osama told Alia. And Alia told her mother, "Now I won't be a widow."

How could they have known what was coming? Just a couple of years later, the Gulf War that would effectively destroy the Iraqi Air Force began.

But before all of that, for their honeymoon, Alia and Osama returned to Mosul, where they had met. They rented bikes and rode across one of the bridges crossing the Tigris. The Nineveh plains spread out to the east, and beyond the plains were sharp-peaked mountains. And that's where Alia had a premonition that one day she would lose her husband. The work he did in the planes he flew, even in peacetime, was dangerous. "I will never leave you," he told her on that bridge, as they paused to take a photo. "Nothing will happen if God doesn't want it to happen. But if something does happen, I know you are strong, like a lion. You can protect our future children and protect my name. I know who you are." Alia, her mind not completely eased, told him, "Please be careful, though, because really, I can't believe myself without you."

The two pilot friends with whom her husband had strode through the lobby of the Nineveh Oberoi Hotel that morning in 1988 when he first spied Alia were both, like him, assassinated. In 2014, when ISIS captured Mosul, the Oberoi became their base. The bridge where the newlyweds took their photo was destroyed by militants trying to halt the Iraqi army's advance. In 2017, when the Iraqi army retook Mosul, the hotel, littered with casings, became their outpost.

Alia says now, remembering telling Osama on that bridge that she couldn't conceive of herself without him, "I lied. I did live after him." And half to me, half to herself, she goes on: "What is life without a partner who loves you and you love him? Right now, it is only a story that I tell."

· • ·

A few weeks later we are back, checking in with Sara, who has found a new job since Alia's first visit, working in the stockroom of a nearby

99 Cents Only Store. What Sara really wants, though, is to get certi-fied as a lab technician. Being a stockist hurts her dignity, she says.

Once business has been conducted, Alia and I nestle into the faux leather stadium seat sofas. We have come to Sara's today to gather more of her story. As we hold our clear tea glasses by their delicate handles, Sara begins.

This is not a love story.

When she was fifteen, Sara fell in love with an artist. When he ar-rived at their home to propose an engagement, though, her father, an engineer, would not accept the match. When she was sixteen, she fell in love with a doctor. But he was older than her father. He, too, was summarily dispatched. Sara cried and cried after he left. "Every day you are crying about someone," her mother told her. So when Sara's uncle suggested a young man who worked for him, her mother in-vited him over.

Mohammed arrived with his mother and four sisters, all wearing black burkas, their eyes peering through the slits. Black gloves cov-ered their hands in case of accidental contact with men who were not their relatives. Sara refused at first to meet them. The burkas were a bad sign to Sara. But her uncle pressed her. "Go inside to meet them," he urged. She pulled off her hijab, rebelling with what tools she had, and went into the living room and served coffee to Mohammed and the sisters in their black burkas, her rich auburn hair swinging freely.

Maybe Sara's freedom intrigued him. Because although his mother and sisters did not accept Sara, and Sara did not accept him, Mohammed persisted. So when the engagement offer came, Sara's mother pushed her. To be married might provide protection, given Sara's love of freedom, which, in the increasingly conservative world of Syria, could be dangerous. Her mother would not leave Sara alone. "Only engage! Please! Only engage, and if you don't want him after that, we can break the engagement," her mother pleaded. So finally, Sara relented.

She tested Mohammed. She wore her scarves shorter than he thought proper. She smoked narghile. For Sara, those water pipes filled with flavored tobacco, inhaled in cafés with friends, were the defining symbol of her freedom. She told him she loved narghile, to see what he said. To see if he, too, was free. He was trying to understand her, but she made him crazy. She was nothing like the women he knew—women who bowed down to men, subservient. Again and again, Sara gave back the engagement ring. But he kept returning it to her.

In a way, it was Sara's rebelliousness, her refusal to be constricted, that ultimately tied her to him. Two months into the engagement, Mohammed's parents invited Sara's family to lunch in their home. In Sara's family, everyone sat together at meals and at gatherings. And in her home, no one ate until her mother sat down. But at Mohammed's that afternoon, men were separated from the women, and the men never called the women by name. Instead they yelled out, "Girl," when they wanted something—more water or another dish. When Sara and her parents left, her father said, "If they don't respect their women, he will not respect his wife." At home, they had Sara pile everything Mohammed had given her on the table. Then they called Mohammed. When he arrived, they said, "We are sorry. Maybe you all are better than us. But our tradition is different from your tradition." And they broke off the engagement. "Please," he told Sara's parents, "give my family time for you to understand us."

Sara felt sad about Mohammed when she saw him, come to take back all he had given her. She didn't love him, but she felt sorry for him, humiliated in this way. And she was furious with her parents. "From the beginning, I didn't accept him," she shouted. "Why didn't you listen to me?" Sara turned her face from them and said, "This is my punishment for you: I will marry him today."

The beatings started right after their wedding, in the bedroom of the family home in Al Kadam, where they lived with his parents and sisters and brothers and spouses. "If a man doesn't slap a woman, that means he's not a man," one of her sisters-in-law observed as they were all sitting together one evening. The first time Mohammed hit her, Sara jumped up on the sofa so they were eye to eye. "We are equal now," she told him as she hit him back. She was scared of him, but she hit anyway. "Change your clothes," he ordered her. "We are going to see your family."

But he clearly didn't understand her family.

"Has your wife ever slapped you?" Mohammed demanded of her father when they got there. "Do you allow girls to do that to men?"

"No," her father replied. "But why would my wife hit me? And my daughter never hit anyone. So why did she hit *you?*" When Mohammed tried to stutter out a reply, Sara's father told him, "Men don't hit women. If you were a man, you would not do that."

This is not a love story.

From the beginning she had told him that if he wanted her to wear a burka like his four sisters, he should just divorce her. And he told her, "I will never ask you to do that." But after they'd been married a few months, Sara's family planned a party to congratulate the couple— grilled kabobs and platters of rice and fresh salads with parsley and mint. Sara had planned to wear a white scarf over her hair. But when she went into their bedroom, Mohammed told her, "I will take you to your family if you put on a burka." His mother had even given Mohammed one of hers for Sara to use. So then Sara knew who was really behind the request. And maybe it was a small request, something she could do just to appease them. But she had made it clear to Mohammed that she would not wear a burka and he had been okay with that. This wasn't right and, easy or not, she wasn't doing it. "Divorce me. Divorce me right now if you want." Mohammed relented.

But after the party was over and they were preparing to leave and return to his family's home, he told her to put the burka on. Sara refused. "I will divorce you right now in front of your family if you don't," he threatened. And this alarmed Sara's mother. A divorce this early in the marriage would bring shame: people would think there was something wrong with Sara, that she had not been a virgin when they married. So her mother told Sara, "You chose him. You need to accept everything."

Sara put on the burka, so when they arrived back at the compound, Mohammed's mother thought that she had won. But she was wrong. Inside, Sara knew that no one controlled her.

That night, Sara called her aunt and begged her to come pick her up. When her aunt arrived with her sons in tow—out of propriety—Mohammed took the sons to sit in the living room with the men. Privately, Sara's aunt told her, "Your home is beautiful. Your life is good. It's only a burka. Put it on. Accept it." But then, from the living room, they heard Mohammed's mother yelling. She had gone in among the men without a scarf on purpose—a deranged echo of Sara at their first meeting. "Is it normal for people to come to our home in the middle of the night?" she shouted. Her sons were getting nervous. Sara's aunt, seeing the insanity of the situation, told Sara, "You are coming with us."

As the sons of her aunt began gathering Sara's things from the bedroom, Mohammed pulled Sara into the kitchen and started to cry. "Please don't leave," he said.

"Your life is too different from my life," she replied. She felt happy to see him crying. She knew his family didn't love her. "I can't continue with you in your life." Sara was holding the offending burka in her hands, and as they left, her aunt took it from her and threw it at Mohammed. "Give it to your mother to wear."

Later, back at her parents' home, Mohammed called Sara. "You broke our home," he told her. "I don't have a home," Sara responded. And that's when Mohammed decided to build her one, with the gold he had given her at their engagement. He carved out a small apartment, if you could call it that—just a kitchen, a bathroom, and a bedroom—inside the family home, with only a thin wall between them and his family. And for a while, their life evened out. Sara got pregnant. It would be so much harder for them to divorce now, Mohammed thought. He grew nicer because of this new security he felt. He loved her. But his family did not. And so they grew meaner.

This is not a love story.

Their son, Adam, was born. And Mohammed hit Sara again. He hit her a lot. That was his problem: he loved to hit. All of the men in that family did. It was their way, and the women just took it. But Sara was different. She started to hate Mohammed. Once, after he'd beaten her, he sat on the floor and kept saying over and over, "Please don't leave me." He wasn't stable—hitting her one minute, then begging her to stay. It was then that Sara decided: no more babies with him.

And for three and a half years, she managed to not get pregnant, even though he refused to let her use birth control. So instead, she would always get up quickly from their bed and shower, washing herself inside, which worked somehow. But Mohammed, who wanted kids—lots of them—started to grow suspicious. "Why aren't you pregnant yet?" he would ask. Then, that one time, he kept talking to her afterwards, telling her, "Don't go. Don't go."

Later, when she went for a sonogram and the doctor showed her that she was having a daughter, Sara begged for an abortion. "I'll kiss your *feet*," she pleaded. "I know the way that they treat girls," she said of her in-laws. "They don't treat them like human beings!" One of the brothers had started addressing his wife as "Animal," and she would actually come when called. "This girl," Sara said of her unborn daughter, "will not be free."

Jojo was born around the time that people were beginning to be abducted and imprisoned, when the government imposed an emergency program, quashing the peaceful protests. If they saw you on the street, if they became suspicious of you, they could take you, and nobody would ever hear from you again.

In the neighborhood of Al Kadam, some of the men had formed a patrol, watching out for government forces to warn people when they were coming. That's ostensibly why Mohammed was arrested and taken to prison. Because the neighborhood patrol, the government said, was aligned with the Free Syrian Army, bent on taking down the government of Bashar al-Assad.

He was in prison two months. When Mohammed came home, he told Sara, "Next time, if they come, I will kill myself before they take me there again." What he saw, what they did to him, he could not explain. And he also couldn't stay in Al Kadam. So he sent Sara and the kids to live with her family in Barzeh, in the north of the city. And then he did that which, before he'd been jailed, before government tanks began trundling through the streets, was unthinkable: he joined the opposition to overthrow the government because of what the government did to him.

This is a war story.

. • .

"Oh *gelby*," says Alia, Arabic for *my heart*, a term of endearment. Sara's heart is Alia's heart is suffering. On the coffee table, we have made a huge pile of leathery pistachio shells, which we've been eating while Sara tells her story. Sara is furiously stirring sugar into a fresh cup of tea.

"So did you know where your husband was fighting?" I ask Sara. "Sometimes he would contact me," she answers. At one point he was in Darayya, a suburb southwest of Damascus that for awhile became a Free Syrian Army stronghold. "Pray for me," he told her. "I think I'm in a bad situation."

And then he called Sara to give her the news that his cousin had died in the fighting, that the young man was a martyr now. "I told him, enough!" Sara tells Alia and me. "Don't stay with them! Don't keep fighting!" But Mohammed asked Sara, "Why are you saying that? I wanted to be a martyr before him, but he was taken before me. I will tell you something, Sara, and keep it in your mind," Mohammed warned. "Do not forget it. When you hear something has happened to me, say *Hasbiyallahu*," meaning "God is sufficient for me"— a prayer placing all one's trust in God. He begged her, "Please promise me you will say that?" And Sara said she would. Then for two or three days after that she kept calling his cell phone, but couldn't reach him.

Sara pauses here and takes a deep breath. "My mom would sleep with me and the kids," she begins again. "That night, we were all in bed. I had my hand on my daughter's hair. And then, at midnight, my daughter pointed up to the ceiling and said, 'My dad is there.' I looked at my mom and my mom looked at me. My daughter said, 'He sent me kisses.' And I was scared because I thought something had happened to Jojo's mind. Two hours later, I got a call from my sister-in-law and she said, 'Did you talk to Mohammed today?' I said no, not today and not yesterday either. My sister-in-law said that they had heard two hours before—I swear—that he had been injured. And when I heard that, I said *Hasbiyallahu*." This was in 2013.

Is this a war story? Is this a love story? I don't know anymore.

"So that means her daughter, her baby, recognized the truth before anyone," Alia says. And then she adds, "It is the opposite for me."

Alia tells us about a dream she had after her husband died. He had come to her and told her that the baby she was carrying would be a boy. "He will be *barakah* to you," Alia remembers her husband saying—a blessing—"and he will bring you happiness, something good in your life." Two hours later, she went into labor. But the government had imposed a curfew across Baghdad, and no one was allowed out on the streets for several hours yet. When Alia called her cousin's wife, the OB-GYN, she said, "I can't deliver you!"—because of the curfew—and then: "What happened to you, Alia? It is not your time!" The moment that the nighttime curfew ended, Alia's driver helped her into the car and they made their way to the hospital, where she was delivered of the baby who would never know his father but whose father had announced his arrival in a dream. "It is the same thing, but the opposite," Alia says to Sara, thinking of the daughter who would never know her father, but who saw him in some kind of liminal space between two worlds.

Some relic of Sara's husband might have lingered in that space for months, but in the meantime, his body lay in an improvised hospital in a basement in a bombed-out cinder block building in Yarmouk, an unofficial Palestinian refugee camp a few miles south of Damascus. Yarmouk and al-Hajer al-Aswad, which bordered the camp, were home to over 100,000 Palestinians from the Golan Heights, who had been claiming a tenuous sanctuary in this informal city-within-a-city for sixty years. Now these Palestinian refugees were at the forefront of the movement against the Assad regime. If his fellow fighters had brought Mohammed to an actual hospital, he would have been arrested. But at the makeshift hospital in Yarmouk, which was under the control, by then, of the Free Syrian Army, he was safe from prison at least.

Sara passed through the narrow streets where, only the day before, a mortar had hit. But when she arrived at the address that her in-laws had given her, the fighters guarding the building didn't want to let Sara in. "Let me just see him, at least," she pleaded. When they eventually relented, she went down a short flight of stairs and found herself in a cavernous room jammed with tables, with men lying on them or on the floor. Many were shrouded in the standard-issue gray blankets given to soldiers when they enlist. There was blood everywhere. A man cradled what remained of his arm that had been severed. The room swarmed with flies.

Mohammed was stretched out, unconscious, on a saffron-colored sheet on a table too short for his long legs, which dangled over the edge. A thick woolly brown blanket was pulled over his bare chest. His head was wrapped in white bandages and medical tape. The doctors had done their best, in these crude conditions, to remove the shrapnel that had hit him.

But because this was a makeshift hospital in the basement of a building in a refugee camp, the doctors did not know that they had missed some internal bleeding somewhere, and blood was filling Mohammed's lungs. When they realized this, because by now Mohammed was on government watch lists, his brother, who was not, brought him to Al Bassel Hospital in Damascus. He told the authorities there, "We found him injured on the street and we're just bringing him in. Nobody knows who he is and nobody knows his family." And then Mohammed's family warned Sara to stay away—in order to protect him.

As Alia listens to Sara, she wipes her eyes with a napkin that Sara has handed her and then translates some more. After Sara's husband was transferred to Al Bassel, she had gone there and taken Jojo and Adam with her. Standing outside the doors, she would try to peer in whenever they opened. Finally she asked a doctor if she could just take a look at the injured inside, that maybe there would be someone she knew. Sara could tell that the doctor saw through her, that he understood she was looking for someone specific, someone the regime would not want in its hospital, but he pretended not to pick up on any of this. And she pretended not to see what he had chosen to ignore.

Mohammed was on a ventilator. That was the only thing keeping him alive. The doctor told Sara they could detect no brain activity. And yet, with his wife and children there in the hospital beside him, Sara noticed tears seeping from Mohammed's eyes, and his heart rate on the monitor beat quicker. "His mind came back to him when he knew his kids were there," Alia says after translating Sara's story, her nose stuffy from crying. *Oh gelby, my heart.* There is a sisterhood between them, these mothers of fatherless children. One father who had been murdered because he fought on behalf of his government. The other mortally injured fighting against his.

Eventually, the doctor recommended that Mohammed be transferred to the Islamic Hospital in Amman, Jordan, away from the war zone, and his friends began making arrangements. Mohammed's mother would travel with him by ambulance. He'd cross the border on a ventilator by using his brother's passport, so that he wouldn't be apprehended. Just before he left, Sara went again to see Mohammed, this time with her own mother. Bending over him as he lay unconscious, she whispered into his ear, "You'll be all right. They will take care of you. They will take you to Jordan." And again, tears welled up through his eyelashes.

Sara left Syria two months after that, because she saw no way to continue alone in her disintegrating country with two small children. Other people stayed in Syria; if Sara had not had two small children to protect, she would have stayed too, she says.

Perhaps this is a love story. But it's complicated.

. . .

From Damascus, Mohammed's family had made arrangements to cross into Jordan with a man they knew in Daraa Governate, a region in southern Syria near the Jordanian border whose capital city is where the uprising against Bashar al-Assad had begun two years before. It was now July 2013. Sara told her parents that she would take her brother, Mustafa, with her. He was nearing the age when he'd be pressed by the regime into military service. "I would take care of him, and he would take care of me," Sara remembers thinking. "We would take care of each other."

In Kiswa, south of Damascus, a couple of men from Daraa met Sara and Jojo and Adam and Sara's brother, along with two sisters-in-law in their burkas, their eight children, and one of the sister's husbands. The other husband refused to leave Syria. The men from Daraa ferried them 100 kilometers along the Damascus-Amman highway in a livestock trailer, then across the fertile but treeless Hawran plains that stretch into northern Jordan. The men from Daraa, a Bedouin region with a tight clan structure, would likely have had ties that transcended the border between Syria and Jordan. The plains, like the people in that region, don't adhere to political boundaries.

For two days, they stayed in a farmhouse on the outskirts of the small abandoned city of El Taebah, controlled by the Free Syrian Army. "Alia, it was like a city of ghosts," Sara says. Then the Daraa men loaded Sara and their group back into the trailer and they traveled an hour or so to another city where everything everywhere was shattered. Through the open trailer, Sara could see the rubble and smell the smoke and rotting flesh. They passed some children playing in the dust, and when the kids saw the trailer, they ran after it. One of the boys, understanding that the group was leaving Syria, made a "V for Victory" sign. They were getting out and the boy was cheering them on. But Sara's sister-in-law started weeping. "No, that's not us! That's you," she yelled back to him. "You win! We are cowards. *You* are brave. You're staying here. We're leaving." Soon, the trailer had left the kids behind.

The men from Daraa brought them to a building in that broken city whose name Sara never learned. Or just the outline of a building, really, framed out in cement blocks and mortar. In the basement, they joined a growing crowd of hundreds of Syrians: mothers, fathers, children, babies, single young men, grandparents, cousins, aunts, uncles. But hovering around the crowd, milling about outside, separate from the FSA soldiers with their flak jackets and guns, were men dressed all in black. "They were people we didn't know, people who didn't look like us, people who were not part of who we are," Sara says. Their Arabic was not Syrian. Sometimes their Arabic, like this strange city, was broken.

Around 10:30 or 11 that night, two huge trucks pulled up and the FSA soldiers channeled this flood of humanity out of the basement—women and children in one truck, men in another. When they had driven some distance on the dark desert road, a string of white headlights suddenly appeared, far off but coming toward them. The two trucks stopped some meters apart, and the women were herded off and down onto the cold, hard ground. A woman beside Sara held a baby, and the baby was crying. One of the soldiers rushed over to the mother, put his hand over the baby's mouth, and told her, "You either make him stop or you kill him! They will kill all of us if they hear him!" Sara pleaded with the soldier, "Bring me my brother! If we're going to be killed, I need my brother by my side!" But eventually, the string of lights halted, and turned around, and they could see the red taillights diminishing in the distance. Only then did the truck with the men begin moving until it joined the women. Soon after that, when the trucks stopped for good, Sara's brother was beside her again and they could take care of one another.

"Do you see that tree?" the soldiers were saying now, walking through the crowd, pointing off into the far distance where Sara could barely discern an obscure silhouette illuminated by a pale light. "You need to head there. We will not go with you, but we will be watching you from here. That's the border with Jordan."

"It is like the day of judgment," Sara was thinking to herself. All these individual souls in this vast, desolate void moving together, both particle and wave, converging toward that uncertain light. Sara had a handbag over her shoulder and she was carrying Jojo and drawing a rolling suitcase behind her. Her brother held Adam's hand in one of his and pulled a second suitcase with the other. Sara was also carrying a gallon of water that her mother had given her before they left Damascus. Even though her feet started to bleed from the rocky ground they were stumbling over, Sara's heart would not give her permission to leave this water in the desert, this parting gift from her mother, whom she might never see again in this life. Around her, other mothers' little children were tripping on the stones in the dark, and the night was so black that she could not see her son's hand in front of her. How easy it would be to lose him in this abyss. When a man stumbled and fell down beside her, Sara turned reflexively to try to help him, but her brother yelled at her to *Leave him! Leave him! Go, go, go!* And they walked on, she had no idea how long. They were not thinking about time. There was no time anymore.

And then they were at the border and time and space began again.

At the crossing, they found themselves being funneled through a narrow gate. Sara was holding her kids and her suitcases. "And at that moment, when they opened the gate, Alia," Sara says, "I turned my face back toward Syria." Sara's voice is wavering now. She must pause between words in order to catch her breath to say them. "And I felt like someone had reached into my chest and pulled my heart from my body and thrown it on the ground. And only my body entered."

A security guard welcomed her, saying, "You're in the land of the Nashama"—meaning those Bedouin of this region before borders divided it, men who host their visitors honorably and protect them. But when he saw the tears in Sara's eyes, he asked her, "Did you lose your husband? Did you lose your children? Why are you crying?"

The Arabic word *watan* is often translated as country or homeland. But it signifies so much more than that. Your *watan* is the place where you belong, the place which gives you dignity, the place where everything that you love dwells. Sometimes husbands use this word to describe their wives. That's the word Sara used in response to the man from the land of the Nashama, when he asked if she had lost something. "We lost our country," Sara told him. "We lost our homeland. We lost everything." And then her body moved with all the other bodies through the narrow gate into a foreign land.

4 *The Storm inside the Story*

In August 2008, my husband and our three daughters and I camped our way through the canyon lands out west—the Grand Canyon, Arches, Bryce, Zion, Mesa Verde—nomads for a brief season, carrying everything essential in our station wagon. At a farmer's market in Moab, Utah, a place named for the biblical territory east of the Jordan River, I remember how a geologist who looked like the desert prophet Edward Abbey explained to me that the landscape we were driving over, with all its striated stone formations, had once been the floor of a sea. Which I took as a warning, a reminder to remember how small we are.

We came home from that trip, my journal indicates, the day before Alia arrived with her three children in Houston. Just over a month after that, Hurricane Ike hit Galveston and roared inland toward us.

By then, Alia and the kids had been here just long enough for Haneen, Alia's teenage daughter, to grow thin and weak with despair. She was getting Facebook messages from her friends at the International School in Jordan, where she'd been at the top of her class. She spoke Arabic, obviously, and also French. But here, though her English was better than that of many of the kids in her school in southwest Houston, where their resettlement agency had placed them, she didn't speak Spanish like them. Haneen cried every day. "I'm lost in America!" she told Alia. "This is not *my* dream." One afternoon, Haneen fainted. Her blood pressure was very low, and the doctor who examined her told Alia, "Please take care of her. Inside, she is broken."

And then, Hurricane Ike. The day before it hit, her caseworker had stopped by to warn Alia that a hurricane was coming and to drop off a plastic bin filled with cotton balls, Band-Aids, antibiotic ointment, aspirin, a flashlight. "If anything happens, don't leave the apartment," he warned her. "Take your kids and sit in the closet together." But the closets in her apartment were barely big enough for one person. From the small window, Alia could see her neighbors carrying bags to their cars and then the cars leaving until the complex seemed desolate. Alia had no car, and even if she had, she knew no one and would have had nowhere else to go.

The other Iraqi refugee family had stayed, though, and when the rains started, Alia called them, hoping they'd invite her over to sit with them, the way, during the shelling and bombing in Iraq, she had sat together with her in-laws and their children. But they only told her, "Keep the phone by your side. You can call us if you need something." The night came. And the winds. The lights went out. Alia kept her kids close. Mustafa slept, but Haneen was shaking. Alia had asked God to give her a sign that she should come to this place. But now she was asking herself if she had run from death and traveled over those seas only to die here in this cheap apartment in an America she could not recognize from the version that had been in her head. Lines from the Qur'an about the end of the world kept washing over her:

When the sky is torn
When the stars are scattered
When the seas are poured forth

When the tombs are burst open
Then a soul will know what it has given
   and what it has held back

Then the roof above them gave way and water from the upstairs neighbor's bath came pouring in.

. . .

As soon as she had arrived, Alia's resettlement agency helped her get a Social Security card and apply for food stamps and Medicaid, and they were paying her rent for now, but she knew she was supposed to be self-sufficient within four months of her arrival. The hurricane and the subsequent power outages had brought the city to a standstill, but the clock for her was still ticking.

Meanwhile, the English classes her agency enrolled her in took place at her apartment complex, which was convenient, since she had no car, but most of the other students, refugee women too, from Burma, Nepal, Congo, Afghanistan, didn't seem to have had much education and many were just now learning their ABCs. Being placed with them made no sense to Alia, so she stopped attending. But she had no skills to make up for her lack of language. In Iraq, other people did everything for her. And her degree in business administration had been more or less for show. Here in America, without English, her education was essentially useless.

The director for her resettlement agency called Alia in as the four-month deadline approached. For the meeting, Alia put on an elegant black tunic and pants, and a silky black and white jacket. But when the director sat her down, she told Alia bluntly, "You need to work. You need to learn English. By next week, you need a job. We can't continue to pay your rent after this month." And she was right. That was the deal. That's how the refugee resettlement system worked, whether you came here with a husband, whether you were young and unattached, whether you were a single mother with three children: you had to work here in America. Alia understood it all—intellectually.

"What about babysitting?" suggested the director. "What about housekeeping?" But this had been the rub up until now. It paralyzed Alia to think about working part-time for minimum wage, taking a bus two or three hours round-trip, leaving Mustafa in the daycare center her agency had recommended, where the children had runny noses and the rooms smelled like dirty diapers—to do all of this and still not be able to pay her bills. It made no sense to Alia.

But it was more than that. In Iraq, Alia had had housekeepers and babysitters. She'd had gardeners and cooks, drivers and tutors. She'd stayed at luxury hotels where they served continental breakfasts in the lobby. But she didn't have the language to explain now who she was—who she had been—in Iraq. And the chasm between *that* Alia and the Alia this director seemed to see was like a gash in her dignity.

"I can't," though, was all Alia could say.

"If you can't, then I can't pay any more checks for your rent," the director replied, irritated.

"It is hard," Alia said, because that was all the English she possessed to try to explain her family's place in the Iraq that no longer existed. "I can't." And then she just cried.

The director reached into a drawer and pulled out a box of tissues. She came around from behind her desk and hugged Alia. "Don't cry," she said, more gently now. "Let me explain how the resettlement program works."

But Alia knew all of that. "Don't explain," Alia told her. "But you ask me to do something that is very hard for me. I can't do it."

All that she had been through before—the invasion of her country, the assassination of her husband, the bombings, the body in the plastic bag that she'd run over in her driveway where once all her nieces and nephews had played, a body without a head, dumped there by whom and for what purpose she did not know, though the lights from the American tanks kept it illuminated all night, just outside the huge glass windows of her house, making it impossible to look away—all of that trauma was on one side of the equation, but the trauma of life in America was on the other. In Iraq, if she lost everything, she could live with some cousin or other. But here, there were no cousins. Here there was no one, and she'd be put out on the streets. America had been a terrible miscalculation. She called her brother, Ahmed, in Jordan. "Shred your asylum case with the UN," she told him. Why should he suffer, too, as a refugee in the United States? "Buy an apartment in Amman. It is a big mistake to come here!"

On the plane over the waters of the Atlantic, Alia had prayed to God to give her someone to guide her in America. And in the dream before she left Jordan, her husband had told her to go. "I will be with you," he'd said. "You're not alone." But she was alone.

.   .   .

Through the peephole, Alia could see two young men. "*As-salaam alaikum,*" one of them said—*Peace be upon you.* "We have heard that you are a single mother here with three kids," the other said in English, while the first translated what he was saying into Arabic. "We know that you are struggling and we have come to help you to resettle and to acclimate to the environment here."

As Alia stood on the other side of the door, listening to those Arabic words after three or more months of trying to make herself understood in the barest of English, she felt the wall that separated her from everyone else here start to dissolve. She hesitantly opened the door.

Though she didn't know it then, the young men were students at the University of Houston, in the process of founding what would become Amaanah Refugee Services. One of those men was Ghulam Kehar, the nonprofit's first CEO. A couple of years before, Ghulam and a group of college friends, feeling inspired to do some kind of service project, collected money to buy some groceries to donate to people in need. In asking around, trying to find a family to whom they could give what they had gathered, they heard about a Somali refugee family. The students hadn't understood much about refugees, didn't know they were living in Houston. When they went to visit the family and found fourteen or fifteen people living in a three-bedroom apartment in southwest Houston, Ghulam and the other students thought, *This doesn't seem normal.*

They started investigating and learned about the limitations of the federal refugee resettlement program, how it could offer only about six months of assistance at most, and they resolved to do something about it. For a couple of years, they continued to collect food, clothing, furniture, whatever. Then, as they were finishing their degrees, they started Amaanah Refugee Services—*amaanah* meaning trust or responsibility in Arabic, because they felt, as citizens of the city, it was their responsibility to welcome people who were coming here and to help them rebuild their lives, to step in where the aid from resettlement agencies, by necessity, left off.

That afternoon, as Ghulam and the translator sat with Alia, listening, the desperation poured out of her. "Don't worry," Ghulam told her. "We will be with you."

Ghulam called the director of Alia's resettlement agency and had the period of financial support extended from four to six months. Seeing Haneen, emaciated and distressed, not wanting to go to school, Ghulam and his team helped the family to move to an apartment in a complex filled with other Iraqi refugees in another part of town where the schools were stronger. He became a kind of older brother to Alia's son Habib. They found a preschool for Mustafa. They assisted Alia with rent after the six months ended, and helped her through the process of purchasing a car she could afford. They enrolled her in English classes and set her up with a part-time job babysitting. And this time, Alia embraced the work that before had seemed so humiliating, so far from who she thought of herself as.

Her husband had not left her alone after all. And God had sent her a guide. She and the children now had a network of people watching over them. And Alia wanted to build her children up upon this new foundation. "Be something good," she would tell them. "You see the people who helped us to be like this? Give love to all the people around you." This was her philosophy now. And she would repeat it to all three kids. "God, he gave us two hands. One hand is for giving, and the other hand is to receive. If you will not give, you cannot receive. Help someone, and someone will help you."

. . .

One spring afternoon, Alia invites me to help her deliver rental assistance checks to the leasing offices of the apartment complexes where the nearly thirty women of the Transformed Program live. We start in the Gulfton area, the most densely populated neighborhood in Houston and one that city officials have taken to calling the Ellis Island of our era because it's inhabited almost entirely by immigrants. In these three square miles live 40,000 residents—most likely a massive undercount because many are undocumented and fearful of deportation. They speak over fifty languages. But the apartments, thrown up in the 1970s to house single young oil boom workers migrating south from the Rust Belt, are now dilapidated and overcrowded, their cramped asphalt parking lots unsheltered by trees. Playgrounds and swimming pools and clubhouses are almost unheard of. These complexes are not the Lower East Side tenements of the late nineteenth century, but they can, nevertheless, feel pretty bleak.

Still, the entrepreneurial spirit is thriving, and as Alia and I drive the streets of Gulfton, we pass a tiny Ethiopian shop on the ground floor of The Alliance, one of the five resettlement agencies in this city, where I'd once bought a typical Ethiopian street snack of roasted barley and peanuts called kolo, and where they also sell berbere, a spice mixture that is key to the cuisines of Ethiopia and Eritrea, and rounds of spongy injera flatbread. All the restaurants and markets in Gulfton like this one point to another kind of American dream—a landscape of longing and imagination, arcing back toward the irretrievable past while trying to make use of that past in the present.

This idea of the past being carried forward even as it's been left behind seems related somehow to the conversation that Alia and I are having as she drives and I type addresses into her phone and call out directions. I remind Alia of this thing she'd said to me when we were with Sara a few days before, as Sara was telling us about how she had told her son, if soldiers arrived to kill them, to just close his eyes and let them do it. How this had been normal. "In the beginning I think they don't feel it," Alia had said. But over time, they do. And then she'd confessed, "Right now, this is happening with me." Alia finds herself crying more often lately. Her doctor told her, "You went through so many things. And your personality, you are very emotional. If a glass is full with water, just another drop will make the water run over."

The traffic on the street is reflected in the iridescent green lenses of Alia's aviator glasses. She continues. "Right now Sara is busy building a new life here. And it takes all her attention, all her power. She *needs* to forget what happened to her before. But after a while, if she has empty time, she will remember. She will think a lot about what happened to her before, and the memory will be refreshed." Forgetting, or not remembering, "is the secret to the life, to continuing to live," Alia says. "I tried to build my kids with zero memory about the past. But with my clients, every time when I try to not remember, they remind me. I can't forget my story because I see it through their stories. I feel it when they say it. Before, I had only one story. Now I carry twenty-eight stories"—the stories of her current clients. "Twenty-eight stories are with me now."

Alia runs in to drop off the rental assistance check, and then we head back onto the streets clotted with yerberias and hookah lounges and Whataburgers. Alia says that maybe part of the reason, too, that these stories weigh on her, part of the reason she is crying so often, is that she understands what is coming for these single mother refugees: the struggle to get healthcare, the exploitation at work, the snags that come with food stamps and Medicaid, the difficulty in finding English classes that fit their schedules, the lack of childcare even if they do. She sees the separation coming between Mina and her daughter. She sees the hunger and loneliness that will haunt Mendy. Each woman only has the capacity to deal with the problems immediately in front of her. But Alia now has a kind of tragic vision. "Maybe," she speculates, "because I'm outside the story, I see the story better than her. Because she is in the storm inside the story."

. . .

Back in 2008, after the hurricane, after Amaanah knocked on Alia's door, as her English was improving, Ghulam asked Alia to translate for an Iraqi client who was having some issue with her rent. And even though Alia wasn't sure her English was good enough yet, she wanted to do anything she could to help, to pay it all back. And it worked. She got the ideas across. So Ghulam asked her to help again. And again. And again. Whenever he would hear about an Arabic-speaking refugee, particularly those single mothers who were struggling, he'd ask Alia to translate. And when Alia did, she'd hear what they needed, and she began to see what she could do—enroll the women in English classes, try to hook them up with jobs, make a trip to the furniture bank. Soon she was working with other single mothers, women who spoke neither Arabic nor English, and she'd have to grab someone—a child, a neighbor, a caseworker on the phone—to translate from Burmese or Tigrinya or Swahili or Dari into English. And somehow she managed to understand and to be understood. This was empowering, but also healing in some deep way—to help women who had come here alone with their children, strangers in a strange land. In 2011, she became the first full-time employee of Amaanah Refugee Services.

Alia is a woman who believes in signs. When she dreamed that her husband told her "Go," the night before she left Jordan for the US, Alia saw that as a sign that the risk she was taking would be worth it. But when the hurricane hit just weeks after their arrival in Houston, she worried it was a sign that she had made a mistake. This spring afternoon, as we navigate the streets of southwest Houston, our conversation punctuated by stops at leasing offices scattered across land that had once been a prairie, Alia tells me that she sees in her work among the widows and orphans another sign. "When I do something for them, and I see their happiness, this gives me a message," she explains. The message Alia hears is this: "What happened to you pushed you to ask yourself, 'Who are you *now*?'" And Alia realized that she was no longer the woman from Mansour in Baghdad, who could shop for gold jewelry like it was groceries. She realized that her purpose was to help refugee women and their children, all strangers to her. "So it is fair in the life," she says, "what happened to me before."

"Because, Kim," Alia goes on, "what makes a person sad? When he feels something that happens is unfair. And this question is coming to him: *Why?* I remember this happened to me when I came here." The hurricane had hit Houston, Alia was out of money, her kids were not happy in school. "And it came to me, that situation," she concedes.

"The feeling that this is not fair, this is unjust?" I clarify.

"I couldn't say it. It would bother me a lot, if I said it. But I felt it."

"You didn't want to admit it, even to yourself?"

"Exactly. But what happened after that"—the work with Amaanah—"that is what made me feel it is fair. To become who I am now—seeing the happiness in my clients' faces."

We had left the clutter of Gulfton behind and made another drop-off at a complex near Braes Bayou, which had flooded the year before during Hurricane Harvey. I remember driving through the area afterward, the lawns obscured under piles of matted insulation and water-logged sheetrock, moldy furniture and household belongings.

"I love your way of talking with me," Alia says as we head back north up Fondren, passing her first apartment in the city. "You know, when you're asking me questions, you help me know myself more. I go back to remember who I am. Because sometimes I forget myself."

As we drive on, Alia continues to think about the happiness she can see in the women she guides, the way the work has shaped her. Back in Iraq, in her mother country, she had lived in that house with crystal chandeliers and mirrored walls and floor-to-ceiling windows, the house that was protected by virtue of the power of the people in it. Within that house, everyone did everything for her—the cooking and cleaning and laundry, the driving, the tutoring, the gardening, the shopping. She did nothing for anyone else. She lived a life of privilege among the privileged, never crossing borders. Then that life was obliterated. And she found herself in Houston.

"When I came here and I started looking around," Alia continues, "I saw many people who were different from my color, different from my religion. They were nice to me. They called me *sister*. All of us, we are equal. The only difference is if someone is nice or bad. I got this point from here and I respect it and love it. This point makes me who I am—positive, happy, nice to people. Nice inside. Because before, I feel I was not nice inside. Now, I am more human."

In the Book of Deuteronomy, Moses delivers a sermon to the Israelites on the plains of Moab, east of the Dead Sea, overlooking the Promised Land, as their forty years of wandering in the desert are coming to an end. "Do not deny justice to the foreigner or the fatherless," he exhorts them, "and do not take the widow's cloak as security. Remember, you were slaves in Egypt and the Lord your God redeemed you from that place." Widows and orphans and strangers. In the Hebrew Bible, in the Gospels, in the Qur'an, in all the holy books, it's the same: these are those that God demands, again and again, that people care for and protect. Catastrophe may be looming, though we think we're safe, whether in a mansion in Saddam Hussein's Iraq or in an old house in a quiet neighborhood in Houston. One day soon, we could ourselves be the foreigner, the fatherless, the widow, dependent on others' justice and generosity for our salvation. That's what it means to be human. We are all created equal in that fragility. *Remember.* A modern Pharaoh was overthrown in Egypt during the revolution in 2011. And the plains of Moab that once pointed the Israelites to the Promised Land are in present-day Jordan, home to refugees from Palestine, Iraq, Syria, Yemen, Sudan, Somalia, Algeria, Libya, Ethiopia, and so on. And there is a Moab in America too, which was once the bottom of a sea and is now a desert. But the America to which Alia had come, which to so many strangers had been the Promised Land, seemed to be forgetting, in 2018, what Moses said God said.

II Between the Ground and Sky

"You're not in the sky. You're not on the ground.
You are in between.
This is the worst part of the whole story."

5 *In the Garden of Bitter Fruit*

It was May, just before the start of Ramadan, and Alia had traveled to Amman for the wedding of a niece, her brother's daughter, who had been a little girl in the SUV when their families fled Iraq for Jordan. While she was gone, I passed the time by tagging along with Deeshown, another Amaanah case manager, as she visited some of her clients. On this muggy morning, I wasn't quite sure where I was going. Deeshown had texted me the address—a public housing project bordered by the light rail line just north of downtown Houston, far from the epicenter of refugee resettlement on the southwest side of town—and when I pulled in, all of the squat buildings in each of the sectors looked pretty much the same. But when I saw the African wax cloth fabric draped over a clothesline—hypnotic geometric patterns and stylized images from nature, a vibrant dream world coming into creation—I figured I was in the right place. As I turned onto the cement walkway leading to the stoop of Elikya's apartment, I noticed something else distinctive among the drab brick units with their yards of fraying grasses, barren except for satellite dishes: a tiny, riotous vegetable garden.

Elikya, dressed in a tunic and matching pants of more red and blue wax cloth embroidered with gold thread, hair cut in bangs and a bob, was cooking chicken in an aluminum pot in the cramped kitchen, only wide enough for one person, onto which the apartment opened. She turned down the heat and led us into the adjacent living room, its furniture overstuffed and oversized for the small space, with a dark, imposing cabinet that covered up the only window. A garland of red silk flowers strung high on one wall, bordering the ceiling, added a touch of brightness to the otherwise claustrophobic space. On the couch and chairs, cornflower blue embroidered fabric squares had been laid out neatly on the seats and armrests. A lamp stood in the corner with branching lights, a fountainhead of crystal.

That day I listened as Deeshown, through a Swahili interpreter on speakerphone, went over details for the English classes Elikya was taking at her resettlement agency, the pain in her shoulder that wouldn't go away, the bill that she'd received from the hospital for emergency care, her work cleaning office buildings downtown at night for $7.50 an hour. Elikya didn't like working nights. She had a house full of children and grandchildren she was trying to raise, and she needed to be home to watch over them. She also needed beds and mattresses.

As Deeshown and I left the apartment and stepped out, blinking, into the sunshine, I looked again at the garden, sprouting from this otherwise desolate scrap of hard-packed clay. In the fecund jumble, I could tease out okra and some kind of squash and peppers. The other plants I did not recognize. But Elikya had said, when I told her about my writing work with refugee women in Houston, that I could come back to talk with her, so I'd have another chance to ask. I could not have known it then, but over time I would come to understand that the story of Elikya's garden in this housing project beside the train line is also the story of her displacement and wandering, of everything she lost along the way. And it's her answer to that story, too—an act of reclamation.

· • ·

"She's asking if you want to hear the story from when she was still in Africa?" says my translator, Pierrine, herself from a town on the border between Rwanda and Congo. We are sitting across from Elikya and I have just explained again about my work following the stories of some of the women in the Transformed Program, how I'm not with Amaanah or the government or a news organization, because I sense there is some confusion. And then Elikya hands me a laminated UNHCR Proof of Enrollment paper from the Bwagiriza refugee camp in Burundi, a document she has clearly retrieved before our arrival in order to show me, as if she needs proof somehow of the story she will tell. It lists the names and birth dates and has photos of the eight children and grandchildren that she brought with her to Bwagiriza, and their address in it: Camp II, Quartier 29, Cellule D. I wonder how many times with how many officials Elikya has had to go over the harrowing details of her story, to prove her desperation.

"Wherever she wants to begin," I say.

"When she was young, before she started school, war began," Pierrine translates. This was in Bukavu, the capital city of South Kivu province in eastern Congo, on the shores of Lake Kivu, one of the African Great Lakes strung along a rift valley. On the other side of the lake lies Rwanda. Her father worked as an accountant, and on the land they owned in the city her mother grew beans and cassava to feed the family, as well as fruit trees—orange, papaya, guava, avocado.

The country had, in 1960, gained its independence from Belgium, and by the time Elikya was born in 1966, it had been renamed Zaire by its president, Mobutu Sese Seko, who took over in a coup supported by the United States, and then promptly had his Soviet-backed predecessor assassinated. Elikya thinks that she must have been about six or seven when the war started, because back then, before they counted ages in years, you didn't go to school until you could lift one arm up and drape it over your head, then touch your other ear with your hand. ("I remember that," Pierrine says to me as she's translating. "That's like forty years ago. I remember that too.") It was about a month after the rebels had come and ruined everything where they lived, and stolen what they had—it was about a month after that that Elikya started school.

Elikya's father came from the village of Mumosho, south of the city and just a mile or so from the Ruzizi River that formed the border with Rwanda. Her father's father was the chief of that village, whose families lived and farmed among the lush green hills that fanned out from the market center. Because banana trees produced in such abundance there, often when her father would take his children to visit, the people would make kasiksi, the traditional fermented banana beer. But the liquor being only for the elders, her father would ask the brewers for glasses of fresh squeezed juice instead for Elikya and her brothers and sisters.

Elikya loved to go to Mumosho during the seasonal planting of beans and corn. She loved when her aunts and uncles, the people of the village, would take her with them to help, loved to watch what they were doing and to try to learn. When they dug up the cassava roots out of the ground, she could see how they peeled the tubers with knives in order to dry it, and how later they would grind it into flour. When they harvested the corn, they would bring buckets full to cook over a fire, and they'd all eat their fill there in the village among the green mountains. When it was time for her family to go back to Bukavu, they'd be loaded down with more fresh corn, along with all kinds of fruit, and chicken meat and eggs.

Not all of the children liked to help as much as Elikya. But they had a saying: "If you don't like to help, you will not enjoy the blessings from the elders." Meaning, if your grandfather, for example, sends you to do something, and you stomp your feet and resist, you will never receive the fruits that come from the ground. But if you gladly obey, your grandfather will pull you close. "Oh my sweet child," he will say and he will spoil you rotten.

When she was in the sixth grade, Elikya's father told her that she would be marrying a captain in the army twenty years her senior, the son of a friend of his. The man had offered a dowry for her. But this didn't make any sense to Elikya—he was so old, and she was so young. She couldn't get her mind around it, though she knew that sometimes even babies, nestled within the wombs of their mothers, were already betrothed. But before the wedding with the soldier could take place, Elikya ran off to her uncle's home and he took her in and enrolled her in school. That's where she stayed until, at fifteen, her grandmother and an aunt came to bring her back. They said she must follow the orders of her father. That was in 1982. Her first three pregnancies she miscarried.

Soon after she had at last given birth to a daughter and a son, her husband, a colonel now, was deployed on a military operation in Kibarizo in South Kivu province. Even then, back in 1986, Mobutu's dictatorship, precariously propped up on cronyism and corruption, could barely maintain state control in the east. Instead, a confusion of militia groups and warlords and rebels struggled for power, often in an attempt to command some source of mineral wealth—gold, copper, diamonds, coltan. Elikya's husband's unit wore braided violet cords around their shoulders as part of their uniform. And they had among themselves a secret code, spoken in Lingala, a Bantu language and the official language of the military, to suss out potential enemies: "Mokili"—*The world*—a soldier would start. "Mokili ngonga"—*The world's time has arrived*—was the proper response. But the rebels must have got to some of the soldiers. Maybe beat them until they gave away the secret code. Stole the violet cords. Seeped in among the unit. They wanted the ammunition and satellite equipment that the soldiers carried.

Her husband had, under his own command, twenty-six soldiers as well as four escorts. Ten soldiers died in the initial gunfire. They were the lucky ones. The rebels executed her husband's escorts, then bound her husband's hands and legs. They said they would make of him an example for his people back home, and they castrated him so he could never have any more children. Then they cut off his ear. After that, they cut off one ear from each of five of the soldiers too— because they didn't listen, the rebels said, with brutal logic. When the soldiers refused to eat their own ears, the rebels killed them. The remaining soldiers they forced to perform sexual acts upon each other. Many of these men died soon after. *Mokili. Mokili ngonga.*

He was in the hospital four months. Elikya was still young. She couldn't handle living with no husband. But then afterward, when he was home, they were always fighting. They were like two women. "What can I do? It's the rebels that ruined me," he told Elikya.

She was barely twenty. What was she supposed to do, married to a man who had no functionality? He said what had happened to him had to be kept between them. But he gave her permission, if she wanted, if she felt the need, to sleep with another man. He told her to go to a bar, get drunk. But she said no. She was not accustomed to that. So she ran off again, this time back home to her family.

But her in-laws tracked her down and all of them, even her parents, told her that because she had agreed to take her husband when he was healthy, she could not abandon him now. No other woman would ever have him. And besides, there had been no problem between Elikya and her husband, or between the families, but if they divorced and Elikya married again, there would be. They said it was her burden to remain. But they did agree to pay a second dowry.

It was a devil's bargain. In order to have more children, in order to hide her husband's shameful mutilation, she would have to let his brothers rape her—though they didn't call it that. And when they raped her—and she knew that's what it was, even if she couldn't call it that—she had to hide that too. Life continued. Four other children arrived to join the first two that she'd had with her husband.

It was in those years that the land again rose up to offer a kind of consolation. After the atrocities that her husband suffered and the way they maimed him, he could see that Elikya was not happy. So he said to her, "We should try to figure out our life, plan our future. We can't rely on the military. Tomorrow I might die. If we prepare today, that will help our children tomorrow." And together they drove south out of Bukavu a hundred miles or so to Kipupu, the village of his family, among low mountains surrounded by deep forest. They traveled with a military transport because the roads were largely impassable. Although Zaire, as it was still called then, possessed more wealth in untapped natural resources than any other country in the world, it could not take care of some of the most basic needs of its citizens.

In the village of Kipupu, Elikya cooked the food they had brought, and her husband's people showed her one of the mountains and said that was where she could farm. So her husband and some of the other men took their machetes and cut down the trees and burned them. And after two weeks, when the ashes had cooled, Elikya prepared more food, along with kasiksi, the traditional beer. They invited people from all around to come and plant seeds. And when the seeds sprouted, her husband returned to his military camp and Elikya stayed in Kipupu.

Mostly she grew corn. She raised cows and goats as well. At harvest time, she would again cook food and serve beer to those who came to help her. Another day it would be another person's turn to cook, another person's fields to pick. And after the harvest came the grinding, all by hand, after the corn had been fermented in water for four days, then laid out to dry on mats made of woven reeds or banana leaves. After grinding, they'd fill cloth sacks with the flour.

Nearby, men working in the gold mines, patrolled by armed groups as well as by the Congolese military, would come to Kipupu for supplies. In exchange for their small flecks of gold, Elikya would sell them bags of the flour she and the other women had ground. From time to time, she'd travel to the city of Uvira to exchange this gold for currency. In those years, Elikya made a lot of money.

Sometimes Elikya would visit her husband in Bukavu, and sometimes her husband would come to Kipupu. He was coming, at least in part, to check on the mines and his farms. Elikya's husband, the colonel, would get permission to travel to Kipupu from the commander in Bukavu. He knew he could not return to his boss empty-handed—having been told, in fact, by the commander the kinds of resources he should bring back.

The thing is, the system of corruption that governed the country, and South Kivu, the province where Elikya was from, that system was embedded in everybody's minds. The colonel would lean on the village heads in and around Kipupu. They had the information he wanted on the ground there—where to get what he would need to bribe the commander. He had to treat them right.

The corruption infiltrated everything—a cancer feeding on the country, rotting it. Elikya would often travel with her husband away from Kipupu on missions throughout the east. The children would be scattered among relatives or else brought along as well. Because when rebels came to a village, they demanded to know how many military families lived there. *How many? How many? If you don't tell us, we'll kill you—all of you.* That is why Elikya tried to camouflage her children among her husband's brothers' families.

Once, she went with her husband to Kilembwe to collect ivory, the way the military collected gold from the mines as well—all part of the system of payoffs and protection. It was probably 1987 or 1988. In Kilembwe, they were sitting in an open-air shelter beneath a mango tree when a guy on a motorcycle stopped and said hello, then talked for a while to some of the higher-ranking officers. Later, after he rode off, they realized the guy had been Laurent Désiré Kabila, the once and future president of the Democratic Republic of the Congo (DRC), but at the time a revolutionary rebel fighting to overthrow Mobutu.

They sent the ivory on to a military transport center and ordered a group of soldiers off to get supplies. By the time Elikya and her husband arrived at the center, those soldiers radioed in that they had ambushed rebels in the area. Elikya's husband had them brought in and interrogated. They confessed they were working for Kabila. They said that they had heard that working as a rebel against the government paid more than being a soldier for the government, where they had to fight the rebels and dig in the mines. They told Elikya's husband that when the rebels would run out of ammunition, they'd bribe a local military commander, who would then let the rebels pretend to move in and overpower the government soldiers, and the soldiers would pretend to flee. Then the rebels would collect ammunition and supplies. Afterward, the commander would communicate with his superiors about the "attack." In that system, the one embedded in everyone's mind, no one could do the right thing. Even though you worked, you didn't get paid. Or if you did get paid, it wasn't enough. And it wasn't just soldiers. It was also teachers, doctors, nurses, police. So you did what you had to do to survive.

Eventually, after the 1994 Rwandan genocide, a million Hutu refugees streamed into eastern Zaire and launched attacks from the refugee camps there against the Tutsi government across the border in Rwanda. The corrupt Mobutu regime, aligned with Hutus, was a conduit for arms shipments to guerilla fighters. But in 1997, Kabila, with the support of Tutsis in Rwanda and Uganda, captured the capital, Kinshasa, and declared himself president. And then the renamed Democratic Republic of the Congo became the site for wars that pulled in countries from across the continent. Millions died—more than in any conflict since WWII. Kabila was assassinated in 2001, only to be replaced by his son, Joseph. The wars officially ended, but the killing, the rape, the forced starvation, the destruction of whole villages, the constant displacement continued.

And over the years, the region around Kipupu, that remote village where Elikya and her husband had their farm and cows and goats and mines, had become an epicenter for scores of rebel groups. They wanted control of the mines. They wanted power. They wanted vengeance. And they needed supplies to continue their attacks. These desires often intersected. Perhaps that was the case when, in 2005, they killed Elikya's husband.

By then, Elikya was no longer living year-round in Kipupu, so after the death of his parents, she and her husband had traveled back over the treacherous roads, to be with his brothers and sisters. The night they arrived, Elikya hid her six children one by one among various in-laws so that, if they were attacked, it would only be her and her husband. But even then it was already too late. Somehow some rebel group had found out that the colonel was in town. Like a cinched belt, they circled the house where Elikya and her husband and his security detail were staying.

The world's time had arrived.

They pounded on the doors and broke in and, guns waving, woke everyone up, ordered everyone *Down on the floor, Down on your stomachs.* They demanded cell phones. Then they dragged in the sister of Elikya's husband and tried to force her to have sex with her brother. "Are you joking?" Elikya's husband said. "I can't! I can't! Do whatever it is you want to do." So they shot him. And then they came for Elikya. "We'll do whatever we want with you. If we kill all of you, who's going to send news back where you came from? There won't be anyone." She was saved only by a soldier who arrived and fired warning shots into the air.

Here is what Elikya did not know:

That the aunts in whose care the two eldest of Elikya's children had been placed, upon hearing about the ambush, ran away with the teens to try to save them.

That they took them north to the city of Uvira.

That from there, they crossed into Burundi, thinking they would go to the refugee camps in Tanzania.

That it would be years before she would find those two children again.

The soldiers took Elikya to the military camp in nearby Minembwe and housed her with war widows from across the region, telling her that, for now, there was nowhere else she could go. But she saw that it was no place to keep her four remaining children. So she handed them over to various aunties to protect.

In the camp, she waited. She waited for the papers that would give her the rights to her husband's full salary, which was her due. But if the government didn't pay the living, why would they pay the wives of the dead? Even if she could have returned to Kipupu, with her husband gone the land she had farmed no longer belonged to her.

Months passed. Because the camp in Minembwe, in the high tropical mountains, was so vulnerable to attack, the women had a strategy to try to save themselves from rape. If they heard the rebels coming, they would slather their private parts with mayonnaise and try to convince the attackers that they had gonorrhea. The night they came for Elikya, she tried that trick. "I'm ill," she said, and showed them.

"We saw you walking in the market," they shouted.

"I was just forcing myself," Elikya pleaded.

As they battered her face, they said, "You used to think you were all that when your husband was alive. But now you are nothing." And with the butts of their guns, they beat her until she passed out.

For days afterward, Elikya stumbled on footpaths heading east through the mountain forests towards Lake Tanganyika and the highway north to Bukavu, accompanied by military escorts. She had to get to a proper hospital, but she could barely walk. The world's time had arrived. And the harvest was bitter fruit. She was nothing in the middle of nowhere.

·　●　·

That summer, I spent a lot of time on my own with Elikya while, in the background, the Trump administration continued its full-scale assault on immigration. One stifling morning, she and I boarded the Metro train that stops beside the public housing complex where she lives, just north of downtown, and rode past the office buildings that she cleaned at night, making about $350 every two weeks. ("What am I supposed to do with $350 every two weeks with a house full of children?" Pierrine had translated.) We were headed to an English class run by Catholic Charities, her resettlement organization, and for the occasion Elikya was wearing a floor-length purple satin dress embroidered in yellow, with matching yellow patent leather pumps, a black velvet head wrap studded with faux diamonds, and lots of gold—earrings, bracelets, a necklace, a watch. In the classroom, she smiled widely and greeted her classmates, all Congolese, with "Jambo, jambo!"—*Hello, hello!*—and hand slaps. The men wore dress shirts and jackets, the women tailored dresses made from wax cloth. Some of the women bore scars on their faces. All throughout class, cell phones rang and buzzed or, in the case of Elikya's, played a zippy jazz tune ending in a trill of piano keys. She was getting calls from one of her daughters in Houston, from her son in a refugee camp in Burundi. Her reading glasses were stamped in zebra stripes.

Elikya and her partner that day, an elegant man with salt-and-pepper hair wearing a guayabera shirt, the two of them more advanced than the others, were given a passage to read entitled "Who Is Like You?"

There are a lot of people in the world. They all look the same from a long way off. They all have a head and body. They all laugh and cry. They all think about things. They all feel things. They all dream about things they want to do. People all need air. They all need food and water. They need to sleep. They need someone to love them. In these ways, people all seem the same.

But they are not the same. They don't think the same way. They don't feel the same way. They dream different dreams. And they want different things. No one is the same as anyone else. So, who is like you? No one in the world is just like you. You are special. There is only one you.

As the instructor explained those last lines to them, Elikya laughed with what seemed to me bemusement or skepticism, though I could have been projecting. Then, while their classmates practiced different "k" sounds—*qua-, qui-, quo-, ca-, co-, -ck*—Elikya and the man in the guayabera shirt debated their answers to worksheet questions about the passage. Even though I couldn't follow their conversation in Swahili, I found the questions and their possible answers deeply confusing. "Write *a* or *b*," said the directions: "What does this story show? (a) That many people are just like you OR (b) that each person is special," went one question. "Why isn't anyone else just like you? (a) No one else needs the same things you need. (b) No one else thinks or feels the way you do," read another. I tried to understand the source of my confusion. On the one hand, this passage, being used to teach English to refugees in Houston, Texas, USA, appeared to be about the brotherhood and sisterhood of human beings, their equality—*"people all seem the same."* But on the other—*"No one in the world is just like you"*—it appeared to be about the primacy of the individual. And then I saw that the confusion wasn't just in me. The confusion is a central tension in this country. Are we the pilgrim collective or the lone frontiersmen?

. . .

Back when I had visited Elikya with Pierrine, as we were making our way, single file, through the narrow kitchen to leave, Elikya told us of her struggle to find healthcare to treat her diabetes and high blood pressure. Working only part-time, after all, she could not get health insurance benefits. And although her children and grandchildren were still eligible for the national Children's Health Insurance Program (CHIP), Elikya herself was not covered. Elikya pointed to the fleshy aloe vera leaves and flat prickly pear pads piled on top of her refrigerator. "She says that is what she uses for medicine," Pierrine translated.

So when Elikya asked me, weeks later, if I would help her enroll in the Harris Health System, which offers care to the one million residents in Harris County who, like her, have no insurance, I found that I couldn't say no. Even though, as a matter of journalistic integrity, I perhaps should have, so as not to interfere in the story. And yet, I had told Elikya that I wanted to understand the specifics of her life here. Not having health insurance, that was her life. Also, Elikya can be a bit bossy.

When I arrived at her apartment the first time we arranged to enroll Elikya, she told me through one of her teenage grandsons that, because she had just begun a new job a couple of weeks before, still cleaning offices downtown, she didn't have pay statements yet, which she would need for the application. There was one pay statement, but it was online. And she hadn't enrolled in the company's online portal because she didn't have a computer and she couldn't figure it out on her phone. And in any case, it was all in English. She would try to get a paper copy that night at work.

The next time we met, she had the paper copy. I sat on her over-stuffed couch with the enrollment instructions and called out the list of all of the other documents she would need—work permits, ID cards for her and each child and grandchild who lived with her, lease agreement, electricity bill, that single pay statement—while Elikya rummaged for them in her bedroom, a little alcove off of the living room separated by a silk embroidered tapestry. When we were certain we had everything together, she stuffed all the papers into her gold-trimmed black patent leather handbag and went to change clothes.

Elikya's teenage daughter, Lydia, came in then. I must have been complaining about all of the paperwork required to get basic health-care in this country, and Lydia said that a lot of Congolese—"a *lot*"—talk about wanting to go back to Africa. Even her older sister. "If you have a farm in Africa, you can live," Lydia told me. "Yes, a lot of people say they are going back. But I am not going back. Why should I go back to Africa?" She wants, she told me, to finish school here. In Africa, after elementary school, you have to pay for your education. Though here, at this school, she doesn't really have friends. Not like in southwest Houston, where they lived among other refugees and immigrants when they were first resettled, before someone from their church helped get them into public housing, which makes rent so much more affordable for Elikya, but which has come at the cost of increased isolation. Here, Lydia eats lunch alone. But she doesn't mind. She doesn't want to have friends who smoke and drink. And as long as she has her cell phone, she can talk to her old friends in south-west Houston and she will be fine, she says.

As we drove to the Harris Health enrollment office I said to Elikya, making small talk, "Lydia is a good girl."

"She is lazy," Elikya replied. And we both laughed.

Lydia was supposed to cook dinner for the family—it was her day. All the kids take turns cooking. She needed coconut oil to cook, but they had been out, so Lydia just lay on the couch, texting. Elikya walked over, then, to the Family Dollar store in the strip center next to her apartment to buy some oil so Lydia could cook. And she bought plantain chips for us to snack on. As we drove, Elikya's phone rang and she talked to her sister in Congo.

At the enrollment office, Elikya's application was rejected. She needed to include a second pay statement from her current employer. She needed, because she did not yet have two pay statements from this employer, to have her former employer acknowledge that she no longer worked for them. Except that Elikya doesn't know where to find her manager to get this acknowledgment. That company had been bought by another company. The best option, it seemed, would be to wait until she had two pay statements and reapply.

Back at the apartment, Lydia was cooking a stewy sauce made from cassava leaves plucked from the garden, while a gaggle of boys played a card game they didn't know the English word for. They called it "metate."

Another day, I drove Elikya and Lydia out along the southwest fringes of the city to visit some Congolese farmers I had written about the year before who worked with an organization called Plant It Forward. Elikya's small garden was growing as the summer deepened, and she'd been teaching me the Swahili names of the plants in it, some of which I knew—okra, squash, peppers—and some I did not—*lenga lenga,* an amaranth cultivated for its greens; *ngai ngai,* a type of hibiscus we call roselle in English; and *sombe,* which is the leaf of the cassava. Elikya and I got by on my college French and her basic English, with Google Translate filling in for Swahili. While Elikya talked to Constant, a refugee farmer from the Republic of the Congo, which shares a border with the Democratic Republic of the Congo, Lydia and I marveled at the sugar cane flanking Constant's beds of arugula and zucchini and long beans, organic vegetables that he sold to restaurants and at farmers markets. Standing in the shade of the thick green stalks, Lydia remembered how, on her grandmother's farm in Bukavu, they would cut and peel the cane and suck the sweet juice. "When I tell my brothers about this," she told me, "they'll say, 'Oh, you're so lucky!' Because we never saw this here in America."

· · ·

There is a period in Elikya's life that I have had difficulty piecing together, a time of Odyssean wandering between the moment that she stumbled, battered, out of a dense forest in eastern Congo and an afternoon, seven years later, that she drove into a refugee camp in Burundi in a caravan of buses with four children, four grandchildren, and a basket of live turkeys. The elements of the story are the same, but certain key details shift with each telling. Fragments appear and disappear. The narrative rearranges itself. Was this how her memory worked? Had the trauma confused everything? Was the confusion a coping mechanism? Or had certain connective links been lost in translation? When I asked Elikya once, through Pierrine, about dates, trying to pin down timelines, Elikya told me, "Back then I would never ask what day it was. Everything was blended." So I began to think of this part of Elikya's story like a Cubist painting in which multiple perspectives exist simultaneously, and all are necessary to get at the essence.

In the city of Bukavu, Elikya had surgery to repair internal bleeding in her abdomen following the soldiers' beating.

After the surgery, she left for Burundi, a country that borders the DRC, to claim asylum because, as she was told by a military colonel, a friend of her husband's, if she stayed in Congo, she would be in danger.

After the surgery, she traveled to Goma, a city north of Bukavu, to visit her mother.

After the surgery, she thought to herself how she was all alone and she had no idea where her two older children were in the world.

After the surgery, she went to Uvira, a city south of Bukavu. For two weeks, the colonel, the friend of her husband's, who was stationed there, tried to radio to colleagues throughout the region searching for news of her two older children. The colonel bought her and her four remaining children tickets to Tanzania, where they traveled by boat across Lake Tanganyika, because she had heard that the missing children might have traveled there with their aunts to claim asylum.

The colonel paid for her transportation to Burundi. She went to Burundi, to the city of Rumonge, to the market on the shores of Lake Tanganyika, because a woman she knew thought she had seen her oldest daughter there.

Elikya had gotten pregnant in Uvira. "You understand how military people work," she recalled.

She had the baby girl in Tanzania, where she had gone to find her children. She asked the heads of all of the neighborhoods of the town of Korogwe in Tanzania if anyone knew of them. No one knew of them. The baby died on the boat home.

She had the baby in Rumonge, in the home of Leonie, a woman she had met at the market where she had gone, with her four remaining children, to try to find her daughter. "I'm sitting here," she had told Leonie when they met, "because I don't know where to go. I came to look for my children who are lost." Leonie took her to her house and cooked her fish in palm oil with a sauce made from tomatoes and celery and bell peppers, which they ate with fufu. Elikya showed Leonie the scar from her surgery, while Leonie told Elikya about a son who had died. "There is a lot of suffering in the world," said Leonie. Leonie was like her mother. Leonie was like her sister.

The baby girl was one month old when she died.

Time passed.

Elikya and her four known children, gathered to her now, lived with Leonie, and Leonie introduced Elikya to the workings of the Rumonge market, where Leonie sold fish. With a little savings from her farms in Kipupu—all her life, even in the hard times, Elikya kept a rainy day fund set aside so her children wouldn't go hungry—she began making arrangements with the fishermen plying Lake Tanganyika. She would buy them gas and they would bring her their catch before selling to anyone else. She had three groups of fishermen in whom she invested. Elikya would dry the fish, then sell it at the market in piles like quicksilver. When Tanzanian boats docked, she would ask the travelers if they had seen her children. Once, a man arrived on a boat who said he was from Korogwe. Elikya asked him if he knew any refugees who had run there. "There are a lot of them," he answered. "Which ones, specifically?"

"My children," Elikya replied. "I lost my children." And she gave him their names and asked if he would ask the locals in Korogwe about them.

Time passed.

One day, Mama Aldi, an old friend of Elikya's, turned up at the market in Rumonge. After Elikya finished selling for the day, they sat together drinking a beer. Mama Aldi's husband had been a soldier too, and had died in the fighting in Congo, and she, too, had come with her children to Burundi. Mama Aldi had been watching a young woman for a while now, she told Elikya that evening, in the nearby city of Bujumbora, where Mama Aldi had a place in the market. This young woman looked so much like the daughter of Elikya, Mama Aldi went on, whom she remembered as a child. But she couldn't be sure. That was such a long time ago and in a place so far away.

"Do you know Elikya?" Mama Aldi tentatively asked the young woman one day.

"How do you know Elikya?" the woman replied.

"I think I know your mother," said Mama Aldi. "Your mother exists. She's not dead yet. I know where she is," she told her.

But the woman was frightened. "Don't bother my brain," she told Mama Aldi.

As Mama Aldi told Elikya this story, Elikya listened more and more closely. "Is this a dream, or is it true?" she wondered.

Elikya bought food and left her children in the care of Leonie and traveled to Bujumbora. And there she found the lost child, her daughter, Aline. But when Elikya arrived, she entered a house of lamentation. Her daughter, now a mother of four children, had just lost her husband, and the house was full of relatives and friends gathered there for the traditional week of mourning. When her daughter recognized her mother, she laid her head upon Elikya's feet. For a moment, Aline forgot the death of her husband and remembered instead how they had killed her father, and all the lost years since then that she and Elikya had been separated. "I didn't know my mother was still alive," she said. "Maybe we are dreaming."

Time passed. Time always passed, no matter which version of the story. The boats from Tanzania docked in Rumonge and departed. Elikya would ask the travelers about her son, Patrick. Aline told Elikya that one of the aunts, who fled with the children that night in Kipupu when Elikya's husband was killed, had said she would take Patrick and try to get to Tanzania. Afterwards, they had lost contact with them.

Elikya would send money as well as corn and fresh fish coming off the boats to Aline in Bujumbora, who was now in a precarious situation with four young children and no husband. "Now I'm here," she told her daughter, "I will be by your side. If I have food, you're going to eat it. If I have clothes, you're going to wear them." She taught Aline to weave on a homemade loom—table coverings and coverlets for beds and couches. She taught her to embroider. She taught her to sew hair wraps from the bright patterned wax cloth. She taught her how to cook samosas as well as deep-fried mandazi donuts sweetened with coconut milk and cardamom. These were items Aline could sell at the market. "I can die tomorrow," Elikya thought, "and you will know how to raise your children."

But Elikya's heart was not at ease, because she did not know where her son was. So when a soldier from the DRC, passing through Rumonge, told Elikya that he worked in Lemera, a city in Congo known for its coltan mines, and that her son and the aunt had gone there—not Tanzania—Elikya knew she had to return back across the border to try to find him.

When she got to Lemera it was evening and it was raining. The soldier she had met guided her to the house where her son was living, and when her son saw Elikya, he came running. And, like the sister from whom he had been separated, when he saw his mother, he remembered his father, who had been killed.

That night, over a feast of grilled meat from a goat her son had bought at the market and had slaughtered to thank God and to celebrate their reunion, Patrick told his mother that his aunt, who had saved him, had herself been killed in Lemera, shot by the military. The mines, the vying factions, the guns made Lemera a perilous place. But the mines also made it a magnet, and the pull of the money that a young man with a strong back could make there was hard to resist. Her son, in the end, refused to return with Elikya to Burundi.

"Your aunt was killed," she tried to argue with him. "You could be killed, too."

"If I see something dire, I will run," he tried to reassure her.

She knew this son was an adult and couldn't be forced. So she said to herself, "Let me fight for the others."

Maybe it was after that visit, the second lost child having been found, that Elikya told Leonie she was ready to claim asylum officially in Burundi and enter a refugee camp. Maybe it was after the death of Aline, who had gone in for surgery on a goiter on her neck, which had begun to make breathing a labor. When Aline died during the operation, besides an inconsolable grief, she left Elikya with her four children. The life that Elikya had cultivated—buying fish and then drying and selling them, raising turkeys, wheeling and dealing in the Rumonge market—began to unravel. She couldn't care for twice the number of children now, and run her business too. And she couldn't pay for all of their schooling—the tuition, the uniforms. As it was, she was burning through her rainy day savings. Nor could she return to Congo, where she still had family. It might be her home, but there, she would never be at peace. She had lost so much, and so many people. In any case, she would not be not safe. When her husband was alive, he had been able to shield her with his military power. But someone had given him up, most likely, and she knew if she returned to Congo to live, she and his children could also be betrayed.

So she told her story to ONPRA (the National Office for the Protection of Refugees and Stateless Persons), the UNHCR's partner on the ground in Burundi. And on the morning of April 5, 2012, eight months after she claimed asylum and almost a year after her daughter's death, Elikya and the four children and four grandchildren left Bujumbora on an ONPRA transport with a multitude of other families, in six cars and three buses, for the interior of Burundi. Through the window, she could see Lake Tanganyika receding. The road cut through the dense trees, and from time to time it would open onto a village. Sometimes, if there was a market, the caravan would stop and the refugees would buy bottled water and oranges. At the temporary accommodation center where they slept that night, everyone was given pots, plates, cups, bowls, blankets, jerry cans for collecting water—and, for all girls over twelve, underwear, a bucket, soap, and feminine hygienic pads. Elikya herself left nothing to chance. She had already brought mattresses, a generator, a bag full of the small silvery dried fish, and a large woven palm frond basket with a lid in which she'd placed four live turkeys.

When the caravan entered the camp, the people there cheered and clapped, calling out "Karibuni! Karibuni!" *Welcome everyone!*

And as the newcomers disembarked, they got on cell phones trying to reach relatives or friends who they knew were there already. Elikya collected the things she had carried, but it was her woven basket that attracted the most attention. Many people had never seen turkeys before. "Oh my God, what is this?" they asked. And from that day forward, Elikya was known in Bwagiriza Camp as *Maman Dindon.* Mama Turkey.

. . .

One morning I drove over to Elikya's apartment so she could teach me to cook *ugali na sombe,* fufu with cassava leaves, the unofficial national dish of Congo, as well as a chicken stew. Elikya's neon blue braids were wrapped round her head and pinned near the crown, and she was wearing her red button-up uniform shirt. By the time I arrived, she had already harvested a large aluminum bowl full of cassava leaves from the plants growing in the plot outside her front stoop. In the kitchen sink was a red bucket filled with two whole chickens, defrosting. And, like a Martha Stewart for the coming world, Elikya had arrayed the other ingredients we would be using on her small countertop: garlic heads, green bell peppers, onions, pale green chayote squash, raw peanuts, tomatoes, bouillon cubes, and palm oil the color of a setting sun.

Cassava, which had grown in her mother's garden, her grandfather's farm, and in every place Elikya has cultivated, is a plant sufficient unto itself—its roots provide starch and calories, its palmate leaves protein and fiber. But cassava also contains cyanide, and so it must be prepared properly. As the leaves steamed in water on the stove, Elikya flipped and swirled them, in between butchering the thawed chickens and slicing the onions and peppers. Then she peeled a whole head of garlic and pounded it in a mortar and pestle.

Out on the porch, she lit a small grill called an *mbabula*—a tin pail lined with a thick band of terracotta clay that she'd filled with a handful of charcoal. As the pot with the chicken and vegetables and garlic and bouillon began to steam and then boil over the fire, Elikya and I sat on the stoop beside her garden, pounding the cassava and chitchatting in broken French and English. Actually, I should say, Elikya was pounding. When I tried, she just laughed. To some interior rhythm I clearly could not hear, she beat the cassava leaves along with garlic cloves and the peeled chayote in another massive mortar, this one with a stout wooden pestle a yard or more long.

At Bwagiriza Camp, Elikya had at first cooked outside over firewood set within stones and shielded on one side by a low brick wall that Elikya built herself. The UN had provided massive tarps, which were then set up to create a shelter. The floor was hard-packed earth. Their rations—oil, rice, flour, sometimes beans, sometimes peas— was never really enough. And the beans themselves were old and dry and wouldn't soften, no matter how long you soaked and then cooked them.

Near the camp was a small farming village. At the market there, Elikya bought a *mbabula*—the clay grill—with some of the money from her rainy day fund. The women from the village would come to the camp to sell charcoal. One of the farmers, Mama Delice, would sometimes bring cassava leaves, and the leaves of beans, and avocados. Elikya told Mama Delice, "Come, I will buy some from you. Sit down. Maybe drink some tea. Eat some fufu." And later, when Elikya visited Mama Delice in the village, she brought some of her dried fish as a gift. Later, Elikya brought clothes the kids had outgrown. Sometimes Elikya would visit Mama Delice with her children. Sometimes Mama Delice would visit Elikya with her children. They had a friendship now.

One day Elikya asked, "Mama Delice, can't you give me a place to farm?"

"No problem," she replied. So Elikya, as she and her husband had done in Kipupu, prepared kasiksi, the homemade banana beer, and carried it in a massive hollowed-out gourd—a sign of respect for Mama Delice and her husband, on whose land Elikya wished to grow. Then the husband of Mama Delice called over the village elders to inform them that he was giving Elikya some of his land to farm. Elikya paid the husband to help her cut down the grasses on the land and burn them. A week later, they prepared the rows. Elikya had secured cassava cuttings from another woman who farmed in that village, and then Elikya cooked rice and beans and sweet potatoes and brewed more kasiksi and called the people in the village to help her plant the rooted cuttings. They also planted a field in beans and another in peanuts. From time to time, she would make a batch of kasiksi and invite her friends and they would weed the fields.

Life continued.

In addition to the farm, Elikya had planted a garden in the area around her shelter in the camp—a shelter that she was transforming. Over the bare earth floors she laid down small stones, and constructed walls made of wood and mud. The UN installed a solar system for electricity along the camp's tidy streets. And in her garden, bordered by the fence she also built, Elikya planted a banana tree, along with amaranth, yam, squash, roselle, okra. She penned her turkeys, and to that small flock she added ducks and chickens, which she would use to feed her family and to sell.

Elikya also started a cinema, in a small annex she built beside her house, where she would show movies from India and Tanzania on a VCR that she had brought from Bujumbora on one of her buying trips back to the city. She would travel there to purchase dried fish, as well as used clothes and shoes, which she would clean and trade from her house in the camp, measuring out kilos of the fish for other refugees in exchange for their UN rations of oil, rice, beans, peas, which she would then stockpile. Even some of the local Burundians would buy from her. And when the refugees ran short at the end of the month, Elikya would sell the UN rations back to them.

Life continued. Life was good in the camp. Elikya loved farming, loved eating the food she had grown, loved feeding it to the children. And she had money now to buy them clothes. She no longer had the stress of not having money. When you don't have money, your mind is turning all the time—*What next? What next?*

The night before they left Bwagiriza Camp in July 2015, after all of the security interviews in which she told her story again, after the background checks, after all of the immunizations and the physicals, Elikya threw a party. She had already sold off the turkeys she was raising, but she still had ducks and chickens, so she cooked those along with rice and cassava leaves. She served beer and sodas. Many people came to say goodbye, and they feasted and drank and sang and danced and they said, "This is our last shared meal." Some people lingered all night.

Elikya sold the house she had built with the stone floor she had laid to a guy in the camp for $25. He loved her banana tree and the garden and the gate. She sold everything else, too, that they couldn't carry in their suitcases—all her stores of dried fish and rice and beans. But in her bags, Elikya packed the cuttings and seeds of the foods she didn't think she'd be able to find in America: cassava, corn, roselle, amaranth, squash, tomato. She had heard that American tomatoes taste like paper and that everything is grown with chemicals. Then, as the party dwindled, she gave her pots and plates away.

Elikya was Mama Turkey in the camp, but to her neighbor next door, Elikya was Mama Vitamin because of her energy. This neighbor loved to make people laugh. He used to love to drink kasiksi, but by then he'd stopped drinking. His children were her children's friends. When he had a problem with his wife, he'd come complain about it to Elikya and they'd end up laughing together. When she left for the US, he carried her bags all the way to the entrance of the camp.

And their other neighbors, too, escorted Elikya and her children and grandchildren to the cars that would take them to the plane that would take them to America.

.   .   .

That day I cooked with Elikya, before we ate, she filled a plastic tub with water and offered me a cake of pink soap. We washed our hands, then sat in the cool quiet of the living room. I watched Elikya carefully as she pinched off fufu with her right hand, smoothed it flat, and gracefully used it to scoop up the stewed cassava and chicken. Then I clumsily tried to mimic her.

Back in Congo, the wife of Elikya's son Patrick, pregnant at the time, had been harvesting cassava with some other women in their village when they'd been abducted by rebels. Some of the women were shot right away, but the others, including Elikya's daughter-in-law, were shunted and shoved through the forest to the rebels' camp where they were made the rebels' wives. Then the rebels did whatever they wanted to them. After a few weeks, the rebels grew tired of the women. "This one is lazy," the wife of Elikya's son heard them say about herself. "Let's kill her." But one of the other rebels said, "No— leave her. If you kill her, you're killing two people. Even if this one is bad, the one inside her might not be. Just let her go." And they did. When they led her back home, they took a winding path to make sure she wouldn't remember the route.

Back in the village at last, she stumbled into her own funeral. Everyone there thought that the lost women were dead. "How is this possible?" they asked her. And they imagined at first that the others must be alive as well. So, like the biblical messengers who come to Job, she had to tell them that she alone had escaped. "God is the one who helped me," she said, "and that's why I'm here." That night, she and her husband did not sleep, and the next day, along with their three children, they fled to Burundi. And that's where they are now—in a refugee camp, though it's not Bwagiriza.

Elikya's son feels like he is losing his mind when he thinks about how they kidnapped his wife, and what they did to her. He has started drinking and insults her for sleeping with the rebels. Elikya tries to advise her son from across the Atlantic. "You need to understand: a lot of women died the way she was almost killed." Sometimes he listens. Sometimes he doesn't. "Once a woman has had more than one man, she isn't a woman anymore," he'll say.

"That's how it is in Congo," says Elikya to me.

Elikya asked her daughter-in-law if she wanted Elikya to pay for her to return to her family. "Where can I go?" she asked Elikya. "You'd be sending me back to a place where people have to sleep in the forests because their villages aren't safe. It's only hunger and gunfire every night. I have nowhere to go."

So the son of Elikya and his wife remain in the camp in Burundi with their children, not knowing if they'll ever go home again to Congo, or if they'll have the chance of a life somewhere else.

"Just be patient," Elikya consoles her son when he tells her he wishes he could be with her in America. "God will help you and you will be able to come here." But even God doesn't appear to know when that might be.

Elikya once told me and Pierrine that, because there is so much upheaval in Congo, people often don't get a chance to plant, to farm. "If they do, they are planting for the people who will come after," she said. Even at the refugee camp in Burundi, it was the same.

At their first apartment in Houston, Elikya and her children and grandchildren lived on the second floor. One day, Elikya was looking at the seeds she had brought with her, and, not knowing what else to do, she went downstairs and began to dig in the compacted earth where a few squared-off boxwoods were subsisting. Then she planted four bean seeds, and she watered them. Eventually, miraculously, they grew, and Elikya, whose name means *hope,* harvested the leaves and cooked them. And even though she knew this place was not yet her home, "I thought," she told us, "here in America, you can plant something and it will grow."

6 Haneen

We have come to Zara's to cook shakriyeh and molokhia. In her hometown of Hama in Syria, shakriyeh—chicken cooked in yogurt—is sometimes made with yogurt from the milk of sheep that graze in the pastureland west of the city. Hama is known for its sheep's milk products. This hot summer afternoon, Zara has propped her phone up on the counter and her mother's face is there with us, beaming in via WhatsApp from Jordan, as Zara chops onions. They are chatting back and forth in Arabic while Katia, my translator, a Syrian-American herself, is listing for me the various Arabic stores in town where I can buy frozen molokhia, the greens that give the dish its name. In the past, when she would travel to Syria to visit her own mother, Katia would bring dried molokhia leaves back here with her, packed into her suitcase like an illegal substance. "You can buy it fresh here, and it's delicious" she tells me, "but it's not the same flavor." This is because, she explains, the land here in Houston is not the soil of home.

Zara is a single mother of four—three daughters, ages 15, 13, and 9, and a son in pre-K at the nearby public school. She and her husband divorced after coming to the US, but that is a story I do not yet fully know. Zara, whose profile reminds me of some Roman Fayum mummy portrait I once saw in a museum but can't now quite remember, is wearing a hot pink t-shirt with the word LOVE in sequins across the chest. She laughs easily and seems both totally at ease and intent as she cooks.

"So Zara, when you're cooking this food now, what do you remember from cooking it in the past?" I ask her. Katia and I are leaning against the counter while Zara measures out ghee and rice, which she'll serve with the shakriyeh. The molokhia, meanwhile, is stewing down, mucilaginous like okra, with the cloves from several heads of garlic. "She remembers her kitchen in Syria, in Hama, and how much she loved to cook there," Katia translates. "She helped build her apartment and lay it out and everything was new. Cooking this brings her memories of being there."

I think about my own kitchen in another part of this city, and all the dinners I have cooked, the photo of my husband and me on our first anniversary perched on a shelf above where I chop vegetables; all the pie crusts my daughters and I have rolled out beneath the window that gazes out on the backyard, with its ancient pecan tree and threadbare grass where they used to run around barefoot when they were little. "What kind of *emotion* is connected to this food?" I wonder out loud in Zara's kitchen. She thinks for a moment. "*Haneen,*" she replies. Katia fumbles for the proper translation from the Arabic. "Longing," she begins. Alia and her husband, I recalled, had named their firstborn for that form of love which they felt for one another. But *haneen* is not always a hunger for the beloved, Katia muses. It can also be a kind of nostalgia for one's home. "It's the feeling," Katia goes on, "of longing for her home in that part of the world."

A couple of months before, when Alia and I had visited Zara early on, she told us about that home in Hama, or rather the one in which she'd grown up and where, every week, she and her brothers and sisters and their children, who all still lived in the same neighborhood, would gather with their parents and grandparents in the back garden among the pomegranate trees and the sweet-smelling jasmine vines. They had laid down stone for a terrace, and they would dash water over the stone to clean it, then sit, all of them, in the shade in the afternoons, eating pomegranate seeds, playing dominoes, drinking tea, the whole family, just as they had done when Zara and her siblings were younger, before they had married. Zara's mother's dream, Alia was translating, had always been to live among her children and grandchildren, one big gregarious family, just like they had done before the war in Syria. "Right now," though, Alia said, "they live not only in different neighborhoods, but in different countries." Zara went on in Arabic. "We lost our home, we lost our home, we lost our home," Alia translated. "The worst thing now is that we are very far from each other, after the war."

On that visit, Alia and I had catalogued Zara's family's displacement and separation. Her parents, along with two brothers and two sisters and their collective children, live in Jordan. Another sister lives in Turkey. Two brothers, both single, separately made it to Europe. One lives in France and the other in Germany. Zara is here in the US. Only a sister, with her husband and children, remains in Syria. As Alia and I sat with Zara in the courtyard of her apartment complex, fuchsia-colored azaleas in bloom, it occurred to me that all those children, growing up in different foreign countries—Zara's own as well as her nieces and nephews—will soon be fluent in languages other than Arabic and will no longer have a common language that binds them together.

Cooking now with Zara, as I had cooked before with Elikya—which is to say, standing around watching as they deftly peeled and diced and whisked and basted—it seems to me that this simple, daily task carried with them from their homelands could be seen as an act of resistance against their displacement. Or more than that: as something holy, almost sacramental. When Elikya brought cassava cuttings and bean seeds with her on the plane to America, when she planted them in this soil here, when she pounded the vegetables she had grown, she was doing more than feeding her body and the bodies of her children and grandchildren. She was resurrecting a past and a place and her identity within them so that they could live, momentarily, again. And Zara, in cooking shakriyeh and molokhia, with her mother's face watching over her on WhatsApp, is recreating a home that no longer, technically, exists. With this act she can enter into sacred time where there is no beginning and no end and where nothing has been lost forever.

· · ·

Zara was a baby of two months during the Hama Massacre in 1982, when the Syrian Army, attempting to put down an uprising against the government led by the Muslim Brotherhood, besieged the city and slaughtered upward of 40,000 civilians—though no one has been able to document the exact number, and it could be much higher. One hundred thousand were expelled. Seventeen thousand remain missing to this day. Whole neighborhoods were obliterated and then cemented over. It was the deadliest attack by an Arab government against its own people in the modern Middle East, and it was ordered by Hafez al-Assad, father of the current president, Bashar al-Assad. The orders were carried out by Bashar's uncle, Rifaat.

Zara grew up in the shadow of that catastrophe. Katia, who was translating the day Zara mentioned the Hama Massacre, recalled, by way of explaining to me about the lasting effects of the carnage, her husband's cousin, who had also grown up in Hama. This cousin had been taking shelter in a basement with the women and children of her neighborhood when soldiers swarmed in and shot everyone dead. The bodies crumpled around this cousin, and she was buried beneath her own mother, which may have saved her. Then the soldiers cut off the women's hands to get at the gold they were wearing. "And she was the only living thing," Katia told me, "the only living girl among the dead in that basement." Katia had met this cousin several times. She's highly educated, a professor at the university. "But you can tell how she . . . on the inside . . ." Katia couldn't quite complete the thought. "What happened in Hama is something no one ever . . ."

So when the protests started in the city's Assi Square on Fridays during the summer of 2011, Zara felt a deep unease. By early July, 500,000 protestors were taking part in the rallies—bodies moving together like meadow grasses bending beneath the wind. Watching them, week by week, Zara could almost foretell what was going to happen. And soon enough, the Fourth Brigade moved in. It was headed by Maher al-Assad, the president's brother, a brutal enforcer who set up a blockade around the city and cut off electricity, water, and all communications in Hama and surrounding villages. Tanks randomly shelled homes and buildings. Snipers shot scores of young men coming and going from mosques. With the Shabiha, the private militia of the government, turned loose, nothing would be off limits. *Shabiha* means "ghosts."

Over the next year, as the Free Syrian Army moved into Hama and an armed opposition took hold, Zara and her family were caught in the middle of relentless government forces on one side and the FSA on the other. The bombs would inevitably land on the people living in between. Three times, she and her husband gathered their little daughters and fled to a village in the countryside, where her brother-in-law had found an abandoned house next to a cemetery for all of them. But out there, without water, trying to cook over wood on an open fire, sleeping under mosquito nets, threatened by scorpions, Zara said, "I felt like a refugee in my own country." They were always on the move—even traveling as far as Raqqa in the eastern desert—out of fear. But the peace and safety they tried to find outside the city was nowhere to be found.

Back in Hama, the threats were both actual and existential. Sometimes, out of nowhere, regime tanks would surround a neighborhood, cutting it off, those inside not knowing whether they would be kidnapped or killed or raped. Parents whose children were trapped at school outside the cordon didn't know if they'd ever return. Then, just as suddenly, the tanks would leave. Zara constantly felt she was bracing for the moment a bomb would hit and take away her children. She took to sleeping in her hijab in case soldiers broke into their home. "This was my life," she said. "After what I told you, about how happy we were before, how we were very happy, if you could see our faces . . . We lived in the horror. I could never have believed before what happened to our country." It shouldn't be called the Arab Spring, Zara believes, but the Arab Fall, because that is the season when everything dies.

The most shattering part of all of this was that the horror was being perpetrated by fellow Syrians. The betrayal originated with the government, but it was carried out by the frontline soldiers. Paranoia infiltrated daily life, invisible but suffocating, like chlorine gas or sarin. Neighbors who had always lived as friends, who had taken tea together in backyard gardens day after day, now wondered who was with the opposition and who was with the regime. "You couldn't trust anybody anymore," Zara remembered. Someone you had known forever might turn around and inform on you. If you were always expecting a traitor to stab you in the back, you couldn't feel safe. You could never be free.

Zara knew people who had been betrayed. A young man, the brother of her sister-in-law, who was evading forced military service, for example. Close friends offered to hide him, but then reported where he was. He hasn't been seen since the army hauled him away. Or an older woman Zara knew, who would move through the neighborhood at night with another woman, the two of them tending to the badly wounded left on the streets because it was too dangerous to try to save them. The women would treat them where they lay, or drag them to one of the informal field hospitals in basements of nearby buildings. They were proud of their work. But then someone reported them and the women were jailed for two weeks. After Zara's neighbor was released, she no longer went out at night.

When the Fourth Brigade came to Hama, Zara's father knew it was time to get Zara and her sisters and their families out. He had already gone to Jordan with Zara's mother and their sons, who were in danger of being conscripted into the army. But in late October 2012, he made his way back to Hama for the others. On the bus out of town, on the road to Jordan, he sat behind the driver trying to get the low-down on the checkpoints they'd need to get through, trying to figure out who manned them—regime or FSA—and what dangers might be lurking. As they drove south through the wreckage of Damascus, vast stretches of buildings that had once been homes and shops, now obliterated by her own people, Zara felt as if the soil and the stones were weeping.

At the Jaber-Nassib border crossing—through which Sara would pass not quite a year later as that border was shutting down—Zara and her family waited under the desert sun for two days, among hundreds, maybe thousands of other desperate people, while fellow Syrians screamed insults at those trying to leave. Regime soldiers guarding the crossing beat an old man who was simply trying to ask a question. Zara, pregnant, sat on a blanket with their suitcases and her daughters around her, the littlest one, not quite four, on her lap. Other families had been there for a week, even two. On the second day, though, a high-ranking army officer arrived on the scene. "Why are all these people waiting?" he demanded of the guards. "Get their papers ready. Make them move. Get the women and children first." And then Zara and her sisters stood in line, their children in their arms or at their sides, faces grimed with desert dust and streaked with tears, followed by husbands, no longer in control of anything. They joined the desperate stampede trying to get their papers processed so they could pass through to the other side.

In Hama, Zara had been living for so long with uncertainty and fear. And she had felt scared every moment of the journey from Hama to the border. At the border, too, she had not known what would happen. Would they be allowed to cross? Or would they be turned back to drive again across the desert? Would some clash erupt between the regime and the rebels? But when they stamped her passport, she felt an immediate and almost physical relief. It was only a matter of time now until she would see her mother, to whom she'd said goodbye nearly a year before, not knowing if they'd ever see each other again in this life. It was only a matter of time before she and her family would be safe. For an hour, sitting on the bus on the Jordanian side, she kept taking deep breaths. She felt as if she'd been resurrected from death to life.

.   •   .

A month or so before I cooked with Zara in Houston, with her mother watching via WhatsApp, I had eaten a meal prepared by Zara's mother in Zarqa, an overcrowded city surrounded by desert in Jordan, while Zara's face, framed by a pink hijab, watched us on her mother's phone from its perch beside the TV, which was covered with a prayer rug.

I had traveled to Amman to participate in a program on geopolitics and humanitarian action in Jordan, and to visit the families of some of the Transformed women, including Zara's. The country was, that summer of 2018, grappling with those 1.5 million Syrians who had been crossing over throughout the civil war.

In Zarqa with Zara's family, I could witness firsthand the concrete fact of their version of family separation and the helpless stasis of life as refugees in a country where the future seemed never to arrive. Zara's parents and a younger brother had lived since early 2012 at the dead end of an unpaved lane off the chaotic thoroughfares of Zarqa, where delivery trucks and cars and vans clogged the narrow streets and the skies were cluttered with electrical lines draped overhead. Graffiti were scrawled across the haphazard walls and buildings, all loosely constructed from sand-colored stone, but my Arabic was too limited to be able to read much of what they said as Malek, my Jordanian driver and translator, careened through, trying to find the address.

Upon our arrival, Malek and I sat on the black sofa with leopard print seats, plaster walls peeling, and spoke with Abu Obeidah, Zara's father, 80, as he rolled his own cigarettes and then popped them into an empty Marlboro package. He was lanky, dressed all in white, from skull cap to kaftan to pants, his eyes warm and smiling. His forehead was smudged with the zebibah of the devout, a sooty bruise that comes from relentless prayers made prostrate on a rug, facing Mecca. He told us, when I asked about his family's refugee status, that he travels from time to time by bus into Amman to the UN offices there, but he can never get a clear update on their case. So they wait.

One of his sons, Mohammad, lives with his wife and children in East Amman, a neighborhood in the capital that, like southwest Houston, is packed with refugees and immigrants, many undocumented, living hand to mouth in close proximity to neighborhoods of great wealth and waste. I had visited Mohammad and his family a few days before. The house was cool against the summer heat, with its plastered walls and tiled floors and arched doorways. But aside from the long mats on which we sat, arrayed around the living room, I could not glimpse any furniture. Although the program I'd come to Jordan to attend had helped me see the larger framework in which refugees in Jordan were operating, and some of the ways in which the country was trying to adapt humanely to the influx, the experiences of Mohammad, like those of his parents, revealed the disconnect between public policy and lived reality.

Mohammad told me how, until recently, like almost all of the other Syrian refugees in Jordan, he had no work permit. If he'd been caught working, he could have been arrested and deported back to Syria, which he had left in fear for his life. Maybe the first few days an employer would pay, but then they'd just stop. Or maybe they'd pay, but less than what had been agreed upon. And refugees couldn't complain to the police if they didn't get paid, because they weren't supposed to be working in the first place. "The point is commitment," Mohammad told me—or the lack thereof. Like the future, nothing could be counted on.

However, since getting his work permit six months before, after having been in Jordan for five years, that form of uncertainty had eased. Now, Mohammad works all week in construction and on weekends at a bakery. The rent is still high, the pay is still low, and water and medical care are expensive. But at least now, if he's not paid, he can go to the police and complain.

"Do you ever think of staying in Jordan, rather than trying to go through the UN to another country?" I asked Mohammad as his young daughter leaned against him and his toddler son crawled into his lap. "No, of course not," he said. But it wasn't at all clear that they'd ever be resettled anyway, whether they wanted to be or not. He and his wife had been interviewed for permanent resettlement in France at the same time as had his brother Obeidah, who, single, was now living in Lyon. But when the authorities told Mohammad's wife she'd have to remove her hijab for their official photographs, she refused. "This is just too much," Mohammad said, "to remove the veil just for a photograph." He thinks this is what doomed their chances to be resettled. And now, with the travel ban in place for Syrians hoping to come to the US, there were fewer and fewer options for Mohammad and his family.

When he calls Zara in America and his brother in France and they tell him what they are paid, Mohammad feels sad, thinking of his own wages in comparison. "I don't know," I protested. "Zara is in a program now for women refugees because life is very hard. And the money is *not* enough. And the rent is *too* high." But Mohammad wouldn't accept this. "She makes a great effort," he told me, "but there is a good salary. Here, there is a great effort with a terrible salary." Mohammad wanted to go to America not because of any starry-eyed ideas about freedom and democracy, he said. "I just want to live. I want to feed my children. That's all I care about."

The afternoon I spent in Zarqa, as we spoke with Abu Obeidah, Zara's mother had begun carrying in pitchers of hibiscus tea and a homemade salted yogurt drink, along with platters of food that she had prepared for me, their guest, on whatever meager income they had mustered: fried kibbe made from meat and bulgur wheat and pine nuts; a smoked eggplant dish with ground lamb and peanuts; hummus; a chopped salad of lettuce, tomatoes, cucumbers, parsley; a tray of sliced lemons and whole green peppers. The smoked egg-plant seemed to be a variation of baba ganoush that came, her mother explained as I peppered her with questions, from her hometown. Zara was still there on the phone on the TV stand. "We're sorry that this is not very much," Abu Obeidah was telling me as the dishes kept coming, and I couldn't tell if this modesty was part of the ritual of the guest-host relationship, or if he was serious. "We should have sacrificed a goat or a sheep," he said, apologetically.

· · ·

There are the sisters we are born among, and the sisters that we find, those who carry our stories inside them, and who save us. When she arrived in Jordan with her husband and three young daughters, after the drive on the bus south through Syria, after the border crossing, Zara found an apartment in Zarqa near her parents' place at the dead end of that same unpaved road. The apartment had been abandoned for years, and then, right after Zara's family moved in, the plumbing backed up and the apartment flooded. Pregnant out to here, with her girls, barred from Jordanian schools, running wild, and her husband sick in bed with a hernia, Zara, not knowing what else to do with all the standing water, began mopping it out into the hall and down the stairs. When her brother arrived to help, Zara went looking for another mop. She knocked on her neighbor's door. No one answered at first, so Zara kept trying to flush the water out on her own. But as the water sloshed around her feet, her neighbor's door opened. And there was Emmi.

Emmi had just given birth herself a month or so before to twin boys, and she'd been sleeping in snatches between nursing, so she hadn't heard the knock at first. "Are you looking for a place to rent?" she asked Zara after they had exchanged greetings.

"No, I'm your new neighbor! I've been here for two days. We came from Syria."

Emmi invited her in, and over coffee Zara told Emmi the story of how they had left Hama. Zara had been missing the children of her husband's brothers and sisters, who were still in Hama, so when Emmi's twins woke up and Emmi carried them in, Zara went gaga over them. But, Emmi told her, she had also had a daughter. Only the year before, in October, the little girl had died of cancer. It started in her intestines, and then spread throughout her body. She had been just four years old—around the age of Zara's youngest daughter. Maybe, Emmi confessed to Zara, the beatings her husband gave Emmi, the distress of watching this, had hastened the cancer's rampage through her daughter's small body. And now here Emmi was, just a year after her daughter's death, with two newborn sons. She was, she told Zara, exhausted, physically and emotionally. Still, the next day, she brought over a basket of fruits and vegetables for the new Syrian family. "According to the prophet," Emmi said, "*If your neighbor is in a good condition, then you are in a good condition too.*"

A week passed. Emmi, still in that newborn fog of longing, nostalgia—*haneen*—for sleep, had not been able to check on Zara. But then Zara knocked on Emmi's door again. Emmi thought she looked a little down. Who knows why—even Zara isn't sure: maybe it was the gestures Emmi had made to welcome Zara, maybe it was the way that Emmi opened herself up, telling Zara about her daughter. But in Emmi's apartment above the chaotic streets of Zarqa, with their noise and exhaust and dust, Zara found herself asking Emmi, "Will you be my soulmate here in Jordan?"

Rooheh—the word in Arabic is, literally, "my soul." "Can you be *my soul?*" Zara hadn't planned on asking this. It just came out. The question caught Emmi by surprise, too. At first, she didn't really understand what Zara wanted. So Zara told Emmi how she had left her best friend of sixteen years back in Syria, and was desperate now for someone she could confide in and with whom she could speak freely. "Would you be that person?" Zara asked.

We think of soulmates as foretold by the heavens. They are those, somewhere out in the wide world, whose path we'll cross *as it is written.* But Zara was impatient. Maybe she wanted to control her own fate. So much, after all, had already been taken from her, and there was nothing she could do about that. And so Emmi, with the grace that must have carried her through a brutal marriage, the death of a beloved daughter, and the birth of twins in this suffocating city, said to Zara, "Sure, why not? I'll try to be what you're asking me to be. I hope I'm good enough."

Their households became linked, a tangle of children running back and forth between them. Zara's daughters were always helping Emmi with the twins. They would take turns carrying them around on their hips, the babies bobbing precariously, the girls themselves so young and scrawny. Emmi's older son, too, grew close to Zara's daughters. He had lost his sister, but in them he found three others.

Zara's son, when he arrived a few months after their arrival, was simply folded into the mayhem.

Zara had come to Jordan with nothing. Her brother gave her a few mattresses, and she picked up some worn rugs from a woman who moved to the UAE. But Emmi told Zara, "Anything you need, my home is always open to you." So Zara, who didn't have a washing machine, did her laundry at Emmi's. In exchange, Zara cooked. Money was tight, with Zara's husband sick, though even if he'd been healthy, he wouldn't have been allowed to work as a refugee in Jordan. They survived on the food stipends from various agencies they were registered with, and, at least at first, their landlord helped them out by not charging rent because they were Syrians and he felt pity for them.

Emmi was always wanting to try everything Zara cooked, so Zara would send the girls over with samples, like her lemony grape leaves stuffed with ground meat stretched with rice. Zara ruined Emmi with her dishes. Once, Zara was baking the sweet dish called *esh el bulbul*—"nightingale's nest"—made with shredded dough like straw and shaped into hollowed-out circles, dappled with pistachios for the eggs, all of it then steeped in rosewater syrup. It's a laborious recipe and Zara had made them for a family gathering. "Emmi needs to try this," she thought, though, and managed to save the very last nest for her friend and send it over. And if, on occasion, Zara didn't send something, Emmi would call the girls to her and ask casually, slyly, "What did your mother make today?" Once, Zara was frying kibbe. Emmi, smelling the browning orbs of bulgur and spiced lamb from her own apartment, made her way across the hall. Zara was standing over the stove and couldn't answer the door, but when one of the girls came and told Emmi that Zara was cooking, Emmi asked, "Is she frying kibbe? Just go grab a couple and bring them to me."

At first, despite Emmi's confessions to Zara when they met, Emmi held back. At night, through the walls, Zara could hear the violent beatings and the way Emmi pleaded with her husband to stop. In the mornings, after Emmi's husband left for work as an airplane technician, Zara would rush over to check on her friend. "Why would he do that to you?" Zara asked. But Emmi was more reserved. She didn't want to give everything about her life away. She would say to herself, *Okay, you heard. That's fine. But I can't give you any more.* "Why would he do that to you?" Zara would repeat. "That's his way" is all Emmi would say.

Perhaps because beatings were something Zara had known herself, from the earliest days of her marriage, Zara kept coming back, and she and Emmi would make coffee and sit together. Zara would insist, "I'm here for you. You can confide in me. I'll be your confidant. You can tell me."

"Why bother?" Emmi would respond. "I'll give you a headache with my stories."

Slowly, though, Emmi began to reveal to Zara all that she'd been through, even before the death of her daughter—the things her husband threw at her, the way he burned her hand, his need for control, the way he treated her like his possession. It was so stressful. He was the kind of guy who was always making problems, who stirred up trouble wherever he went.

A couple of years after Zara arrived in Jordan, Emmi's husband suffered an injury that required brain surgery. After that, the seizures started, and the beatings worsened. He angered so easily. He couldn't take the noise—and there was always noise. With no one else to blame, Emmi and the children had to take it.

Zara became the voice in Emmi's head that she needed to hear, the one that reminded Emmi of her own forbearance in the face of such brutality, but also of the insanity of the situation. "How can you live like this?" Zara would ask. "If it was me, I'd just take my kids and leave." And the more that Zara bolstered Emmi, the closer the two women became—and the more their relationship began to threaten their spouses. Emmi's husband, knowing that his power lay in keeping Emmi isolated, sensed Zara's growing influence on his wife and didn't like it, while Zara's husband warned her, "Stay away from Emmi. That guy is going to make trouble." But for Zara, staying away was not an option. "I will never leave her. We *have* to be together," she would say. Because by now they really were soul sisters.

Still, despite her urging, even Zara knew that, in that country, for a woman to divorce was nearly impossible. There are no civil marriages in Jordan, only religious—those sanctioned by Shariʿa, the Muslim court system. And marriage is an agreement between two families. Even if Emmi could pay a lawyer to make, as was her right, a legal case for divorce and compensate her husband for the dowry that their families had negotiated, there was a deeper force at work, and that was culture. There were no women members in the Shariʿa court system to hear her case. And anyway, there is intense social pressure to resolve these kinds of conflicts outside the courts, within the family. In practical terms, that usually means the woman, guided by a male guardian or elder, is persuaded to act in the perceived interests of the family, rather than for herself. A divorced woman with children would live in the shame she had brought, but so would her extended family. And this had to be avoided at all costs—a cost that included the bruises and burns across the bodies of Emmi and her children.

In fact, Emmi had tried to leave her husband many times, but her family and his family had always pulled her back, like an undertow that she was powerless to swim against. Yet, Emmi believed, God knows exactly what your life needs, and he will send it to you through someone. So even though she stayed with her husband, Emmi now saw that God must have guided her to do so because of the good thing that he would send her way. And the messenger turned out to be Zara.

.   .   .

"She got a restraining order from the judge. Her husband will not come anymore to her house—they told him that," Alia had translated into English for me while taking notes in Arabic when we first met Zara in the early spring. It would take a few months for the story of that restraining order to unspool. In the meantime, in my notebook, I scribbled my first impressions of Zara: *Flat eyes. Deep skepticism.* She had met us out on the sidewalk in her navy blue abaya, a matching headscarf over a white cotton liner pulled tightly around her face. Seeing her, I remembered instinctively my aunts, Catholic nuns in habits, whom I grew up around. But inside, Zara immediately peeled off the layers, freeing her thick, wiry black hair, threaded with gray strands. She wore jeans and a tie-dyed shirt slit open along the sides. *Weary jadedness,* I wrote. *Faded acne scars.*

Zara did not have a steady job. She had been working part-time with a woman who cooked for private Saudi clients and delivered the food to them. Zara was observing her carefully, trying to learn from her experience because she hoped to have her own catering business one day. *Chews her nails. Puts hands on eyes. Holds hands in front of her. Looks at them.* "She doesn't love her husband," Alia translated. "And she doesn't like to remember him. She was married so young." Fruit flies hovered with dust motes in the light above the coffee table. They were having problems here, Zara told Alia, with bedbugs. "She wanted to divorce him six months after she married him."

By midsummer, when Katia and I cooked shakriyeh and molokhia with her, Zara had begun divorce proceedings and, with the help of Alia, found more regular work at a Mediterranean restaurant owned by a Syrian-American near a posh mall beside a highway. A former client of Alia's, an Iraqi refugee woman, worked there as well. "Where did you learn to cook?" I asked Zara as she stirred the cornstarch into the shakriyeh to keep the yogurt from separating. "After I got married," she replied in Arabic. "In my own home."

The wedding took place when she was eighteen, she tells me and Katia, which in her circles was considered old. Her future mother-in-law, who used to come to the embroidery shop where Zara operated one of the machines, had been trying for years to get Zara married to someone in her family—four sons of her siblings at first—but Zara rejected all of those proposals. Finally, the woman offered her own son. And because Zara loved this woman, despite her own misgivings about the son, the way he seemed to run from responsibilities, in the end she married him.

The morning after the wedding, her mother-in-law announced: "Here's the kitchen . . . it's all yours!" Zara had been watching her own mother in the kitchen growing up, but her mother had always insisted on doing the work herself. Zara didn't want her mother-in-law to know she didn't really know how to cook. And yet, Zara understood something more important than the technicalities of food prep. "It's how you put yourself into the cooking," she says. Zara is using another Arabic phrase here that Katia needs to parse for me because the literal translation is meaningless. "It's as if you're blowing part of your soul into the food," explains Katia. "When you're cooking with the desire to cook, it's different than if you don't like what you're doing. This is what she means—you're cooking from your heart. Part of your spirit comes through in the food."

Her mother-in-law had asked Zara to cook *kebab hindi*—ground beef mixed with onion, curry, cinnamon, and allspice, then formed into ovals and baked in a tomato sauce. Zara wanted to prove to her new in-laws that she could do anything she set her mind to. They wanted to see if the girl they had gotten as a wife for their son could cook. "It was like a challenge," Zara recalls.

Her *kebab hindi* was a huge success. The guests her mother-in-law had invited over were asking Zara how she had prepared it—what was her secret? Her mother-in-law was so proud. "That's my daughter-in-law!" she exclaimed. Though part of the thrill may have been her own relief at no longer having kitchen duties. The family had forced Zara to quit her embroidery work, which conveniently freed her to cook for the extended family, who lived all together in the house in Hama. Her mother-in-law would go out in the morning and come home with all of the ingredients and say to Zara, "Here is everything. Just take care of it."

. . .

One afternoon after my return from Jordan, Katia and I meet Zara at her apartment. She has just gotten off work and brought home with her the daughter of her boss, a wisp of a slip of a wee thing, maybe three years old. The girl's mother had left the father when she was only a baby, and sometimes Zara's boss has no choice but to take her to the restaurant. Zara feels for the little lost girl, and brings her home with her whenever she can so she can be with other children. At this moment, though, the girl is battling with Zara's son over control of Zara's cell phone, where Zara has put on a children's music video, an irritating mechanized voice singing to synthesized music.

This afternoon, I am trying to understand more of Zara's life in Jordan—how the family survived when her husband was sick with a hernia. Since he had never liked to work anyway, and now had an excuse not to, the responsibility for their rent fell on Zara.

Back in Syria, Zara had operated a little pop-up shop out of the house selling lingerie, makeup, hair color, and some skincare products she made herself. Sometimes she would acquire household items and resell them as well. During the war, she started selling goods that people couldn't live without—clothing, feminine hygiene products, cleaning supplies. Because soldiers had flooded the city, and to cross from neighborhood to neighborhood required passing through risky checkpoints, people preferred shopping with Zara, who not only was nearby but would also let them pay later. She had left all that inventory behind, but when the wife of an uncle came to Jordan after Zara got settled, she brought her the merchandise, and Zara started selling again, out of her apartment there.

And then there were also the *anasheed* she was hired to sing— chanted religious songs to celebrate a birth or a graduation or a wedding. In Hama, she and her friend Firaq, the soulmate she had told Emmi about when they first met, sang *anasheed* together at parties around the city. Firaq, whose name means "separation," was named by her mother for the void left when her husband was killed during the 1980 Hama Massacre, just before the birth of her daughter. In the intervening years, the city had grown increasingly conservative, and by the time Zara and Firaq formed their duo, when both were in their late twenties, these kinds of parties were very much on trend. Zara treasured the nights with Firaq, singing together. It was hard being a daughter-in-law in her mother-in-law's household, with so little time to herself, not to mention space, with her and her husband and their three little girls crammed into a single bedroom. Zara and Firaq would try to arrive early so they could talk together before the party began. Then they would sing, keeping rhythm on the daf, a massive tambourine-like instrument. Every home they entered, Zara used to think, had a story. Afterward, Zara and Firaq would walk together, joking and laughing, meandering through the peaceful city, in no hurry to get home, and not once dreaming of the war that was coming.

"If you want, she will sing for you," Katia says to me, as Aya, Zara's middle daughter, flops on the sectional alongside Zara and buries her head beneath a cushion, trying to drown out the noise of the reeling children, miniature dervishes, vying for Zara's attention. Tasneem, her eldest, is trying to serve cardamom coffee to Katia, Zara, and me, the thimble-sized china cups clattering on a silver tray, while Soulaf, the youngest girl, exasperated, pleads with Zara to make her brother and this fairy-like interloper STOP BEING SO LOUD. It's a madhouse.

But then Zara, who has gone to the kitchen to get a Tupperware lid, sits on the edge of the sofa and begins to sing. She is a stone in a rushing river. The frenzy flows past her and becomes a low babble as Zara's voice breaks open the space around us. The song begins slowly, and the yearning in her voice seems to ache toward something we can't yet see. The yearning is her voice. Her voice is a rope and it is pulling all of us toward the source of the ache, where we will be consumed. Then Zara begins rapping the Tupperware lid, her improvised daf, and the song quickens. I feel a kind of whirling in her voice now, and beneath the whirling is that relentless beat like feet pounding the earth. Zara is singing in the voice of the companions of the prophet, who miss him, who long for him, who feel like orphan children without him by their side. A cell phone rings. Mohammad, her little boy, leans against Zara and babbles to himself. But all of that is so far away. Because we are in a desert, by a fire, beside a woven tent, listening to this ancient sound. The stars above, small pinholes of light, mirror the sands below and we are disappearing in the immensity. Finally, after an eternity, the beating of the daf begins to slow. Zara's voice grows quiet. When it stops, we find we are in our bodies in this apartment in the city again.

Sometimes, Zara tells me and Katia, at the restaurant near the mall by the highway, among the stainless steel bowls and pots and pans, she sings *anasheed* after closing time, keeping the beat on a cutting board, as she and a woman from Mexico and the Iraqi woman wash dishes.

. . .

At Zara's that day we cooked shakriyeh and molokhia, after we ate and as we sat drinking black tea steeped with fresh mint and sweetened with the requisite overload of sugar, Zara told us how much her husband misses her cooking. When he stops by to pick up the children, he can smell whatever is braising or frying from outside the apartment, and he asks them, longingly, "What did your mom cook today?" His mother will call the girls and reprimand them: "Why didn't you pack some food for your father?" Zara laughed gleefully as she related this story. "This is my revenge: for him to smell the food and not be able to eat it!"

And then Zara poured more tea and recited a flowery poem she'd recently sent to Emmi, as Katia tried to translate the largely untranslatable:

> Two years have passed. Sadness and sorrow prevail because of our
> separation.
> Our friendship has docked on the shores
> of love and longing.
> Our love has reached the highest skies,
> as we beg the Almighty to meet again.
> Oh God, my love has entered deep into the soul.
> We met by chance to become neighbors,
> then friends, then kin.
> We promised each other to keep our love pure,
> no matter how long we are separated from each other.
> We must meet at some point. I miss you, my princess—
> But no: my mother, my friend, my sister.

They had been in Jordan going on four years when Zara got the call in February 2016 from the International Office of Migration offering her family permanent resettlement in the United States, if they chose. So Zara called Emmi. "What do you think?" And Emmi told her, "Go. Just go."

"Are you sure you'll be able to manage on your own?" Zara asked her. Emmi was pregnant again, and the women were together all the time, more than with their husbands. And with a family that ignored

Emmi's suffering in their attempt to solve the complicated equation of violence and honor that was her marriage, she had come to rely on Zara for emotional sustenance. But this time, it was Emmi who was strong.

She reasoned with Zara. "Jordanian citizens barely have enough to make a living and live a decent life," Emmi reminded Zara. "What is here for you and your kids? This will be good for their educations. You have no future in Jordan. You don't even have an ID to prove who you are." Emmi wanted for Zara what she could not have for herself—to get out of that noisy, crowded city to save her children. "Go. Just go," she repeated.

But that wasn't what convinced Zara in the end. Rather, it was Emmi's plea: "Help me be someone. I have provided a lot of good for a lot of people—my family, my brothers and sisters, everybody—but no one is giving me anything or helping me to be me. No matter how long it takes, I will try to join you." Once Emmi put it that way, Zara had a goal. She would go to America and start a new life there, learn the language, prepare the way. This made sense, because she and Emmi were one. Zara would be ready for her and they'd support each other when Emmi finally came.

The IOM gave Zara a choice of departures: July 21 or August 21. Emmi was due in mid-August, so naturally Zara chose the latest possible date. In the months leading up to their flight, there were interviews and paperwork, health screenings, vaccinations, cultural training sessions to prepare them for their new life. And then, ten days before they were set to leave, during Eid celebrations marking the end of the month of Ramadan, Emmi went into labor.

There had been such a flurry in Zara's apartment—family and friends coming to say goodbye, neighbors perusing the furniture she needed to sell, suitcases that awaited packing. In the midst of all this activity, Zara called Emmi to check on her and she could tell something was off. "Are you having contractions?" she asked. When Emmi admitted that she was, and that her husband had taken the twins to Emmi's mother's house, Zara asked, "Do you want me to come over?"

"How can you come over with all those guests in your home?" Emmi asked. But she was almost in tears from the pain, and she was, she admitted, frightened about the delivery.

"I'm here for you. I'm with you. Everything will be okay," Zara insisted. And at the hospital, although only doctors and nurses were allowed in the delivery room itself, Zara gently lifted Emmi's clothes off and held up the hospital gown for Emmi to bow into. Emmi didn't want anybody else to help her.

On Zara's last day in Jordan, on her last day embedded in a network of family and friends, reconstructed in that country of first asylum, she had a million things to do—more shots at the IOM, a final trip to the market. But the chaos outside her was nothing compared to the uncertainty looming within her. Leaving this social web to live alone with her husband and children, what would he be able to do to them there in the US without this buffer, which, in any case, never shielded her completely? Her brother Mohammad in Amman, who had already been left behind by his other brothers, now in Germany and France, could hardly bear to stay while Zara went. But he had no choice. And how could she say goodbye to her mother and father? It had always been her mother's dream to have her children all together. Then everyone had scattered. Part of the family had been reconstituted in this foreign country, but now Zara was leaving for good. If, in fleeing to Jordan, they had consoled themselves by saying they'd return to Syria one day, when the war was over, they all knew this resettlement meant that Zara wasn't coming back.

And how could Zara say goodbye to Emmi? Just days before, the two of them had been sitting with Zara's mother, Emmi holding Zara's hand. Emmi didn't want Zara to leave, but she was pushing her to go. "I know my heart will be burned," she told Zara, "but this is best for you and your kids."

But on this last day in Jordan, Zara still needed to go to the market and finish packing. They had to be at the airport by late afternoon for their 9 p.m. flight. Still, when Emmi called and said, "I'm waiting for you. We need to have coffee together," Zara wanted to give her that. Emmi had made some sandwiches with cream cheese, but when they sat together at her kitchen table to eat, she couldn't even swallow. "Let's cut this up and eat together," Zara had tried to encourage her, "and then I need to go to the market and get back home." When Emmi insisted on going to the market with Zara, even though she'd given birth just days before, Zara had one of her girls stay with the new baby and Emmi's other children, and, one last time, they walked the streets of Zarqa, stopping to grab the things Zara thought she would need but didn't know if she'd be able to get in America. Emmi was with her every step of the way until they arrived back at the door of Zara's apartment. And then they stood there in the hallway, Emmi unable to speak, both of them holding tight to each other on the spot where they had met four years before when Zara came looking for a mop.

"Emmi's body is there, but her soul is with me," Zara tells Katia and me on this summer day a couple of years hence. And for a moment, as she remembers the pain it caused to say goodbye, Zara's voice breaks, and then she, too, cannot speak.

In the silence of that grief-filled chasm, Katia turns to comfort her. "*Inshallah Allah yijma'ak fiah*," she soothes. "God willing, God will bring you together soon."

"It's all for the kids' future," Zara goes on, remembering what Emmi had told her. But her words, like thorns, catch in her throat. It seems she's not so much explaining to us as trying to remind herself, or to convince herself, I can't quite tell which.

7   *Define "Eventually"*

"What I can do? I am mom and dad," Mendy asks by way of explana-
tion for the hardcore summer routine she has put in place for her children, which involves the banning of tablets and television in the quiet
morning hours when they are all studying together, Mendy for the A+
Certification computer service technician course she is taking on Saturdays at the community college, Shahad and Mohammed to im-
prove their English. Mendy's textbook is in English, but when she
shows it to me, it reads like a foreign language. I need an interpreter.
Mendy goes through each chapter, she explains to me, and then listens to a translation that a group of students have posted in Arabic on
YouTube. Then she goes through the chapter again. "I sit there. That
is my corner," she says, pointing to the couch near the window. "I listen to my lectures and the kids sit by me. I used to watch my dad studying, so I am like him." And I recall how Mendy's father, who never
attended school, taught himself Arabic, writing the letters on a chalkboard after he finished working in the cotton fields. "Because I
learned that from my dad, I want to teach the same thing to my children. I want them to remember that I was always studying." When
they arrived here two summers before on a flight from Jordan just as
school started, neither of the children knew any English—not even,
says Mendy, their ABCs. So last summer Mendy drove them hard,

making them practice writing in spiral notebooks, and then practice more. "But this year, I leave off," Mendy tells me, laughing at herself in staccato high-pitched mirth. "I said, *No. Let them play.*" But first, in the mornings at least, they study.

Through the door off the living room is the single bedroom that Mendy shares with the kids. She sleeps on blankets on the floor and they sleep in twin beds. Her friend Dahlia, a Syrian refugee who lives in this complex a few buildings over, tells Mendy she should move nearer to her and get a two-bedroom. "I say to Dahlia, no. I want to take my time with my kids," Mendy says. "Tomorrow they will leave me. I want to share these moments with them. When I sleep with them, when they feel that I am near them, they cannot forget."

In the mornings before school, Mendy and the kids sit here on the carpet, Mendy drinking black tea with sage and sugar, the kids drinking warm milk, all of them joking together. "It is a good time for us," Mendy tells me. In Jordan, in Zarqa, the same crowded desert city where Zara lived, Mendy would drink her tea in the mornings and sit looking out from her apartment, past the clutter of buildings to the low mountains of Amman beyond, taking in the beauty and the stillness.

When they had arrived at the airport in Amman, Mendy asked the driver, a Jordanian, to take her to the Sudanese part of town, and he drove her there, to that building. The manager, also from Sudan, when he heard she was from Kadugli and saw her injured leg, guessed the situation and offered her and the kids a room on the roof with an ad hoc kitchen. The bathroom was not connected. His wife brought Mendy and the kids a mattress and some food. They only charged her for water and electricity. He knew Mendy's suffering, because he had had to leave his country, too. The other Sudanese in the building helped to get her situated. They had all applied with the UNHCR for asylum and been granted refugee status. They told her this was the only way to get her kids in school.

Eventually, that building was condemned and demolished and Mendy went to live in a building owned by another Sudanese man, Aboud, who is from Darfur. Near the top of a hill, in a part of Zarqa with olive trees and pomegranate trees and prickly pear cactus growing behind stuccoed cement block walls that zigzag up the ascending streets, the building seemed a little removed from the grime and clatter below. Mendy and Shahad and Mohammed lived on the bottom floor, just off the street, and Aboud and his Palestinian wife and their six kids lived above. Every Friday they would eat together. Mendy and Aboud's wife would tell each other what they were cooking for dinner. One day Aboud's wife would make some Palestinian dish—maqluba, for instance, with its layers of meat and fried cauliflower, eggplant, and tomatoes, all covered with rice and cooked in a pot, then flipped upside down onto a platter—and send some down for Mendy and her kids. Another day they might eat mansaf, the national dish of Jordan: lamb cooked in a base of jameed—fermented, dried yogurt. When Mendy cooked, it was often Sudanese aseeda, a mixture of flour, salt, a little oil, and boiling water stirred over the stove into a glossy pudding, which she might serve with a tomato sauce, thickened with dried okra ground down to a powder. Aboud's family would wander downstairs and all the kids and the parents would sit on the carpet in the small living room and eat together, light filtering in through the clerestory windows.

The distress that Mendy and her children carried with them from Sudan was partly soothed by the community she and Aboud and his wife and their children made. They reminded her of how it was in her home country, where, Mendy tells me, "If you have anything extra, you share it. You don't sell." In the Nuba Mountains, the Sudanese were always gathering around each other. When someone got married, for instance, friends and family filled the home of the betrothed, eating and drinking coffee for days. At night, the floors would be covered with bodies sleeping cheek by jowl. Often, neighbors' houses had to be requisitioned for spillover guests. If someone died, the bereaved would never be left alone, sometimes for weeks. When Mendy gave birth to Mohammed, she and her husband were living in Khartoum still, a long way from her family. But they all drove up to be with her anyway.

In Jordan, Mendy was rarely alone. Aboud's children were usually downstairs with her and Shahad and Mohammed. If she went anywhere, his kids would trail after her. And she was always luring them over to get them to teach her how to dance the Palestinian dabke, Mendy and the children of varying heights all holding hands in a line, kicking their legs out together in time to the exuberant, reeling music. "We did everything together. We lived life together, as one family," Mendy remembers. But the comfort of Aboud and his wife and children, she goes on, went even deeper. "We lived in one community, not thinking of our country anymore when I found his family. I forgot everything," she says. "We lived the best days of our life with them."

. . .

Shahad has got stuck on a word in her English workbook, and she holds up the page to show Mendy. The word that has stumped Shahad is *eventually*. "Come here," Mendy says, pulling Shahad next to her on the floor, and they lean against the couch and type the word into Google Translate, listening to its mechanical pronunciation. "What does it mean, that?" Mendy asks as they play the word again and then repeat it themselves. "Eventually. Eventually. Eventually." Mendy looks down at Shahad's face looking up, and then she answers her own question. "If you say, *eventually*, that is something that hasn't got any end. It continues," she explains, confidently at first. And then, perhaps aware of my presence as a native speaker, she begins to doubt herself. "This is right?" she asks. "*Eventually?*"

Although I prefer the poetry of Mendy's definition, I gently correct her: "*Eventually* means that sometime, way in the future, it will happen . . ."

"Ah ha," says Mendy, the synapses in her brain linking this English word with the concept in Arabic.

I am thinking about how so much of the refugee experience during that period of displacement must be like a forever receding horizon line you are walking toward. Having fled one's home country and been granted asylum in another, awaiting permanent resettlement in a third—which for 99 percent of refugees will never come—so much life for millions and millions of people exists in that liminal borderland between endlessness and some unknown far-off ending, between hopelessness and hope, between Mendy's definition of *eventually* and mine.

Like for example, the life of Hashem, Mendy's nephew, a sister's son, whom I had met in Jordan about a month before this quiet morning in Mendy's apartment.

Hashem and his mother had been absorbed into Aboud's rambling household when they turned up in Jordan about a year after Mendy. At first, neither sister knew the other was in the country. One day, Mendy had taken Mohammed to Al Bashar Hospital in Amman, where all refugees go and where he was being treated for anemia. Mendy would always say hello to Rawda, one of the Sudanese housekeepers, and Rawda would always ask after Mohammed. One day, Rawda told Mendy that she'd noticed there was another woman coming to the hospital for appointments—a woman who shared Mendy's last name, who was also from the Nuba Mountains. When Mendy heard this, she asked Rawda to find out where the woman was living in Jordan. Mendy wanted to ask around among the Sudanese community about her.

Eventually, with Rawda serving as intermediary, a meeting was arranged at the hospital, between Mendy and this mysterious woman, who had no phone but who had Mendy's last name. *Had our father had another wife whose existence we'd never known of?* Mendy wondered. And then, from down the hospital corridor, she saw a woman in a traditional thoub, holding the hand of a young man Mendy recognized as her nephew Hashem. But who was the woman with him? It couldn't be Mendy's sister—the woman looked so old and thin. Could that be Mendy's mother? But as she hurried toward the pair, Mendy realized that, indeed, it was her sister, a farmer, once strong and straight, but bent sick now with uterine cancer. The sisters held each other and cried. The next day, Mendy collected her sister and Hashem from Amman and brought them to Aboud's building in Zarqa to live with her and her kids on the ground floor.

By the time I visited Hashem in Zarqa, he had been there four years, but his mother had, in the meantime, returned to Sudan, where she had died. She and Hashem had come to Jordan after being brutally beaten in battles with government forces trying to confiscate the family's tribal land in Abu Karshola. Another son of her sister's had disappeared in the fighting and no one knew where he was. Mendy suspects her sister went back to Sudan to search for that son, but she hadn't even told Mendy she was leaving. Maybe, knowing she was dying, she had wanted to return to the land of her birth. Mendy would never have let her sister go if she had known, which was probably why her sister didn't tell her.

Hashem had witnessed all the brutality suffered by his mother and brothers, and it had done something to him. "When you see him, he looks sad," Mendy had warned me. "Thinking more, thinking more . . . ," she said, making furious air circles with her finger near her temple, "like that." Back in Sudan, he'd been a student at the university. In Jordan, like all official refugees, he wasn't allowed to work, and without work, he couldn't afford an education. "But also, we didn't want him to work," Mendy confessed. This was because, at any moment, he might remember what he had seen and break down. Mendy had become a mother to Hashem after her sister returned to Sudan. She did what she knew to do to ease his trauma. "When he was with me," she remembered, "I kept him busy. I gave him things to do." But then Mendy and her kids had been accepted for resettlement, and because Hashem was not her biological child she'd had to leave him behind.

At least Aboud was with him. "He does not leave him," Mendy said. "When we came here"—to the United States—"we told Aboud, 'Please take care of this boy.' He said, 'I will look on him as on my son. There is no difference between him and my kids.' For that reason, Aboud stays close to him all the time."

As with her own kids, who didn't yet know the presumed fate of their father, Mendy had asked Aboud not to tell Hashem about his mother's death. She had thought Hashem would quickly follow her to the US and that she could tell him in person then, ease the blow. "He'll be busy with us and with the children and he won't notice," Mendy told me, explaining her logic in waiting for the reunion that surely, *eventually*, would arrive. "So I kept telling him, 'Soon you will come to be with us.'" But she had made it to Houston just a couple of months before the 2016 election, after which everything changed.

On my trip to Jordan, I sat with Aboud and Hashem in the living room of the ground-floor apartment in Zarqa where Mendy must have danced the dabke with all those children. As registered refugees in Jordan, neither is permitted to work. Aboud receives 265 Jordanian dinar (JD) a month—about $375—on which he and his wife must sustain their six children. His rent alone is 120 JD. His children do attend school, but they go in shifts because the system has become so overwhelmed with the flood of Syrians. Aboud has been a refugee from Sudan in Jordan for many years. He married a Palestinian refugee, who was granted Jordanian citizenship. He wonders if this is why his UN application is being slow-walked. Hashem, too, has heard nothing.

I turned to Hashem, sitting cross-legged on a mat against a white wall, knowing he couldn't work or attend university. "So my question is, just to try to understand your life . . .," I began, helplessly, "what do you do during the day? Can you tell me a little bit?"

"I just go from here to the door," Hashem said, looking down. "No more."

Earlier, while Hashem stepped out to buy orange soda for us all, Aboud told me about how Hashem's mother had died a few years before. "And he doesn't know until now," Aboud said. "He likes to stay with little children. He doesn't have friends." Something had happened to Hashem, Aboud was trying to say. Something had been broken.

And they all missed Mendy. Her cooking—the aseeda, as well as the fried sweet dough doused in citrus syrup called zalabiya. "She liked to teach others, and she could learn very easily," recalled Aboud. She would even teach Jordanians how to make Jordanian food, he told me, laughing. But they also missed Mendy herself. She had such a vibrant personality. "She is the dynamo in her house," he said, then he grew quiet. "When she left the house, it became darker."

Turning again to Hashem, I told him, "I know your aunt loves you very much. She told me that she wishes she could bring you to the US to be with her, and that you could take care of each other." As Hashem continued to look down into his lap, Aboud spoke. "He has no one here to take care of him," he said. "It's a responsibility to have him, because he's sick." Sometimes Aboud becomes afraid that when Hashem leaves the house, he won't come home. People at the UN know about the situation. They have told Aboud to call in case of an emergency. But what can they do? "He is my responsibility," Aboud repeats. "We are living as a family. But if he is sent to his aunt, I will be happy and feel comfortable."

. . .

When we had both returned from our staggered trips to Jordan, I met up with Alia as she zipped around the streets of southwest Houston, pulling into an apartment complex in her red VW, breezing into a woman's home, whipping off her aviator sunglasses like a be-hijabed superhero. Like a breath of fresh air. Like a quenching drink in a desert. That's how Mendy would describe Alia later: "If you are standing in the hot sunshine and someone gives you very cold water," she would say of Alia's work with Amaanah, "you feel you are in a safe place," adding, "I feel that I am with my sister."

But that day soon after my return, as Alia and I cruised the streets of Gulfton, largely devoid of the sheltering live oak trees that shade and cool the more affluent parts of the city, I told Alia about the people I had met in Jordan and what I had come to understand about the situations of some of the women here by traveling there. I told her first about Zara's friend Emmi, the abusive marriage she couldn't escape.

"This is the issue with the rules and the system there," Alia said in response. "That's why I left the Middle East. The woman, she can't live in freedom. She can't get her rights. Always the government in the Middle East is beside the man." This injustice, Alia went on, begins in the home, in the community, where boys are favored and indulged at the expense of girls. "It gives him this impression," she believed, "that he has all the rights. If he wants to marry, if he wants to beat a woman, he has this right. They never," she emphasized, "give this right to the woman." But, Alia argued, "If you go back to our religion, believe me, it would not accept that. The Muslim religion is the same as Christianity and Judaism: women and men are equal."

I also tried to explain to Alia what seemed to be Hashem's traumatic response to the upheaval and loss he'd experienced. I described the relationship between Hashem and Aboud—how Aboud, in a country not his own, watches over this nephew of Mendy's, his countrywoman, because he feels it's his responsibility. But Alia was picking up on something else as well, another thread woven into Hashem's story. "He has refugee status?" she asked, as we stared at photos on my phone that I'd taken that afternoon in Zarqa. Hashem staring blankly into the camera. Aboud gripping UNHCR paperwork. When I told her yes, she said, "The part between when you left your country and you are resettled in another country, this part between these two, this is the worst part of the whole story. Why?" she asked rhetorically, then answered. "Because if you are in your country, you will accept the situation. It is your country. And when you are in the country where you were resettled, you know you should accept it and understand it and learn. You are going through the situation to get . . ."—she was grasping for the right phrase.

"A new life?" I suggested.

"A new life," she nodded. "But this is between two."

"Right. And you never know when it will end, or *if* it will end," I said, following Alia's logic.

"It is confusing," she said, remembering her own time in Jordan, in between Iraq and the US, not knowing there would ever be a life lived in English, working with other women refugees. "It is like . . . you don't know what is the future. What will happen to you. You're not in the sky. You're not on the ground. You are in between. This is the worst part of the whole story."

.   .   .

One Saturday morning later in the summer, Hashem is on Mendy's mind when I drive with her and the kids to her A+ Computer class at a Houston Community College campus housed in a former mall. "A+ Computer" is, incidentally, the nickname Mohammed and Shahad have given to their mom. They tell me this as we pass through the still streets, all in shadow.

Shahad, her hair in tiny braids pulled back into a hot pink scrunchie, carries art supplies in her cross-body purse. She and Mohammed look out the window as Mendy tells me that last night Hashem had called, and afterward she lay awake, unable to go back to sleep, on the floor beside her children. The UN seems to be questioning Hashem's ability to care for himself or to find anyone to care for him. But if he were to go home to Sudan, Mendy tells me quietly, "I'm afraid we will lose him." If she can't find a way to bring him here, where she can care for him, get him into school, get him working, then she would rather return to Jordan than stay here. "He needs me," she says, "and I need him."

Mendy is the only woman in a class of young Black, Hispanic, and Asian men. The room is clean, entirely functional, devoid of all ornament except a poster on a bulletin board that urges, "Learn it. Prove it." I think the message has something to do with getting a job. This is what they are here for, these sons and daughters of immigrants, or these immigrants themselves: a certificate that will land them decent work. Work that will lead to a better life. Maybe, I think, this sterile room at the center of a former mall is the beating heart of the American Dream, such as it is. Or its inception point.

In the hallway outside the classroom, I sit with the kids. Mohammed is playing Fortnite on a tablet, while Shahad paints with watercolors on a long roll of craft paper spread out on the floor. We make small talk. "So when you came here," I ask them, "were there things you thought were kind of weird about America?"

Shahad answers right away. "The language," she remembers. "I was just looking at people, staring at them for a long time. I didn't know what they were saying."

Mohammed concurs. "I thought they were talking like an elephant," he says.

"That doesn't make sense, Mohammed. Nobody gets you," Shahad scolds.

"I know," Mohammed responds, unperturbed.

"I like my country, Jordan," says Shahad absently, painting hearts in purple paint on her arm.

"You think of Jordan as your country?" I ask.

"Yeah, because I lived there three years," she says, matter-of-factly. "I don't even remember how my country looked like. I forgot."

"Do you remember *anything* from it?"

"I remember my grandma's house. The lemon tree. We used to stay under it," says Shahad.

"I still remember my friends," Mohammed chimes in.

"My grandma did not let us take the lemons," Shahad continues, ignoring Mohammed, "so we got so many lemons, and we hid them behind that tree, and in the morning we say, 'Sorry, Grandma, they all fell off.' So we got to eat them."

"That sounds kind of sneaky," I observe, laughing with the two kids now.

"Yeah, we always sneak around," Mohammed says.

"When we were in Jordan," remembers Shahad, "in the morning when my mom gave us money for school, we would sneak to the store and buy ice cream."

"Did she ever find out?" I ask.

"Nope, and I don't want to tell her."

In Jordan, Mendy had told me once, the kids were rarely ever inside. They were always sprinting up and down the narrow lanes, shouting and laughing, with Aboud's kids. But when they moved to Houston, Mendy said, "no one went outside. There was no more running. No yelling. For that reason, they do not love the life here. Mohammed said to me, 'I do not like it here. I am not seeing that it is good.'"

When Mendy comes out of the classroom for a break, she joins Shahad on the floor and picks up a paintbrush and begins to paint, and they all three continue to remember their time in Jordan.

"My mind is kind of mixed," Shahad observes. "When I went to Jordan, I was crying. I wanted to go back to my friends in Sudan," she recalls. "But when I came to America, I cried. I said, *I want to go back to my friends in Jordan.*" And then, as if starting to realize as she is speaking something of what this displacement has cost her, Shahad says, "Even if I go back, I won't know what to do."

Perhaps trying to coax her daughter away from the ache of being always in between, Mendy jokes, "Next year if we go to Australia, will you say you miss the people in America?"

Still serious, though, Shahad replies, "I don't want to live here my whole life."

"Where do you want to live?" I ask this little girl with the purple hearts on her arm, who has lived in three countries and speaks two languages, but who remembers almost nothing of her homeland, except her grandmother's lemon tree.

"I want to go around the world," she says.

.   .   .

Geleta Mekonnen, assistant director for client care and outreach in the Reception and Placement Program of Interfaith Ministries Refugee Services, has invited Mendy and me to his office today to talk about Hashem. I had run into Geleta, whom I knew from some previous work, in the parking lot of Mendy's apartment complex one afternoon, where he had been helping a refugee client submit an Affidavit of Relationship as she formally requested to bring a family member still in Congo to the US through the Family Reunification Program. As we stood on the black asphalt beneath the sun, I mentioned Mendy's worries for her nephew in Jordan, her lack of clarity around how to help him. Geleta suggested I bring her to his office to talk.

Geleta is Yoda-like—balding, with a thinning ring of hair encircling the bottom of his head, his eyes pale, enfolded by gray lids above and deep circles underneath, his forehead wrinkled. Being a refugee himself from Ethiopia, who spent two years in the late 1970s in Sudan before coming to the US, Geleta, like Alia, is a bridge between worlds. The dignity with which he treats people on both sides of that bridge feels, in this era, like lost wisdom, like a balm for the American soul.

Part of treating people with dignity means telling them the truth, and this Geleta does with Mendy right away. The United States Refugee Resettlement Program, he explains, allows certain immediate family members of a refugee to request to come to the United States—unmarried children under the age of twenty-one, spouses, parents. Not, however, other extended family members. This was bad news for Hashem. "It happens to be your nephew is . . . Let's put it in this way: I know he's closely related to you, but in *this* area it is a distance," Geleta tells Mendy gently, but firmly.

"So what else can you do?" he asks. If Hashem isn't already registered with the UNHCR, Geleta answers his own question, he should register, and then he should ask the UN to refer him to the US resettlement program, giving Mendy's name as a possible sponsor. "The reason why is that from time to time the UN refers people for resettlement in hosting countries," Geleta goes on. "Every year they refer cases for Australia, for the EU, for Canada, for the United States—these are hosting countries that welcome refugees. They will see a pool of people and they see that the durable solution for those people is to resettle them, which, in this case, maybe since you are here, may attract the eye of one of those people. One thing working for him is that you are here. You are willing to welcome him if his case is referred to the US," Geleta says. "So that is the only available path I see," he concludes. "Because there is no other."

Mendy has grown quiet and still, her head bowed, eyes closed. She could, Geleta suggests without much enthusiasm, contact her state representative, John Culberson, or the two Texas senators, Ted

Cruz and John Cornyn—all Republicans. She could write them a letter and tell Hashem's story. *But they would never do anything about it, I think, so why even bother?*

"In case I write this letter," Mendy begins, a tightness in her voice, "or in case I meet this person, if he asks me where I work or how I can take care of Hashem . . . He can ask me that?" Perhaps Mendy has heard some of the talk around immigrants not getting green cards if they've used social services—the Trump administration's "public charge inadmissibility test," which said that if the government determined a person was likely at any time to be in need of public assistance, they could be denied admission to or lawful permanent residence in the US. In any event, though, this rule didn't apply to refugees, and Geleta quickly eases Mendy's fears on this front, at least. "No, no," he tells her, "Whether they can help or not, resources may not be a factor. That will not affect your case. Whether they have the interest to help you is a different matter," he continues. "Because right now, things are not rosy, things are not really in favor of the immigrants, the refugees, and they are trying to really cut some of the numbers."

The meeting has so far been, I think, a bit of a bust. But then something starts to shift. At first I don't perceive it. Geleta is urging Mendy, "Anything that you think can work, try it! The only thing they can say is no."

"Yeeeeees," Mendy answers, but without her customary delight, resigned instead to the futile task at hand.

"It may take a year. It may take more," Geleta continues though, warming to his topic. "But don't get tired. Just keep on working. Someday, you may see positive things. Maybe something will open down the line. But don't say, *Oh, I cannot do this.*" Geleta is looking intensely at Mendy now, and she at him. "Every little thing you do keeps *you* going," he says quietly. "Really, we help ourselves. We don't solve anything. There's not really a solution. The solution is:

Do something. When you do something, you are hoping that one day"—*eventually?*—"some good with that will come."

Geleta has offered no false hope. He has hidden nothing. He has not misrepresented the truth, though it is hard to bear. And yet, listening to him, I have begun to feel strangely hopeful. You don't write your senators and congressmen because you think they will listen to you, necessarily. You write them because to write is to act, to not sit still. It is to refuse to be a victim of the vast oppressive machinery that does not even know you exist, that does not see your suffering. *I really don't care. Do U?* said the jacket that First Lady Melania Trump had worn in June as she visited child detention centers along the border with Mexico. You do what your spirit urges, not to bring outward change, but to align yourself with the moral arc of the universe that bends toward justice. Like a Buddhist koan, Geleta's words echo in my mind: *Because there is no solution, the solution is: do something.*

Even Mendy is smiling now. "Is that okay for you?" Geleta asks her. "I'm sorry if I take your time. The reason I wanted you to come is, it's much better to sit face to face, if we can, to have this conversation. Sometimes when you call, something maybe is lost through the air. If we can meet each other, we can challenge each other and we can see each other's views. Any questions, my sister, my neighbor?" he asks Mendy. Then he says, referring to the ancient hominin specimen unearthed by archaeologists in his homeland of Ethiopia, "We are all the children of Lucy."

· • ·

Back in June, when I was traveling in Jordan, on the day I visited Zara's brother, Mohammad, in East Amman, that neighborhood packed with the displaced who lived now in the uncertain space between the ground and sky, I had seen, spray-painted on a low wall, its stucco veneer crumbling, this word: بكرا. Despite my rudimentary Arabic, I was able to read what it said: *Bukra. Tomorrow.*

In Houston, I had a private Arabic teacher for a while, an older gentleman with Coke-bottle glasses named Suleiman, who had fled Muammar Gaddafi's authoritarian regime in Libya after working for the resistance. Suleiman knew I was a sucker for the derivations of words, their roots, the stories behind them, which were never in our workbook. *Yesterday. Today. Tomorrow.* That had been our lesson one week. As I practiced writing the words in Arabic, and then saying them out loud, Suleiman paused on that last one: *Bukra. Tomorrow.* This word literally means, of course, the day that will come after this one. But, Suleiman told me, it has another meaning, too, metaphoric: it can imply a tomorrow that we long for endlessly, a day that will never actually arrive. Suleiman had then recalled an Egyptian proverb that translates roughly as *Tomorrow, when the apricots blossom* . . .—the evocation of a season so ephemeral that it comes and goes before you even know it, leaving you yearning for the next year's harvest even now. "It means a tomorrow that will never come," said Suleiman. "You will wait and wait, but it will never happen." When hell freezes over, so to speak. But, he said, *bukra* also has another usage. It can be a kind of encouragement. *Tomorrow, my sister, my neighbor.* Meaning: a day not too far off, even if we cannot see it, a day that will come eventually, if we can just hang in there long enough for it to arrive.

8 *Cinderella in Jordan*

It's evening rush hour and Sara is trying to get to English class. I am riding shotgun in her secondhand SUV, the glare of the setting sun blinding us. She is blasting music sung in Arabic and moving her hands to the rhythm, singing along, the sound of her voice conveying the emotion of words I can't understand—hurt, longing, chiding, disbelief. Sara is driving as if she's in Syria—speeding up, then slamming on the brakes as she is about to rear-end the car in front of her, honking, yelling at other drivers—all without a license in the state of Texas. The husband of a friend of hers taught her to drive in one day, and she's been behind the wheel here ever since.

"Hate me but don't forget me!" the woman on the radio sings in Syrian Arabic, and Sara pauses her own singing to translate for me. "I don't speak English too much," Sara says, excusing her translation.

"But I understand you perfectly," I assure her.

"My work helps me," she explains, and she tells me she's moved up from stocker to cashier at the 99 Cents Only store, which forces her to talk to customers and practice her English.

But there is more to learning English for Sara than becoming fluent in these transactions, or even than the training as a lab technician that she would like to find. The week before, as Alia and I stood in the doorway to Sara's apartment saying goodbye, Sara told Alia in Arabic to tell me, "I want to write a story about myself, so help me." Then Sara turned my way. "I want to learn English very good so I can write it," she said.

"Don't worry," Alia told her, "we will help you."

Sara is struggling in this English class she's taking, but she likes her classmates, mostly young men from India. They help her with her homework. The other day, she tells me, she asked one of the guys, "Why every people from India do like this?" and she bobbles her head, doing her best imitation of the gesture, then laughs infectiously at herself. "He tells me, 'Sara . . .'"—and she shakes her head as he must have done. Then she bobbles it again.

. . .

The first day I met Sara back in February, before I knew the story of her engagement to her husband in the suburbs of Damascus, his sisters draped in black burkas, or the beatings that he gave her, the basement field hospital where he was taken after being injured in fighting against the regime, before I knew about Sara's flight out of Syria, through empty, burning cities and across the desert plains, Sara had told me and Alia about the apartment in Jordan where she lived for a time after her husband died of his injuries—an apartment within a complex of buildings for the widows of Syrian martyrs and the wives of the imprisoned.

"She was living in a building named One Body Complex," Alia had translated that morning. The name referred to the *ummah*, the collective community of Muslim believers. "She lived with them. Each woman had a story different from the others." When the UN accepted Sara to come to America, the women said to her, "We want you to write our stories in a book. We need someone to write all these stories. Don't forget us!" And Sara, who had once wanted to be a journalist, told them, "I promise you! I will be a writer in the future and I will write them down."

Then in May, as I was preparing to travel to Jordan, Sara again brought up this One Body Complex. "This is one of the stories that I passed through. This is the most important one." And she started to tell me the story, which was the story of those sisters who begged her not to forget.

I think Sara understands intuitively, as all storytellers do, that there is something life-affirming in the act of telling one's own tale. When you tell your story, you are saying *this*—and not *that*—is how it was. You are in control, bringing order out of the chaos of experience. You are giving your past a shape and breathing life into it. You are a kind of god.

Or maybe you are not a god. Maybe you are a refugee woman from Syria. And maybe for this injustice you have suffered—the uprooting, the way you lost your country, the way you lost everything, while the world stood idly by—you want a hearing. Because maybe if you can learn English, maybe if you can tell your story, you have the potential to turn the heart of a listener, to awaken in that other soul some understanding of your humanity, which might become an acceptable stand-in for the justice you will never actually know. Someday, I hope that Sara can write her story in English herself. For now, this is what she wanted me to write down.

When she had first arrived in Jordan, she and her children and her brother, Mustafa, had lived with her husband's family—his mother and brothers and sisters and all their kids—in an apartment that the Free Syrian Army had helped to arrange. But even before her husband died, Sara had wanted out. Her mother-in-law didn't like having Sara's brother in the home. He was only fourteen, but she told Sara, "He is a man, your brother. I care about my son's wives"—as if their honor was at risk with him living in such close proximity. So when someone told Sara about an apartment for Syrian single mothers, she and three of her sisters-in-law took a taxi, all of them in their black burkas, to check it out.

They met with the manager, Abu Suleiman, a Palestinian-Jordanian with salt-and-pepper hair and square-rimmed glasses, who wore the traditional long white jalabiya and constantly worried prayer beads through the fingers of his right hand. They told him, not quite being truthful, "Our husbands have passed away." But he replied, "Don't lie. Where are they?" Sara told Abu Suleiman that her husband was in the hospital. Two of the sisters-in-law said that their husbands had been arrested in Syria. Samah, the third one, who was very beautiful, confessed that she was divorced. That same day, when they told Abu Suleiman the truth, he gave them two apartments to split among them. Later, after Sara's husband died in the hospital from his injuries, Sara's mother and sister came from Syria and lived in that apartment too.

The owners of the complex were Saudis, and rent was free. The women were even given extra money for living expenses. But the rules to which the women had to adhere were oppressive. And also kind of weird. No smoking. No loud music. No makeup. No perfume. No tight clothes. No short clothes. You had to be covered. You couldn't leave without permission. You couldn't leave after sundown. When you did leave, Abu Suleiman would look at your eyes to make sure you weren't wearing eyeliner or eyebrow pencil. Sons over twelve could not live with you. If you had a male relative visiting—even a son—you could only meet with him in the reception area. All of these rules had been put in place, ostensibly, to protect the women, who had nowhere to go and no money to spend, so they felt they had to stay, despite all the restrictions. There were cameras everywhere, watching them. As was Abu Suleiman.

That wasn't the worst part, though. The worst part was Abu Suleiman, who was running a one-man marriage racket at the One Body Complex. He would engage himself to various widows without following proper Islamic procedures—young women with young children, living far from home and in such precarious circumstances as to make consent impossible. He married them in sham weddings conducted informally by a local sheik but he never registered the marriages with the state. Then, a few months later, he divorced them, which was easy to do since there was no public record. Sara had been hearing rumors of this after she moved into her apartment. And then it happened to her sister-in-law, the beautiful Samah, with whom Sara was living.

That day in May that I visited Sara, I reminded her that I'd be heading to Jordan shortly. "Are there people you know who I can visit at this complex?" I asked her. And Sara, eyebrows drawn on thickly, rebelliously, as if daring anyone to object, replied, "You can visit if you want, but don't say someone sent you, or that you have any idea what's going on there. Just act like you don't know anything." I asked Sara for the address and she wrote it in Arabic in my notebook. *One Body Complex. Abu Nasr neighborhood,* she read for me, her finger traveling beneath the words. Then she wrote, *Abu Suleiman.* "This is the guy. He controls everything—Abu Suleiman," she said.

.   .   .

In the end, what I found wasn't exactly the exposé I had vaguely imagined.

One afternoon in Jordan, I visited Sara's sister, Duah, who had lived with Sara for a time at the One Body Complex, before Duah met her husband, also Syrian. When Duah was four months pregnant, her husband left for Germany, via the same route as Sara's brothers and untold other Syrians: Jordan to Turkey by air, Turkey to Greece by sea, Greece to Germany on foot. In the meantime, Duah gave birth to their baby alone in Jordan. Now, three years later, she was still stuck in limbo, waiting on her petition for asylum in Germany. Just the day before I met her, Duah's asylum case had been refused due to a classification error, so she would have to continue to wait in Jordan until the German government made its decision. "She's waiting, but she doesn't know what she's waiting for. She's waiting for things to become better in Syria or to go to Germany. She's waiting for both. She's waiting for nothing." That's how my translator that day interpreted what Duah said.

A Syrian friend of Duah's was visiting that afternoon, and I turned to this friend and asked, "Is it the same for you here as well?" But this woman told me about how she and a group of friends had pooled their money together and bought a car, which this woman drove—a kind of taxi service, their own private Uber. They advertised through friends, who told their friends, who told their friends, and now they had a WhatsApp group and other cars and drivers for women to get around Amman, or for their children to be ferried back and forth to schools, bypassing the city's cabs, driven by men.

I loved this story of movement as a counterpoint to the stasis of Duah's story, this story of female empowerment as a counterpoint to Sara's story of oppression in the One Body Complex, which is where, after leaving Duah's apartment as the sun was setting, my translator and her husband and I now headed.

It was dark by the time we arrived at the complex, whose various buildings rose, clean and white and pure, on one of the hills overlooking the lights of the city below. My translator's husband got out and approached some men hanging around the entryway, where he asked for Abu Suleiman. "That's me," said a man in white jalabiya, prayer beads hanging from his fingers. I almost couldn't believe my luck—that the mission I was on to find this place and this man had been so easily accomplished, with so little drama. Here was at least part of Sara's story made flesh, which up until now had existed for me entirely in my mind, which is to say that it had felt a little like a fairy tale—somewhat unreal.

After some back-and-forth among the men, Abu Suleiman invited us into the reception room. Its walls were lined with couches, which, placed end-to-end, would have stretched the length of a soccer field. I started by trying to loosen him up. After explaining that I was a writer from the US, in Jordan to learn about how the country was dealing with its refugee crisis, I said I had heard that this complex helped refugee women. His answers were curt, and I had the distinct impression that he did not want to talk to me, but he must have done some mental calculation that told him he should. When I asked if there were any restrictions or rules for the women who lived here, he said, "No. Just that only women and children can live here." And then he abruptly asked, "Do you want to see?" And he led us into a courtyard, laid with artificial grass and lit by unnatural halogen lights, onto which various buildings of rough-hewn white limestone seemed to open. Clusters of boys and clusters of girls moved along the walls and across the expanse. Abu Suleiman stood beside me as some shy and gangly Syrian preteens, their long hair pulled back in neon pink scrunchies, came over to practice their English. There would be no possibility of peppering them with the questions I really wanted to ask, or of talking to their mothers, of hearing the stories that Sara had promised them she would tell.

But as we were leaving and I was snapping photos of the girls in the courtyard, which they and Abu Suleiman had given me permission to do, I pointed my phone at one of the signs announcing the name of this place and clicked. The white writing stared out from the center of a royal blue oval, like the iris of an eye watching everything below. *One Body Complex.* And when we got in the car, my translator's husband told me that, when I had taken the picture, Abu Suleiman had turned to him and asked nervously, "Why is she photographing that? That is a Saudi organization. It is on the US terrorist watch list."

· · ·

In the empty hours of the empty days in Abu Suleiman's imprisoning apartment complex in Jordan, as she waited, not knowing what she was waiting for, Sara would scroll through WeChat, looking for a way to escape her reality—a widow at twenty-four with two young children, far from a home to which she could not return. And her sister-in-law, Samah, quote-unquote married now to Abu Suleiman, could not be trusted. Sara knew Samah was feeding information to him about her and her mother and sister, trying to get them kicked out of the complex. In fact, now that her husband was dead, Sara was no longer of any use to his family, and friends started to warn Sara not to leave her children alone—that his family might be plotting to take them. It was through the children, namely, that her husband's benefits, as a martyr, would arrive, and if others had the children, then they'd get whatever money was coming. Sara needed to get new people in her life, because all of the people she'd come with from Syria were fighting with her. But she was stuck in this complex on the outskirts of the city, without any viable reason that would grant her permission to leave. So when her friends told her to download the WeChat app, that it would let her connect to random people, people she'd never met, she did.

His message had popped up on her screen. "Hi! I'm Saam. I'm from Iraq. I love people from Syria. You really helped the Iraqi people during the war. You are very kind people." At first, Sara was not into him at all. *Saam* is a traditionally Shia name, and the Alawites, like Bashar al-Assad, who ruled Syria, are a sect of Shia Islam. Sara had seen what the Alawites were doing to her country and to Sunnis like her and her family, and she wanted nothing to do with someone connected to that. So she asked this random guy who was reaching out to her on WeChat, "Why are you messaging me?"

"I wanted to speak with you because I saw on your profile that you were from Syria," he wrote back. "Why did you download this program if you don't want to talk to other people?"

When Saam explained to Sara that he was actually Sunni, however, she relented. At first they just talked about what was happening
in Syria, and about the neighborhood in Damascus where she was
from. Saam had spent time in that area before the war. He was in Amman now working on a master's degree in political science. Sara told
him nothing, though, about why she was there, nothing about what
she had lost. She didn't tell him she had kids, or that she was living in
this apartment for the widows of martyrs. Instead, she let him think
she was just a woman from Damascus, gold-rimmed Ray-Ban sunglasses perched atop a gauzy hijab, gold-trimmed Gucci bag draped
in the crook of her arm. She told him her father was an engineer,
which was true, but she didn't say that he had stayed behind in Syria.
She didn't tell Saam that she was broke, barely surviving on the food
cards they got from the UN. That she was stuck in this apartment
complex with the lecherous Abu Suleiman and his stifling, self-serv-
ing rules.

After a few weeks of just messaging, Saam and Sara exchanged
numbers and started talking by phone. "What are you doing?" he
would sometimes ask. And she would tell him, "I'm shopping," and
let him imagine her in one of the glitzy malls in one of the upscale
neighborhoods of Amman, as, in reality, she rummaged through
piles of tomatoes at the market. Or, "I'm cooking," and allow him to
assume it was over a stainless steel range in one of the high-rise
apartments that people like her now cleaned for wages. Sara still had
no idea what Saam looked like, and he never forced the issue with
her. "I won't ask you to show me yourself until you say, 'Do you want
to see me?'" he promised her. She liked the time she spent in that
dream world, where she was happy, where her life was beautiful,
where she could forget the truth. She knew she was lying. But it
wasn't to impress Saam. It was for herself. She lied for herself. And
after a while, she found that she had come to need that world. It freed
her. It sustained her. That's why she kept chatting with Saam.

Sara had a friend, Oum Warid, an older woman who lived in one of the neighboring buildings in the One Body Complex. In the mornings, Sara would go to Oum Warid's to drink coffee and talk about Saam. Oum Warid came from Daraa, in that bombed-out southern region of Syria through which Sara had been smuggled on her way to Jordan. Oum Warid knew Sara's story, what had happened to her husband, and she told Sara, "Be careful. This man may bring you problems. He may be no good."

"I'm just friends with him," Sara assured her.

"Tell him the truth, Sara. Tell him you have kids. Tell him you were married. Tell him what happened."

But Sara put Oum Warid off. She didn't want to reveal her internal life to Saam. And in a way, she didn't want to make him real, either. "Not now . . . not now," she said.

One day as they were talking, Saam told Sara, "I'm cleaning my apartment. Open the video and put your finger over the camera and you can see me but I won't see you." At first, Sara shrugged it off, as if she didn't really care about seeing this random guy she'd been talking to. But in her heart, she wanted to know who Saam was. So she opened her phone, put her finger over the camera, and looked.

He was beautiful. And his apartment was beautiful. And his car was beautiful. He had a beautiful life. Later, over coffee with Oum Warid, Sara tried to process what was happening inside her. "Saam is not married. He doesn't have children. He's studying. He has a car and a home. Why is he speaking with me? What is he looking for? He doesn't know anything about my life. Why should I tell him the truth? Why should I tell him I have kids? That I had a husband that died? That I'm living in this apartment for widows?"

But after observing Saam in his world, the imaginary world Sara had called into being just disintegrated. She suddenly saw the shabby truth of her remnant life through his eyes. She saw that his life was perfect, and that her life was nothing. And that she was nothing as well.

The next day, Sara told Saam, "I can't speak with you anymore."

"Tell me why," he demanded. "Did I cause any problems? I promised you I wouldn't ask for a picture of you. I've never seen you. I don't know you. Why are you doing this?"

Sara told him, "You don't know anything."

And he said, "Tell me what's happened to you. Okay? Tell me."

.　.　.

When Sara told Saam she didn't want to talk to him anymore, didn't want to tell him anything, it was because, she explained to me and Alia, "I don't like people to see that I'm nothing. I like to show that I'm something." But when he said to her, "Tell me what's happened to you," something broke in Sara. She was so exhausted. She had no money, and lately her mother had been pushing her to marry someone, anyone, who could take care of her and her children. Sara really liked Saam, but when she had seen how far his beautiful life was from her reality, she realized it was hopeless. It had to end.

And yet. Sara and her mother had been planning to go to the market to spend their monthly rations on groceries, though they didn't even really have the cash for a taxi. So she reached out to Saam again. She told him she needed to go shopping. Did he want to meet her? "Really?" he replied. And then, with a deep breath, Sara told him that her mother and her children would be with her. "Finally," Saam said, "you are telling the truth." He had suspected something was off when, during their phone calls, he could hear her son, Adam, calling out "Mom!" to Sara, but her doppelganger, that woman from Damascus, had told Saam that he was her brother.

Now, veils falling away between them, Sara suggested a plan. "My mom doesn't know anything about you. She doesn't know you are my friend. So I will tell her you are a friend of my husband's—that I saw you at the hospital in Amman and you helped me."

"Okay, Sara," Saam agreed, "but now tell me about your life."

And in the hour or so before they were set to meet, Sara told Saam everything.

"You told him your husband passed away?" Alia asked.

"I told him everything about my life," Sara replied. And then she continued the story. "I couldn't put on makeup or perfume because I lived under Abu Suleiman," she said. "I couldn't wear anything strange." But under her abaya, Sara had worn tight-fitting clothes, and in the taxi she pulled off the burka covering all but her eyes, then lined those in black, thickened her brows with pencil, smoothed on foundation—performing a spell of transformation on herself. Bibbidi-bobbidi-boo. "It's shameful what you are doing," the taxi driver told her, watching in the rearview mirror as he drove Sara and her mother and the kids down off the hilltop into the chaotic center of Amman.

Saam had told her he would be in front of the meat shop, and Sara saw him before he knew it was Sara he was seeing. He was wearing an elegant black suit—a sign of the luxurious life he could afford, so far out of Sara's league. But Sara forged ahead. She needed to know if this was the end of the story, or a beginning.

As he approached them, he said to Sara, playing along with the story she'd concocted, "Hello. Do you remember me? I saw you at the hospital. I was a friend of your husband's." Sara felt, from that first moment, that Saam liked her. After their shopping, he offered them a ride home, which was a good thing because they had spent their last dinars to get downtown. Her mother sat in front, and Sara and the kids in back. He'd left flowers on the seat for her. "Tell me about Damascus," Saam pressed Sara's mom. "I love Damascus."

But in the back seat, Sara, as if the midnight bells were tolling, began unweaving the spell she'd cast upon herself in the taxi, pulling out her burka from her bag, wiping the kohl from her eyes. Saam watched her in the rearview mirror, asked what she was doing.

When they pulled up to the One Body Complex, Sara left the flowers in the car. And as she and her mother walked through the entrance, the blue eye of its sign upon them, her mother said to Sara, "I want to give you some advice: Erase his number from your phone. Delete it."

But then, as her mother was carrying their groceries inside, Saam called Sara. "You are so beautiful," he told her. "Why didn't you take the flowers?"

Later, her mother warned her again, "You are blind. You do not see. You've been married. He has not. You have two kids. He does not. He's educated. You are not. He's handsome. And you . . . you're not the same. Don't go inside his life. It will break your heart."

. . .

Let's back up a minute. Because as Sara was falling for Saam, her position at the One Body Complex was growing more precarious. It's not just that Abu Suleiman's rules oppressed Sara and the other women, widowed wives of martyrs, mothers of orphans without resources. And it's not just that Abu Suleiman used his power to try to legitimize, through sham marriages, what was essentially a form of human trafficking. It's that he had also threatened Sara.

She had recently changed apartments, moving out of the one she shared with her sister-in-law, the woman married to Abu Suleiman. Between their marriage and Sara's husband's family's contempt, the situation had grown untenable. One day Abu Suleiman surprised Sara by coming to her apartment and catching her at the door without her hijab. At first he seemed to be there to announce that he was distributing video games to the children of the complex. But then he persuaded her to move back inside, where he reached down to stroke her hair. "You see, the Syrian people are not smart," he said, unctuously, menacingly. "Why did you leave the other apartment and come here?"

She pushed him away, but after that, Sara could no longer tolerate Abu Suleiman's rules, the control he had over all their lives, the way he was watching her. Though she had a rebellious spirit, she considered herself a pious Muslim who respects the dictates of Islam. She would not accept strange men, cloaked in the garb of religiosity, telling her how she should live. She knew she needed to get out of that complex for good and she started casting around for other options. Predictably, when Abu Suleiman got wind from his wife, Sara's beautiful sister-in-law Samah, of Sara's plans to leave One Body, he let it be known that Sara was being evicted. Samah might have been exploited by Abu Suleiman, but she was also part of Sara's husband's family and, like them, felt no obligation to her. So that's where things stood for Sara when she met Saam at the meat market—caught, like Odysseus, between Scylla and Charybdis.

It was December by now, and the weather in Amman was growing colder. In their apartment, they didn't have enough blankets to really keep warm. Sara managed to find a job working at a cafeteria at the university in the Tarbarbour neighborhood of Amman and had begun looking for an apartment nearby, but Jordanians seemed to be growing leery of renting to Syrians and were requiring three months' down payment, which Sara had no hope of saving. She was getting texts from Saam, but she was busy working and distracted by her fruitless search. Finally he called her. When she told him what was going on, he said, "Sara, you need help. I should help you."

"I'm not asking for any help from you," she replied.

"Forget I love you," he said, a startling admission. "Forget everything. Put it in your head that I'm a relative to you. Please, I want to help."

Sara told him, "It's not time to help me. When I need help, I will let you know." But she had started to love him too.

Time was ticking, though, and by now, Sara had to be out of the One Body Complex in a week. She could find nothing, though she searched and searched. Saam called again, this time telling her, "I decided I'm not shaving until I find you a home and pay for it."

All of this was making Sara's mother deeply uneasy. Out of propriety and respect, Saam had taken her to see an apartment in a building in Tarbarbour nice enough to have an elevator, but Sara's mother said, "We don't have the money for this." Another day he took her to an apartment on the outskirts of Amman, owned by a friend of his. "This is out in the desert—it's too far from the city." Then it was the last day. Saam called that morning and told Sara, "I'm picking up your mom. We only have today. We have to end this."

At that last apartment, Saam counted out the money—three months' rent—and gave it to the landlord. "It's expensive!" Sara's mother started to protest. "I will pay for everything," Saam insisted. All you have to do is sign your name." Afterward, he bought furniture, a refrigerator, a television. But still Sara's mother didn't like the situation, didn't like to accept money or help from people she didn't really know. "This is only a loan. Every month, we will save some money and we will pay you back," Sara's mother told Saam. "Please," Saam told them both, "I don't need anything from you—only accept this favor."

At this point in the story, it is winter in Jordan. But in Houston, as Sara recalls all of this to me and Alia, it still feels like summer—steamy air, hazy sun—though the day before had been the autumn equinox, when the sun shines equally on the northern and southern hemispheres, that hinged moment before everything tilts in the other direction. "I want to ask a sensitive question," I say to Sara. Her story had been interrupted a few minutes before by a knock on the door and the appearance of Oum Mohammed, an elderly Iraqi woman, her lined face starting to sink inward, wearing Terminator glasses to protect her eyes and a black hijab and black abaya. Sara said something in Arabic to her son, Adam, and Adam ambled to the door and then took Oum Mohammed's arm and walked with her down the concrete path toward the parking lot.

"I want to ask a sensitive question," I repeat. "I'm not asking because I am assuming anything. It's just to understand. Were you interested in Saam partly because you knew he could pay, and you had no money?"

No, Sara shakes her head after Alia translates my question. "I loved him," she tells me. "After I saw him, I started to love him. And I started to love his way of life also."

"What do you mean?" Alia asks her.

When she would chat with Saam, she could see how free he was to do what he wanted. Holed up in the One Body Complex, unable to leave at night, she'd call him. "What are you doing now?" she'd ask. "I'm out shopping," he'd tell her. "I'm buying cigars." Abu Suleiman controlled her life, but no one controlled Saam. "This is why I loved being with him," Sara told Alia and me.

"That he had this kind of freedom?" I clarified.

"Freedom," Sara agreed. "He did not follow any rules. No one controlled him. That was different from me."

I once interviewed Ali Al Sudani, director, at the time, of Refugee Services for Interfaith Ministries, the resettlement agency where Geleta Mekonnen, who had advised Mendy, also worked. Ali had come to the US as a refugee from Iraq in 2009, just after Alia. He told me that he looks at America as an idea. He thinks that maybe, if you have a sense of the American way of thinking, though you may not be an American citizen, you are an American nevertheless. And although he didn't get his citizenship until 2014, even in Iraq, translating between members of the Coalition Provisional Authority and the Iraqi military and civilian leaders and tribal sheiks, he sometimes thinks he was an American already, a participant in that idea. And what, I asked Ali, links all of these far-flung incipient Americans together? What's the idea? Compassion, he told me, and hard work and a desire for self-improvement. The need always to be moving forward, building something new in this land of opportunity.

But I am thinking, listening to Sara now, that there is another idea of America, too, one based not on the relentless optimism Ali had described. This other idea of America comes instead from a shared human longing to be free from the oppressive control of others, to wear dark eyeliner if we want, to sing songs in Arabic at the top of our lungs as we drive west down the highway into the eye of the setting sun.

. . .

Sara has invited Alia and me to her apartment this Saturday morning to hear the rest of the story of Saam. The night before it had rained, and as I exit the highway and drive beneath the bubblegum pink crape myrtles, the streets seem cleansed and the air holds the promise, at last, of cooler weather.

When I enter Sara's apartment, the Lebanese singer Farouz is playing on Sara's smartphone, whose case sports a set of fluttering eyelashes. In the morning when Sara wakes up, she tells Alia, she opens the front door of her apartment and the curtains covering the windows. She makes coffee and listens to Farouz. Listening to Farouz in that early stillness, as the sun rises, reminds Sara of Syria, when she would take the bus to school in the mornings and listen to Farouz through her headphones as the city of Damascus passed by. Alia explains to me that Farouz is "kind of like Celine Dion. Celine Dion is number one for me," she says, "but I love Farouz too. Everyone in the Middle East knows her."

"What is she singing about?" I ask, as the three of us sip the tea Sara has prepared.

"It is all about love stories," Alia tells me. "A boy has left her and she is waiting for him to come back. Her songs are about immigrants and refugees—the people who left Lebanon because of the war." We listen to the music for a few keening beats. "I cry when I hear this song," Alia admits. "She is waiting for him, but he left the country. She's waiting winter and summer, day after day. They are separated, even though they are in love. Our singers explain our life. We are emotional people."

"Our language is deep," Sara adds. "It has many words to explain emotion that they don't use here. Or maybe they have them here, but they don't use them. Or maybe we don't understand them, or we don't know them."

Alia agrees. "When we are talking, we talk from the heart, from the eyes, from our face," she says. "Here, they don't have that."

I think about the terms of endearment with which Alia always greets the other women—*my love, my heart, my eyes, my soul*—the ways these greetings go on and on, the warmth that seems to pass between them.

Alia asks me then, "What do you think is the reason for this difference?"

"I think Americans . . . ," I start to try to answer, but Sara jumps in. "Americans are just working," she says. And as I am processing this possibility, flicking through all the hurried interactions I have, even with friends and family, all of us ready to get down to business, to the purpose, or back to whatever it was we were doing, whatever it is we need to get done, Alia, straddling two cultures, says, "Sara, I want to make this point: in the US, they are very humane. The system here, I love it. But the way of the people, I don't love it. They are busy only with their work."

Sara picks up on the theme. Back home, she says, "if you ask anybody, they will help you. Everybody looks after you to see if you need anything. If you have a problem, they say, 'I can help you with your problem.'"

But something had shifted in Syria, Sara concedes. She had noticed this before she left. "Their hearts are more solid now," she says—meaning *hardened,* I think—"because of the war."

"I agree," Alia gently takes up the thought. "The war, it changes the hearts and the ways of the people. When they see people killing in front of them . . ."

But Sara is saying something a little different. "It's showing the true face of the person," she points out. "Because in war, you know everybody—if they are good or not good."

"War takes away the mask?" I try to clarify.

"Before the war, you don't know if they are good or not," Sara answers. "They smile. It's all very nice. But if you have war, and you need something—then, in their face, you can see if they are good or not."

Alia's mother didn't like Saam hanging around—a man whose family she didn't know, someone untethered from any kind of context she could understand. Still, she knew how much Sara loved him, so after they had moved in to their new apartment, she allowed Sara to invite him over. But toward the end of the visit, as Saam was requesting more tea, Sara's mother told her, "Make coffee for him."

Alia turns to me, laughing, and asks, "Do you know what that means?" When I express bewilderment, Alia explains, "When we make coffee for people, it means, *We are done. You can leave.* In our tradition, we do lunch with tea, then in the end, we do coffee."

Sara adds, "My mom told me, 'Make him coffee,' and she is . . ."—here Sara makes a gesture with her eyes casting them urgently back and forth toward the door—"and that means, *Make him coffee and he can go.*"

Like Arabic, Tea-and-Coffee, I gathered, was another language whose depth and subtlety were still beyond my ken.

When Sara set the coffee tray on the table, her mother told Saam, "Thank you so much for everything you have done for us. But I'm a Syrian woman with two daughters. We are refugees here in Jordan, and you know the neighbors are so . . . Please, don't come back. We'll repay your loan, a little every month."

Saam took this in. "Accept me," he told her then. "I'm only serving you. If you need anything, let me know. I'm here."

But he didn't seem to get the picture. He hadn't understood, or hadn't wanted to understand, the language of Tea-and-Coffee. Because a few days later, Sara got a call from Saam. He was in Iraq. "My mom is here," he told Sara. "Can you talk to her?" And he put his mother on the line. Sara was having a hard time understanding her Iraqi Arabic, though. And anyway, it was just weird. Why was Saam calling with his mother?

"He did that to make us trust him more," Sara tells us, "but my mom, after that, did not trust him at all." And she was furious with Sara. "Why did you accept his call? What did he tell his family about us?" she worried. "That he helped us? That he paid us? Did he tell them you were his fiancée? A friend? Like a sister?"

When he returned from Iraq, he came to the apartment to talk to Sara's mother. Sara had been banished to a back room, but pressed her ear against the door to listen. "I know you can't accept for me to come here and talk with Sara," he acknowledged. "I know you're scared for her." Sara's mother said to Saam, "I want to ask you a question: What do you want from Sara? Do you want to keep her heart with you? Or more than that? Tell me, what do you want?"

"I love Sara very much," he confessed. But, he explained, it was December now, and his visa for Jordanian residency would expire the following September. Neither of them were citizens of Jordan, so they could not legally marry there. Although he never answered Sara's mother's question directly, when he left that day, Sara managed to catch him at the door, and he kissed her on the forehead, a kiss that Sara understood was goodbye.

"Sara, I would like to keep talking with you," he messaged her later, "but this is the situation with us."

She messaged back, "It's okay, Saam. If this is what God has sent us, I accept it. If you are meant for me, it will be me. If not, I will be meant for another one."

"You're waiting to marry another one?" he wrote.

Was it the clutch of jealousy that prompted Saam, a couple days later, to call Sara, despite the goodbye kiss? Was it love? "Come down," he begged her. "Let's go outside."

At first, Sara's mother refused to let her go. "I asked him what he wanted with you and he hasn't answered me!"

"I want to go see him," Sara pleaded.

"For two minutes only," her mother relented. "And I will be with you because he hasn't answered me."

In those days, it was snowing in Amman, so Sara and her kids and her mother all bundled up. And as Saam got everyone playing in the snow, Sara's mother melted.

In a secret moment when the others were laughing and distracted, Sara put her hand in Saam's pocket and squeezed his hand. But when he saw Sara's mother coming toward them, he quickly pulled away. Then, as they all trudged through the snow back toward the apartment, Saam stopped Sara's mother. "I want to talk to you. Let me tell you my situation, and after that you can decide what we should do." He loved Sara, he repeated. Perhaps they could be married by a local sheik, he suggested, hesitantly. The marriage wouldn't be recognized by the Jordanian government, he conceded, but later, he could submit the paperwork to the Syrian courts, to have their union formalized.

Sara's mother knew how much Sara loved Saam. And there was a war going on. Some traditions might have to bend. So, though the snow was deep, and dangerous for driving, they found a sheik—and that very night at 8 o'clock, reader, she married him.

. . .

Must the fairy tale always turn grim? For the first few months, everyone, even Sara's mother, loved Saam. He would spend nights at the apartment, and he and Sara would sleep together, husband and wife. But he would always leave early the next morning for prayers at the mosque. He didn't actually live with Sara. He didn't want his friends to know about the marriage. And then there was the time when a friend of Sara's was visiting and Sara could see Saam and the friend flirting, though Saam denied it. "Why would she be looking at me like that?" he deflected, though Sara knew Saam had been looking back. Then there were the messages Sara would find on his phone from other women. Sometimes, in her head, she made excuses for him. But in her heart, she knew.

When his visits started to grow more infrequent, and he turned off his phone to avoid her calls, she understood what he was doing. But she loved him. She told Saam, "Right now, you are seeing the face of Sara who loves you, but if she hates you, you will see a different face." When she loved, it was with her whole heart. But if she stopped loving, things would change.

As his visits tapered off, then halted altogether, Sara's phone calls grew desperate. Mostly he wouldn't answer her at all. Once when he did pick up, he hissed at her, "I don't have enough minutes left on my phone to talk with you." Another time, Sara called from her son's phone, and Saam, not recognizing the number, answered. "Why won't you talk to me?" Sara pleaded with him. "If you want to leave me, say so." But in response, Saam warned her that if she said that again, he would divorce her. Which, under Islamic law, required only that Saam say, "I divorce you." So Sara stopped calling.

By now Saam was no longer paying their rent. He had in his possession whatever paperwork they'd received from the local sheik at the time of their marriage, that snowy night. But one day, when Sara's daughter, Jojo, became so sick that she needed to go to the hospital, Sara's mother called Saam and shamed him into taking them. As they walked the hallway of the hospital, waiting to be seen by the doctor, Sara asked him again, "Why are not talking to me? If you want to leave, just tell me."

"I told you," he threatened, "that if you said that again, I would divorce you." When he dropped them off later, for a long time Sara stood at the window watching his disappearing back.

"So you called Saam many times and he didn't answer you," Alia asks. "What did you do?"

It all came to a head, Sara continues, when she reached out to Saam once again. "Why do you call me so many times? What do you want? I don't want to talk with you anymore," he rebuked her. "So when he talked to me in that way," Sara remembers, "I turned off my phone."

Some time later, Sara was sitting together with her family and some visiting friends in the apartment in Amman when she saw that she'd received a voice message. It was from Saam. "We are divorced," he said.

At that point, everything went quiet, as if a cocoon of glass had been spun around her. She could see the others talking, but she couldn't hear anything. Sara's mother, seeing the blank incomprehension in Sara's eyes, called out her daughter's name, and Sara turned her head to look at her mother, but no sound made it through. One of the friends who was visiting bent over Sara, trying to talk to her, but Sara could only watch him uncomprehendingly. Finally, trying to break whatever spell had mesmerized her daughter, Sara's mother slapped her. "Say something!" she yelled. "Cry! Cry!"

This went on for months. Sara existed in a state of shock. She cried when she was alone. She cried in taxis. She would sit with her family, but she was not really there. At night she would lie in bed, waiting for Saam to come back and say he was sorry, playing out various storylines in her mind. What would she say? Would she hit him? For eight months it was like this—a gestation, a pupation.

And then, Sara began to awaken.

One day, she put her photo on her WeChat profile. That same day, she noticed that Saam had also posted his photo. That was weird. He had never displayed his photo on his profile before. Sara, thinking better of it, removed her picture. Saam did too. Also weird. Then one day he sent Sara a message. "Who is this?" Sara responded.

"You didn't have his number anymore?" Alia asks, momentarily confused at why Sara wouldn't know it was Saam. But Sara makes a *tsk tsk tsk* sound, pursing her lips—*NoNoNo*. "It's to show him, *I don't know you anymore—I have forgotten you*," she clarifies. And Alia and I nod, a light dawning as we understand Sara's ingenuity, her cunning.

"You're right you don't know me, Sara," he wrote back. "I'm Saam."

"I'm sorry," Sara responded, "I don't know any Saam. Can you please not send me any more messages?"

Alia and I are laughing now, delighted at this power move.

Sara smiles knowingly and nods. When our laughter subsides, she goes on. "He told me, 'Sara, you're right. I'm not a nice person. I made a mistake.' But I told him, 'If you say you are sorry from now until the last day of your life, I will not accept your apology.'"

Somewhere in this time, Sara received word that she and her children had been accepted for permanent resettlement in the United States. As her own departure drew closer, Saam told Sara that he, too, would be leaving Jordan and returning to Iraq. "I want to see you before I leave," he texted. "May I see you?"

On the day of his departure, they met at the bus station in Amman. Sara thought about all those nights she had lain awake wondering about this moment, but when she spotted him and they sat down together, she found to her surprise that she felt nothing in her heart. She couldn't connect this body sitting beside her with the Saam she had loved. "I forgive you," she told him. "I forgive everything you did to me. But we are nothing anymore. I loved someone before, but not you right now. You're not that Saam." She wasn't sad. She was empty. "I want to thank you," Sara told Saam. "Thank you for coming back. For eight months, I was very sick, but now I see that it was not worth it, because you are nothing to me."

When she started gathering her purse to leave, Saam pleaded: "Can you wait a few minutes until my time to travel?"

"Before," Sara reminds me and Alia, "I would have done anything for him. But now—no. I stood up and I told him, 'Keep sitting. I'm going to go.'"

Alia and I are caught in the spell of Sara's story, one that, as she spins it this afternoon, on the other side of the hinge of the equinox, feels either tragic or melodramatic—I can't quite discern its nature, its weight, through Alia's translation.

"He followed me out into the street and I stopped a taxi to take me home. He said, 'Please, wait. Wait!' But I said, 'Please, Saam, don't pursue me.'" Then she got into the cab and closed the door.

In a few months, she and her children would be traveling too, to America. At this moment of separation, unlike that other crossing-over she had made years before, when she had turned to look back at Syria, the beloved homeland that was now lost, Sara tells us, "I didn't turn my face to look at him." Instead, she settled back into the taxi as it drove away.

9 *Homeless, Tempest-Tost*

Kırıkkale, the city in Turkey where Mina fled with her daughter after her husband went to buy groceries in their Baghdad neighborhood and never came back, lies 500 miles due east of the ancient coastal city of Troy, which once looked out over the Aegean Sea, but whose ruins, after centuries of shifting sands, now rise up several miles inland. As I listen, week after week, season into season, to the stories of the women with whom Alia works, I find myself remembering shards of stories of ancient Troy. I think of Homer's epic poem about the war between the Greeks and the Trojans, whose citadel the Greeks destroyed after ten years of brutal and pointless fighting. I think, too, about the aftermath of that war, the wanderings of Odysseus, tossed by tempests on the open sea, a soldier trying to find his way home. And I think about the Trojan women of the later poets, like Sophocles and Euripides, who wrote centuries after Homer about that sisterhood—refugee women detained in that liminal space on Troy's shores, waiting to be carried off as slaves and trafficked on some Greek island, their husbands and sons massacred in the burning city behind them.

Mina had nearly killed herself during the years she was waiting in Turkey to know if the UN would resettle her somewhere. *I'm in the middle of the way,* she told them in a moment of desperation. *I want to know where I am.*

But one day, the manager of the apartment where she and her daughter, Tia, were living asked Tia for help translating. Tia had been learning Turkish in school and often translated for Mina. And now a new Iraqi woman had arrived with her four children, and the manager needed to go over some documents with her. That woman turned out to be Maha, who was, at the moment they knocked on her door, pulling out of the oven some sweet treat she had been baking.

Mina and Maha became inseparable, their children like siblings. Tia would play with Maha's daughter after school, when Mina was working. They ate their meals together. "Don't cook lunch," Mina would say. "Eat with us." Or Maha would call Mina to come over for dinner. Mina's menstrual periods could get really intense—she'd vomit so much she'd become dehydrated. Maha would take her to the hospital and stay by her side as an IV dripped fluids back into Mina. Then, when they got Mina back home, Maha would make sure she was strong enough to take care of Tia before leaving her. When Mina ran short of money, Maha loaned her what she needed to get by.

Maha's husband had been murdered by Al Qaeda in the chaotic aftermath of the American invasion. Mina's husband had been murdered by militia, too, most likely. So the women understood each other. They were more than sisters. They told each other everything. In that suspended state between the ground and sky, on the shoreline between their ruined homeland and the uncertain future, at the mercy of the inscrutable bureaucratic wheels of the universe, their friendship provided the mental healthcare to which they had no other access. It became a net that held them safe within it.

But in Houston now, Mina is once again alone. And her desolation has trailed her here, like a restless wraith. "In the beginning, I was thinking a lot," she remembers. "I was confused a lot. I couldn't focus. I thought I was going crazy, or"—the two are often equated by the refugee women I've met—"I was depressed. I couldn't understand the environment or the community." And since her arrival, too, she has been scared to reach out, to ask for help. She doesn't trust anyone. She has no one she loves that she can let inside her, to welcome into her hopelessness.

She worries that she might slip back into that suicidal despair she felt in Turkey, before she met Maha. She hasn't yet met anyone with whom she shares that kind of, as she calls it, "chemistry connection." Sometimes Mina longs to go to a café and sit outside and drink a coffee and talk to a friend. But here, it's only her and Tia. So she just stays home.

But as the sweltering heat in Houston breaks, like a fever, and evenings grow dry and cool, a kind of fog seems to be lifting for Mina. She tells Alia, speaking of that chemistry connection she misses, "I feel it with you." She invites us to join her for a coffee one evening after she finishes work at the fancy hotel where she cleans rooms. She has the next day off, and she wants to do something for once, just for an hour or two, besides going home.

As cars rush past on Westheimer, just beyond the parking lot of the chain coffee shop Mina has chosen, we sit on metal chairs at a table outside and meander from topic to topic. Inevitably the conversation winds round to the war that had forced Mina and Alia out of their ancient city bordered by a sea of sand—the war that hinged them together in an accidental sisterhood in this foreign land. Mina had been saying how, here, there was more freedom for women, that women were equal with men. "'In our community in Iraq,'" Alia translates for me, "'the woman is not respected.' You know when I first felt that?" Alia asks Mina, fiercely. "When I lost my husband." I get the feeling that Alia's fierceness is like a scab covering an old wound beneath.

"Yes," says Mina, nodding.

"After that," Alia goes on, "I decided to ignore my country and to leave it."

"Yes," Mina says again. Then she continues in Arabic, speaking more to me now, Alia translating. "If I had stayed in Iraq after I lost my husband—if I told you how I felt, you might be shocked; you would think bad things about me. If I stayed in Iraq, I would have killed myself. I couldn't live there."

"Really?" I ask—neither shocked nor disappointed, only a little confused.

"I couldn't," Mina repeats in English.

"Why?" asks Alia sharply, as if she knows the answer but wants me to hear it, wants me to know this story, which is her story, too. Almost under her breath, Alia says, "It's the same for me. I didn't want to kill myself, but I couldn't live there." Then to Mina, Alia asks again, "Why?"

"Because," Mina says, "the community's vision of women without husbands: it is not fair."

Alia tells me, "I agree, Kim. I agree."

But I am still trying to get my bearings. "When you say, 'I would have killed myself,' is that because you just felt so confined . . . ," I start to ask, but Mina shakes her head.

"Everything. Everything." Then she speaks to Alia in Arabic.

"I understand you very well," Alia reassures her, "but I want you to tell Kim and I will translate." And again I sense some pain in Alia that throbs just below the surface, something familiar in what Mina is saying that Alia needs to dig up and pull out into the light.

Mina says, "The widow in Iraq, she has no hope. She doesn't have any goals. She doesn't have a life there. She can't do anything. And the community watches her. They keep watching everything she does. They say she is a bad woman. They say she is no good."

By now, Alia is unable to contain herself. "I want to tell you now," she says. "Me."

.   •   .

After her husband had been killed beside her, after Alia had been re-leased from the hospital, the heart of the baby still beating in her womb, her cousin, the doctor, and another cousin brought her home and stayed with her and the older kids in the empty house with the glinting chandeliers and the long dining table and the windows that looked out over the backyard, which was connected to the backyards of her husband's brothers, where Alia had sat during those afternoons before the war with their wives, all the children running wild.

Alia's cousins stayed with her for a couple of nights, but soon enough they needed to get back to their own families. The housekeepers would be there with Alia, they knew. But as they gathered their own belongings and were leaving, the cousins did this curious thing. They took the guns belonging to Alia's husband. In the haze of her grief, this didn't totally register with Alia, but later she started piecing it together. "What did they think?" she asked herself. "They thought I would kill myself," she realized.

Everyone knew the love story Alia and her husband shared. But in the years before the war, Alia had been taking religion classes, studying Islam. In those early days after her husband's murder, she felt strong. Well, not strong. She was weak. But she believed God was in what had happened. It would never have occurred to her to kill herself.

Her cousins were just the first watchful eyes upon her. Following tradition, in the month after her husband's death the family invited acquaintances to pay their respects to Alia, who wore black to signify her status as a widow. But after one such visit from neighbors— friends to Alia for many years—Alia heard them talking. *Did you see her? She seems so normal.* The suspicion and judgment spread to others, and Alia sensed the disapproval. *She lost her husband. He loved her! Why did she not kill herself? Why is she still alive?* It was a malignancy replicating throughout the community. *She's still pregnant? She didn't miscarry?* So went the whispers. *She doesn't care.* Alia had grown up protected by the privilege of her father's status. When she'd married, she was protected by her husband's. But his death seemed to strip her of that respect she'd always taken as a given.

Still, it was her sisters-in-law who really broke Alia's heart. In those days, it had become so dangerous in Baghdad, between the American military occupation and the kidnappings and killings by various militias, that it was treacherous to go out, even for groceries. So it made sense when her husband's brother knocked on her door one day and said to Alia, "I'm going to the market. Do you need me to bring anything to you?" He was only looking out for her.

But after Alia went back inside, she could hear his wife yelling at him. "Why are you going over to her house?" she demanded. The implication was clear: his interest in Alia was suspect. In their country, and under Islamic law, he could take a second wife. Alia was now available, and still young enough, and beautiful. Her sister-in-law must have been worried. And her worry and suspicion must have seeped into the others. It happened imperceptibly at first, the withdrawal. Phone calls unanswered. Invitations unextended. Until little by little, Alia understood that they had constructed a border around themselves, leaving Alia alone on the other side.

But Alia needed people around her. Her whole adult life had unfolded within that community of her husband's brothers and their wives and children. It's where she belonged. Those evenings they gathered together to play poker. Afternoons laughing and eating watermelon, planning the entirely frivolous hours that made up their extravagant days in the upper echelons of Baghdad society. Every morning before she made tea, Alia would call her sisters-in-law: "Who's coming?" She never took tea alone. And now here she was, pregnant, her husband violently murdered, the city burning all around her—with no one. Her parents had both passed away already, so she couldn't take the kids and go home to them. Her brothers were nearby, but they had their families. "There is no sister to me here," Alia thought.

The isolation scared her. Although she had cleaned out her husband's closet by now, she had kept some of his clothes that still smelled of him, and one night she pulled them out and buried her face in them. Alia felt a presence, then, like her husband's soul was near her, and she began to talk to him, though he was dead. She started to wonder about her own sanity. But when Alia reached out to her sisters-in-law pleading for someone to stay with her in the night when she couldn't sleep, no one came. She would lie instead with her older children, trying to control her fear.

"I was shocked," Alia says to me and Mina. Outside the café, the air has grown chilly. Vaguely Italian Muzak, signified by a synthesized accordion, drifts out of the door as it opens and closes, then dissipates in the noise of traffic. Somewhere above us in the dark sky there must be stars, but all the light down on earth obscures them. "I was shocked. I was shocked. I was shocked!" Alia repeats, her voice crescendoing. "I wasn't crazy because I lost my husband. I was crazy because of the community."

This is the real reason Alia left Iraq, she tells us. She left Iraq out of the perpetual fear that at any moment her sons could be killed by the Mahdi army that had murdered her husband, of course. But she and her kids had become more vulnerable on the other side of the border, without the community to protect them. The community forced her into this position of having to leave. "I didn't know I would come to America at that time," says Alia. She just wanted to go to a place where no one knew who she was, where no one was watching her. "I didn't want people feeling sorry for me," Alia trails off. "And I could see it in their eyes."

Mina—who has been listening quietly as Alia lays bares this old pain of her shunning—says to me, "You asked why I was thinking of killing myself? That is the reason. This community. It's different than here."

"You can live here free," Alia acknowledges, picking up on Mina's thoughts.

"And no one doubts your grief?" I suggest tentatively.

"Yeah," Alia swiftly agrees.

"No one is questioning you?" I go on.

"The *opposite,*" she says. "They take *care* of you—the rule and the system. I love that. You're a widow? We will help you! You are a single mom? Our hand to you!" I think about something Alia had pointed out to me once about the origins of her work with single mother refugees, as she had been. In all of the world's religions—not just Islam— there is an injunction to help the weakest ones. "And who are the weakest?" she'd asked, then answered: "Women. Kids."

For a while after she arrived in Jordan, Alia was just grateful to have been welcomed in, though at the same time, she didn't want anyone to know who she was. She fell in with the wealthy Iraqi expats who had decamped to Amman to wait out the war. But Alia was burning through the money she got for the jewelry she wore when she crossed the border. She paid for a year at an international school for the older kids, but then the money was gone and there was nothing else to sell.

By the time Alia presented herself at the UNHCR offices to a Jordanian lawyer named Amal, knowing she needed to try to claim refugee status, she felt backed into a corner. "Go ahead, Alia," she had coached herself. "What can you do to start a new life? You must find a way." For the Iraqis she knew in Amman, though, to become a refugee was shameful. But Alia couldn't go back to Iraq, or they would kill her or her children. And she couldn't continue to live among the rich in this city—the expensive school, the private clubs, the designer clothes, the cars, the money. Amal's team was able to pull together a small monthly remuneration for Alia. They helped collect the paperwork Alia needed as she went through the asylum process—her husband's death certificate, proof of his position in the Iraqi Air Force. "For me, to become a refugee was like a gift from the sky," she says. "There was no other way in front of me. Only to accept this and go with it."

As they waited for news on their resettlement case, Alia's teenage daughter, Haneen, especially, was struggling. Kids at school would ask her questions about her father. Or wonder at her mother, alone without a husband in this foreign city. Or question where their money had gone, why she was wearing what she wore. "We will leave," Alia soothed her. "We will go somewhere that will be our home. And we'll have freedom. People will see only who you are, not who your family is. You will build your life. You will get your degree. You will do something great. You and your brothers. I promise."

But day after day, their life in Jordan was growing more untenable. At night, when the kids were asleep, Alia would stand out on the balcony, the warm breeze on her face as she looked out over the lights of the city. "Please, please find for me a way," she would pray. "I can't continue. It is hard and I don't know what to do."

. . .

Stuck in Turkey with her daughter, Tia, not knowing if they'd ever leave, Mina was always looking back, remembering what she had been through, crying. When Alia first visited her in Houston in February, in her loneliness and isolation, Mina told her, "I want to forget the things that make me tired and sad."

Memory can be poisonous. Forgetting, Alia told me once, "is the secret to life, to continuing to live. Sometimes," she went on, "when I remember what happened—my husband passed away, he was young, people killed him, not God, God didn't take him in an accident—this makes me sad. I wish he was here to see his sons growing. I need sometimes to have his advice, to talk with him. So I try to forget. To not remember what happened to him, to not think about why the war happened, why everything happened around us." From time to time, Haneen will start to ask Alia, "Mom, do you remember . . . ?" And Alia tells her, "Forget. We are here. We built our life here. And we have success here. The community around us is very nice. We are lucky here. We are not there."

Back in June, for the Eid celebration marking the end of Ramadan, Alia had organized a party with donated toys and lots of food for the Transformed mothers and their children in a clubhouse room at one of the apartment complexes. But in the midst of this festive occasion, Mina's daughter, Tia, inexplicably collapsed. Then just as quickly, she recovered. As Tia came to and Alia talked to her, she suspected it wasn't anything too serious. But she arranged for someone to take Mina and Tia to the hospital, while Alia talked to the doctors on the phone and calmed the other mothers and children at the party. Tia would be fine.

Later, when Mina was back home, lying beside Tia in the bedroom they shared, Alia called Mina. "Mina, is Tia close to you?" she asked. "She's asleep," Mina answered. "Go outside and close the door so she can't hear you," Alia instructed. She wanted to talk to Mina alone. Mina had been so distraught at the party, hysterical really. "Mina," Alia told her, "don't be sad in front of your daughter. Don't talk negatively in front of your daughter. Pretend you're strong—the happiest woman in the world in front of her. I know it is hard for you, because it is the opposite situation. But this is what makes your daughter sad— you provided to her everything, but you are not showing her your positive side." And then Alia suggested that Mina take Tia away somewhere for a little vacation—maybe to see Maha, the Iraqi friend she had met in Turkey, who now lives in Lancaster, Pennsylvania.

So she did—she arranged to meet up with Maha. And together with their kids, Mina and Maha day-tripped to New York City. They posed for selfies in their black t-shirts and tight jeans with bedazzled pockets, eyes darkly lined, long hair swaying down their backs, looking like 1980s rock groupies. They took the ferry through New York harbor and past the Statue of Liberty, which they knew from TV, as wind whipped their hair into their eyes.

Disembarking at Ellis Island, the former immigrant inspection station, now a museum, they wandered through the cavernous vaulted hall where newcomers, after disembarking from cramped ships, once lined up for medical checks—looking for trachoma and TB and scores of other diseases and disabilities—before being shunted on to answer an inspector's questions: *Where were you born? What is your occupation? Have you ever been convicted of a crime? How much money do you have? What is your destination?*

Mina could not understand the placards in the museum describing all of this. She did not know the Emma Lazarus poem on the base of the Statue of Liberty:

> Give me your tired, your poor,
> Your huddled masses yearning to breathe free,
> The wretched refuse of your teeming shore.
> Send these, the homeless, tempest-tost to me . . .

But she looked at the sepia photographs of the lines of immigrants with their suitcases and trunks and cloth bags slung over their shoulders, their faces weary with whatever trauma they were escaping, the ache they must have carried in them for those they left behind, the uncertain life that waited for them. And she saw that she was not alone.

She saw that she, who had moved from Iraq to Turkey to America, was not the only one who had known so much upheaval. A lot of people had been through that same suffering—maybe even more than she'd been through. And, she thought, a lot of people wished they were here, like she was now. She didn't know their story, the people in the photos, didn't know what they had endured, where they were going. But she could see herself in them, standing in that line, carrying their luggage, which was everything they had. And now she's here and she's trying to look forward to that life that she was wishing for before she came. She's trying to look forward, just like them.

III *Home*

"If we don't build love inside them,
they won't give love to this place."

10 *The Treasure of Syria*

The plane was filled with other refugees, mostly, like Zara and her husband and children, from Syria. Not all were headed to Texas— some would fly on, after stops in Paris and New York City, to other states. Zara had never flown before, and all of it was a miracle. One minute they'd been on the ground in Jordan, and then suddenly they were in the clouds. They'd taken off in a desert, and now they were passing over the green forests of Europe. Zara loved the tiny liquor bottles on the Air France plane, though she didn't drink, and the way the aircraft hit bumps, like on a road. As they descended into Paris, the Eiffel Tower, which they had always heard about, rose up from the city beside the river. And then, after changing planes, as they lifted off again, Zara thought she could see, through the window, a deer bounding through the trees. She could not tear her eyes away, so in awe was she of God's creation—the beauty of the earth below, but also all of the knowledge that human beings have channeled into such technology. If it weren't for Mohammed curled up on her lap, she thought, it would be a good time to lean back in her seat, sip her coffee, and try to write it all down, everything she was seeing and feeling and thinking.

Finally back on solid earth at the airport in Houston, the families were herded all together so they wouldn't get lost and handed their

I-94s, which documented that they'd been granted asylum indefinitely in the US. Then, after collecting their overstuffed suitcases from the carousel in the cavernous baggage claim at George Bush International Airport, they passed through the glass doors into the waiting area, where their case managers greeted the tide of families and funneled them into separate vans.

As they drove through the flat, sprawling city, Zara was taken with the green spaces, and the vast highways stretching across six or eight lanes. When they got to the apartment on Ocee Street that August day in 2016, Zara was thinking that now she could breathe easy because they were finally in their new home in the US, that now they could rest from their wanderings, that now the new life could begin—here, in this apartment that had been prepared for them by volunteers she would never know, with furnishings and food meant to make them feel at ease. But then their case manager tried to teach them how to operate the A/C unit and Zara was struck by a new thought: "What am I going to do now? I don't speak a word of English."

So many Syrians were arriving in Houston in those days. And after an initial flurried contact with their case manager—signing the rental contract they could not read, getting their social security cards, enrolling in Medicaid—he grew too busy for a week or two to check in on them. By then they were running low on food, and Mohammed, the toddler, needed something to eat, some milk, a little bread. So Zara told her husband, "I'm going to go out and see what I can find." But he only mocked her. "Where do you think you're going?" he asked. "You'll be lost out there." And it hit Zara again: they were here in this strange country, where they knew nothing and no one. What had they done? But she gathered her pink faux alligator-skin purse anyway, put on her navy blue abaya, and headed out. When she saw a couple of women in headscarves, she followed them, trying to get up the nerve to ask for help.

Zara had wanted a divorce before they came to the US. The abuse had been going on since Zara was pregnant with Tasneem, her oldest daughter. But back in Jordan, her family had convinced Zara to give her husband one last chance. Maybe, an uncle reasoned, away from his family and the culture that tacitly supported the abuse, her husband would change. Maybe the States would put a stop to it, if he tried to hurt her there.

But instead, the uncertainty here seemed to accentuate his inadequacies, which, in turn, intensified the badgering and the abuse. Early one morning, a few weeks after they arrived, before her husband or the kids woke up, one of Zara's sisters called, and Zara went out onto the balcony to talk. But as she was talking, he tore open the sliding glass door and began yelling, "What are you doing out here? Get inside and clean up the house!" When Zara told him she was talking to her sister, he kept pressuring her. "Turn off your phone!" Even when she came inside, he wouldn't let up. "I'm suffocating here," Zara was thinking. No matter where they went, their problems followed. So she covered herself and started to leave the apartment. But he followed her to the door, grabbed her hair, and dragged her back inside—and, before Zara knew what was happening, he was choking her. She thought she was going to die. The kids had to push their father off their mother, and as Zara dragged herself outside, she saw that Tasneem, shaking, still in her underwear, was now frantically trying to pull on a pair of pants she must have grabbed in her terror.

In those first few months, while they still had financial help from the national resettlement program—rental assistance, welcome money—Zara knew that it was important to learn English. Although she had taken French back home and could at least read the Latin alphabet, she didn't know how to pronounce those same letters in English, much less how to string them together into garlands of words and sentences. But her husband refused to take the classes that her case manager tried to enroll them in as part of their resettlement package. "There are translators," he told Zara.

Learning a language leaves you vulnerable. You have to be willing to sound silly, to not be understood. Maybe he was afraid of the humiliation. When Zara insisted on taking classes anyway, he brushed her off. "Just don't expect me to do anything for you. If you want to go, go alone." So Zara did, sometimes walking with other women from the complex down Richmond Avenue, cars barreling past, grackles whirling and settling down on the electrical lines strung above, like notes on sheet music. When she'd walk back home, she'd find her husband in the apartment, just sitting there, doing nothing.

There was so little time, though, to learn English before they needed to be working to pay rent on their own. And when a woman from the Syrian American Club—which had been trying to organize informational sessions for the newcomers, and to assess their needs and to help—offered to connect Zara with a job in a suburb outside the city, working for a tailor who needed someone to operate the complicated embroidery machines she had used back in Syria, Zara jumped at the opportunity. "Why are you going there?" her husband sneered. "It's so far away. The gas will be too expensive." But that was just a lie to try to keep Zara down.

Maybe he felt that the control he formerly had when a whole culture supported him was slipping away here in this country. He cursed the older girls for wearing makeup. He slapped little Mohammed.

The hair that broke the camel's back, as they say in Arabic, came almost a year in.

Lately he had begun spreading rumors around the apartment complex, saying Zara was going to other men, or that she loved someone back in Jordan. The other Syrians had begun to follow after Zara as she walked across the asphalt parking lot. "Tell us, what is the truth?" they pestered her. And then one day her husband grabbed her phone from her, trying to unlock it to find proof of the lies he was spouting. When, of course, he couldn't, he threw the phone at her head, gashing open her skin. Then he began punching her. Blood was everywhere.

One of the girls' friends called 9-1-1, and the ambulance came and rushed Zara to the hospital. After the emergency room doctors stitched her up, the police came in and, with an Arabic interpreter from her resettlement agency on the phone, took down Zara's report and snapped a photo of her swollen and battered face. When they asked her if she felt safe going home, she said she did not, so they took her to a women's shelter.

No one there spoke Arabic and no one called an interpreter. By the time she arrived, it was after midnight. She was shown a stack of mats and some blankets, and she carried them into the open hall where they led her, while police stood, hands on their holsters, around the perimeter. Zara lay on the mat, going over the beating in her mind, worrying about what was happening with her children. Maybe she slept an hour. Early the next morning, the women were all awakened and given supplies to sanitize their mats, which they had to stack back up. It felt humiliating—like a prison, not a refuge. She started to feel desperate to get home.

She tried to ask one of the shelter authorities to help her call a taxi. But she had no money with her to pay for one. "I'm sorry," the woman said. Zara tried to ask one of the other women in the shelter if she could use her phone to call her daughter. "No, sorry," the woman replied. Zara wandered out onto the street, hoping to find someone who spoke Arabic who could help her find a taxi. She didn't know where in the city she was. With only the rudimentary phrases she had learned in the English classes she'd had to abandon—*My name is Zara. I am fine. How are you?*—she could not make herself understood, which was another kind of prison. Finally, a woman gave her some change and pointed her to a pay phone, and Zara called Tasneem. As Zara was trying to ask her daughter to send someone to pick her up, her husband took the phone and told Zara, "We're not sending anyone to get you. Come back the way you got there."

As the shift changed over at the shelter, Zara approached one of the entering workers and asked again, "Can you help get me a taxi?" This time she told him she had money at home, so he agreed to call her a cab. And the cab driver called her daughter to verify that he'd get paid. Then he drove Zara through the strange city, and from the parking lot of the apartment, Zara called her daughter, who brought down her purse.

Ten days later, she went to a nearby mosque to request divorce papers. That was the first step. She would also have to go through the American court system to be legally divorced. "Be patient with him. Just give him another chance," the imam pleaded. "You have been together for seventeen years. You should not throw this away. Don't pursue this. Let it go. Have him stay and help you with the kids, just to provide." It all felt so familiar. Men covering for each other so that no one would be insulted, so that no other women would be encouraged to follow Zara's example and leave the men who mistreated them. Men ignoring the interests of women. Men trying to control women. Stifling them. Suffocating them. But Zara was not in Syria anymore. She was not in Jordan.

"Before, we lived in a Muslim country, but we didn't follow the rule of Islam," Zara told Alia, after sharing the contours of this story. "Now I live in a country that is not Muslim, but it follows the Muslim rules." In America, she went on, men must respect women—not hit them. And women are equal with men. Even the poor are taken care of with taxes paid by the rich. All of these ideas had been written into the Qur'an centuries ago. "I feel the Muslim religion is here," Zara said.

. . .

When Zara opened the door to her new apartment, situated between Memorial Drive, which winds past posh neighborhoods on Buffalo Bayou, with its lush overhanging trees and their shrubby understory, and I-10, lined by strip centers, ferrying its ceaseless river of traffic, she felt that she had finally broken free of other people's wishes and demands. It was the first time that she had decided what *she* wanted, and then had set out to get it. So when she opened that door and looked across the expanse of taupe-colored wall-to-wall carpeting and out through the sliding glass door to the grassy courtyard between the two-story apartment buildings, she felt the satisfaction of having reached that goal. And she knew that she would keep going.

That's what she tells Alia this August afternoon, as Alia prepares Turkish coffee in the long-handled aluminum pot on the electric stove. Zara is unwrapping a plastic package of tiny ceramic coffee cups and saucers, a soft jadeite green with gold polka dots. "She got them at Walmart today," Alia explains as we all delight in them. "She's happy to have us here, so she bought coffee and these cups because we were coming to see her," Alia translates as the words bubble out of Zara. Zara has left all of their possessions behind in their old apartment, with the exception of her cookware—an effort to escape the bedbugs that had plagued them there. Alia pours us each a thick steaming shot and puts the cups on a tray. "We can sit on the floor," she says, carrying the tray into the living room. "I love it!" And we sit down on the carpeting, light pouring in through the sliding glass doors and across the new apartment, which, though empty, feels full of possibility. This is not southwest Houston, not Gulfton, the new Ellis Island where the majority of refugees are placed in apartments smashed up against each other, with almost no green space.

Alia turns to Zara and jokes, "Tell me if we helped you to change your life or not, and if not, tell me to leave you alone and I won't come to visit you anymore." And Zara, in mock terror, pleads, "No no no!"

But then she grows serious. "You helped me a lot with your program, for sure," she tells Alia. "When I came to America, I felt alone. No one was with me. But you give me more confidence from the inside to be strong, to show me that nothing is too hard for me. You give me this impression that I can be something." Then Zara picks up the lease agreement that is lying on the carpet between her and Alia. "Do you see my signature?" she asks Alia, pointing. "It reminds me that if I can do that, I can do everything."

When we had arrived half an hour before, Zara had given us a tour of the 2BR/1BA apartment. Earlier, she'd gone to the 99 Cents Only store and bought a red shower curtain liner and poufy fleece blankets patterned with massive mauve roses on purple backgrounds. Alia was arranging for a donated couch to be delivered. So far there were no beds yet, and as we stood looking at the pillows and blankets tidily rolled up against the wall of one of the bedrooms, Zara explained that they were all sleeping on the floor for now. "We are lucky," she said, that same joy overflowing. "I feel very happy when I sleep between my kids and they are around me."

When Zara left her home in Syria, she had not taken anything then either. At the time, she was rushed, and she had the hope that she would return. But she also knew that there would be checkpoints all along the way, and that you could never know who you would come across and what they would take from you. She wanted to bring her family photos, but they had been snapped inside homes among those she knew and trusted, and thus she hadn't been covered. Not wanting to be exposed to a regime soldier or some rebel fighter rifling through their possessions, she left the photos behind.

The kitchen in this new apartment reminds her of her kitchen in the house she built in Syria. Birth after birth of each of her three daughters, she and her husband had continued living in a single room in his family's home, on a side lane off a busy street in Hama. Originally it had been a one-story house with a garden, until her husband's brother added a second floor for his wife and kids. For years, Zara saved money from her embroidery work and from the *anasheed* she sang, and then she built a home for her family above her brother-in-law's, brick by brick. She even carried the tiles and cleaned up after the construction workers and cooked for them. It was finished in 2011, just a year before they fled. There was the kitchen, and a living room and bedrooms, but the rest of that floor was an expansive veranda, from which you could see out over the city to the hills beyond. Zara loved that open space. Every morning, she would wash the floors, and around sunset every evening, she would lay out mats to sit on. And she and her in-laws would take their tea out there, or Zara would serve the food she'd prepared for dinner, and they would gather together and eat in the open air. But as much as she loved that house that she built, emptied out, she told me, it was "just walls, bricks. It doesn't have a meaning anymore, once you leave your home country."

Now she is here, starting over again in this bare apartment, with a restraining order in place against her husband. But this time, in this country, which recognizes those inalienable rights, endowed by her Creator, to life, liberty, and the pursuit of happiness, starting over has been her choosing.

As we sit cross-legged on the floor of this hard-won home, fine grit of coffee grounds littering the bottoms of the polka-dotted cups, Zara tells me and Alia that her mother-in-law has been calling her, begging Zara not to leave her husband alone. "But I said no," Zara says, "because he hit me many times. Before, no one else helped me, no one listened to me. But I am lucky here, in the USA. I don't want to go back to him. I will never go back to him. Never. He broke my confidence. He broke me inside. He stopped me from doing things. Right now I feel like I am strong and I can continue. Right now, I feel like I'm human.

"He called me last week and told me he wanted to come back. I said no. He keeps sending people to ask me to accept him back.

I cannot accept him. I told him that he broke things between us, so he should take responsibility for what he did. He will be alone, without his kids, no matter how hard it is for me to take care of the kids alone. I left one year ago and a few months, and I'm not dying. I'm better than before. So why should I go back? I have my freedom now and I will not accept him giving orders anymore.

"Now I reached my first goal—home. Next, I want to raise my salary and to be what I want to be in the future with my job. After that I will study English. I want to do everything quickly. I don't want to waste time."

.   .   .

Around the time that Zara moved into her new apartment, she received word from the United States Citizenship and Immigration Services agency—this was about two years after her arrival in the country—that her green card was in the mail. So she kept anxiously checking with the leasing office at her former complex to see if it had arrived. On the day that she finally received her permanent residency, the first person Zara called was Emmi in Jordan. As Zara Facetimed with Emmi, jumping up and down and shouting, Emmi cried. Because now, Zara could legally leave the US and visit Emmi in Jordan. And Zara's family. But Emmi.

For Alia, getting her green card and traveling back to Jordan for the first time to visit family there had a different effect, and it wasn't what she expected. By then, her desperation to go home to Iraq, even if it meant her own death, and the feeling she had that America was not her country, had subsided. This was due in large part to the kindness Amaanah had shown in helping find her a job and enrolling her in English classes, but it also had to do with the feeling of belonging she had when people at the organization told her, "I'm your son. I'm your brother. I'm you're sister. I'm your friend."

Even on the plane to Jordan with her kids, Alia had the sensation that she was leaving something behind. She tried to dismiss the feeling. "I should go," she thought. "I need to see my family." Then, when the plane was landing in Amman, another thought welled up, unbidden: "This is not my home."

Still, the first week, she enjoyed herself—eating together, visiting. But the second week, though she was still happy to be with her friends and family, a confusion set in. By the third week, she had begun to feel deeply troubled. "I'm not in my home, I'm not in the right space," she kept thinking. "I want to go back to my country!" But she was afraid to say this to her family. Maybe they would think she did not love them anymore, or that she did not love Iraq. That wasn't it, though. She was missing the American system. "Kim, here the human is number one," she would tell me, trying to explain that trip to Jordan and what she could see from the perspective of that distance. "In our country it is not like that. I'm sorry I feel that. But I found this here." She was a single mother without a husband, and in America, no one bothered her at all about this status or made her feel ashamed. In fact, it was the opposite—sometimes she'd be given even more aid because she was alone.

After that trip, she resolved to help her two sons and her daughter to love America, despite its imperfections. "Because no place is one hundred percent good," she told me "Only paradise. And we live on the earth."

For Alia and Zara, the American system had served them, and in telling their stories from the vantage point of their own safety and security, they could give them these tentatively happy endings. But there were many other refugees I met who found themselves in a more uncertain space here. I think often of one of the first Syrian families I encountered, back in 2016, an older couple from Sahem El Golan in the southwest corner of Syria, a landscape of grapevines and olive orchards. The wife raised cows and goats, while her husband, a chemical engineer, farmed fish in a small pond on the side. Together they raised their ten children in a house that sat on the main thoroughfare. In their front yard they grew fruit trees and Damascene jasmine and roses. In the afternoons, people in the town would nap. In the evenings, they'd gather in the street to talk and laugh and smoke. Life felt easy, uncomplicated. It was, the wife remembered, a paradise.

Though they had been given refuge in America along with three of their grown sons, for the father, there was no future here, no hope. This uprooting, this journey, had been imposed on them by some force they could not see. They did not choose it. Having to leave their country and their life—it was as if, he said, they were trying to complete someone else's will. It was inconceivable, what had happened to them, what they'd lost, and they were still trying to understand the powers behind all of this destruction and displacement. It was like the ancient Marib Dam in Yemen, he said. It stood for 1,200 years in the kingdom of the Saba people. When that dam broke in 570 CE, the water took everything in its path. Similarly, everything he had built in his life, everything they lived for, everything they worked for, was wiped out, simply gone.

When I asked the father what he wanted to be called for an article I was writing about his family and other Syrian arrivals to Houston, he chose the name Abu Bedawi, referring to the Bedouin, desert nomads. The life he shared in Syria with his wife and their children and grandchildren was turning into memory, he explained. He didn't want to forget it, but it was being forgotten nevertheless. And now, though he had been permanently resettled here in America, he nevertheless felt himself to be a wanderer on the face of the earth, someone without a home.

.   .   .

When I met Emmi in Jordan earlier that summer in the Zarqa home of Zara's family, she had only recently returned to her husband, who had beaten her during Ramadan. At the time of the beating, Emmi was wearing a necklace with Zara's name inscribed upon it. He had grabbed the necklace from around Emmi's neck, and the chain cut her.

Emmi had always felt weak in the face of her husband, always bending to his will. When Zara was in Jordan, Emmi started to resist. But since Zara came to the US, Emmi has grown even stronger, and it's because of Zara, who pushes her to stand up for herself. Zara is like Emmi's backbone, Emmi says. Her husband has noticed and does not like this new Emmi. He wants her to be the way she used to be—a blind person, being led. That's why he tried to keep Emmi away from Zara.

When he beat Emmi during Ramadan and cut her throat with the gold letters of Zara's name, Emmi took their little boy, Wisam, and left the older kids with her husband. "I'm not coming back," she told him. "I want a divorce." She was gone for weeks. He kept apologizing and begging her to relent. He sent people who had an influence on both her and her family. In the end, she returned because of one of the promises he made: that if she would come home, he would let her visit Zara in Texas.

One day, as late summer is turning to fall and afternoon is slipping toward evening, I give Zara a ride to the Department of Public Safety office so she can change her address on her driver's license. Zara drives a used PT Cruiser that her kids call "Mr. Bean" after the British sitcom character, but the car is in the shop right now. There are always problems with it. That she has a vehicle at all in this car-centric city, though, puts Zara in a better position than so many refugees. As we wait in the rows of metal folding chairs for her number to flash on the screen, we lean over her phone and she shows me photos on Instagram of Arabic food. She looks around at all of the people, at their eyes. So many shades, she says, that God created.

Besides her usual navy headscarf, navy abaya, and pink faux alligator-skin purse, today Zara is wearing, on her index finger, a bright blue plastic counter that she steadily clicks with her thumb to advance. When I ask her what she is doing, she tells me she is counting prayers. At the moment, it reads 868. There is no set number she is trying to reach, she says. But if she wants something, she tries to pray more. And on that unknown day in the future when she goes to court to have her divorce finalized, she will count extra, and the prayer will be one of thanksgiving.

When her turn comes, Zara and I approach the counter and the DPS officer takes Zara's photo. As Zara opens her wallet and tucks in the temporary license he prints out, I notice Emmi's photo, safe behind a plastic protector. Emmi had pressed it into Zara's hands when Zara left Jordan and told her to take it with her to America. Now, this photo is the first thing Zara sees each time she flips open her wallet.

Prayer count as we get into the car, grackles whirling, black silhouettes against a salmon sky: 1,127.

. . .

Those late summer days, my translator, Katia, and I continued to gather Zara's story little by little. Usually we'd start with how Zara was feeling that week, and usually she'd be worried about her hours at the Mediterranean restaurant, which were haphazard and, at $10 an hour, never really enough to pay rent. Her boss was always holding out the lure of more hours at a downtown restaurant he also ran if she would just be patient, but those hours never materialized. Zara knew he was struggling and leaning hard on her, and she knew her position was precarious, so she hated to press the issue. The assistance from the Transformed Program was helping for now, but by the end of the year that would be finished, so she was trying not to count on that money anymore, to plan as if it didn't exist. Maybe she'd try to find another job—one that paid cash—that she could work in her off hours. When I asked about English classes—like the one Zara had taken against her husband's wishes, when they first arrived—Zara would bring up her erratic work hours and her son's half-day pre-K schedule, the combination of which made it essentially impossible to enroll, even though the classes were free for refugees. "But to tell you the truth," she told me one day, "I learn a lot more just working in an English-speaking environment. I know I'm gonna get there."

When Zara first came to America, she told me and Katia one afternoon, she did not feel like a foreigner. Maybe this is all just her personal revisionist history, her past seen now through the more hopeful lens of the last few months, but Zara insists that, unlike when she crossed the border from Syria into Jordan, where she even spoke the language and shared the culture, from the moment her plane touched down here, she felt like any other American. She had the right to rent an apartment or buy a home. She could open a bank account. Her kids were enrolled in school and became part of the system. She was authorized to work. "I'm just remembering all of those tough times where no one gave me a break," Zara said of that period of displacement in Jordan—when her family was kicked out of an apartment they had been renting, without any legal recourse, when her daughters were not able to attend school for a year because there was no space for them. "If I lived all my life there, I would never be able to accomplish anything," she told us. "No matter how hard I worked, I would never be able to have a home of my own and to build a future for my kids."

These tangible rights gave Zara something more fundamental than a work permit and an apartment and a school for her kids, though. They gave her a feeling of home, which is exactly what she had lost in Syria.

I had come across an essay by the political philosopher Hannah Arendt—"We Refugees," written in 1943—about the desperate attempts of Jews at assimilation, and their loss of identity in the places where they sought refuge. Parts of the essay reminded me of Zara's earlier struggles, like when not speaking English had felt like a prison, but other parts seemed to conflict with Zara's newfound optimism about America. I wanted to know what she thought. So one day I jotted down a passage from the essay in my notebook, and I shared it with her. "We lost our home, which means the familiarity of daily life," I read aloud, while Katia translated. "We lost our occupation, which means the confidence that we are of some use in this world. We lost our language, which means the naturalness of reactions, the simplicity of gestures, the unaffected expression of feelings." I was wondering, I said to Zara, if any of this resonated with her.

There was some back and forth in Arabic between Katia and Zara, then Katia turned to me. "Before they lost their home, she lost a country," Katia relayed, "and the feeling of safety within that country."

It was deeper, Zara went on, deeper than losing your job, or losing your language—although, she said, she still wants to scream sometimes because she cannot convey what she needs, what she wants, what she feels. But this wasn't the real problem. Katia explained, "She felt that once the revolution started, she lost her country, because she lost the feeling of safety and belonging. When your own countrymen are intruding and assaulting you, you lose that feeling that you are home, that you are safe. And once you lose that feeling, you have lost your country." Katia paused and Zara went on, talking about the shock, the betrayal she felt when she understood that government informants lived all around her in those days. "We lost our sense of safety and freedom in our own home," Katia translated, "and instead we were always expecting some traitor to stab us in the back. We weren't safe in our own home," she repeated, "and not from foreigners, but from other Syrians. And so once you lose that, losing a job is really meaningless. Being a part of a society—this is the essential thing that you want to feel. That you're home. Once you've lost that, you've lost everything."

. • .

One day I asked Zara, "When you think of yourself, who you are at the core, is there an image that you have in your mind of what that is?"

"She sees herself in nature, with lots of greenery, and she is walking a straight path," is what Katia said she said.

Another day Zara told me that, back in Jordan, she could see how hesitant Emmi always was, with nobody supporting her and her husband treating her so badly, how Emmi was forever looking back with regret. "Come on," Zara had suggested. "Let's take a walk." And they passed through the raucous streets of Zarqa until they came to a bridge. "Look," Zara said to Emmi. "See how the cars are moving in one direction? They don't stop." They stood looking at the river of traffic. "Don't go against the current," Zara told Emmi. "Life is going *that* way. Move forward. Never look back."

But sometimes, Zara does look back. And she sees that, if she had remained in Syria, or even in Jordan, a lot of things would be different for her. Going through a divorce there—assuming that she even could have—she would not have had any support, she says. She'd have had a lot of pressure psychologically. She would have been drained. But in America, she has felt encouragement from women like Alia. *You're on the right path,* she hears people telling her, and *You can do it.* "Over here, everybody gives you the confidence, and they push you to count on yourself," Zara believes. "Even if you're not fully qualified, you have that sense that you can make it."

This attitude aligns with the insistence by the federal refugee re-settlement program on self-sufficiency, and I know that the dark underside of what Zara is saying could be an America that abandons the vulnerable to fend for themselves. It seems that for Zara, though, the independence and self-reliance upon which this country insists has instead freed her. It has opened up a sense of possibility on which she is rebuilding her life. But Zara's self-sufficiency has been bolstered by the post-resettlement support, both emotional and financial, of Alia and her organization.

Regardless, in Zara's newfound freedom—from her husband, from the strictures around what a woman was allowed to do in that small sphere of conservative Hama—she feels that she has been able to become a more useful part of the Houston community. "Back home," for example, "I was working from my house," she told me, "and when I would sing *anasheed* at those parties, it was all women. So my connection with the world was very limited. But here, I'm just like any other man or woman, and I'm connected to the community more. There's this reciprocity, and I feel a lot more useful."

Zara dreams of owning a food truck, of maybe parking it next to a mosque or a school. Or even of opening her own restaurant someday. She'd decorate the space with flowers and greenery, soft lights, a fountain. She'd serve the foods of her homeland—fresh salads, hummus, falafel, kibbe, eggplant with pomegranates, stuffed zucchini, grilled meats, molokhia, freekeh, shawarma; and afterward, sweets with hot tea and cardamom coffee. She would try to recreate the feeling she remembers of the meals her mother would make for the family in the backyard garden, the ease of those Syrian nights. Zara might call her restaurant "Ya Mal al-Sham," the title of an iconic traditional song by Sabah Fakhri from Aleppo that means something like "Oh Treasure of Syria." In the song, the singer is filled with *haneen*, with longing for his lover, the treasured beloved, from whom he has been separated, though he doesn't say why. "It was a dark day where we said goodbye," the song ends. "Oh God, how I wish you could bring us together again, / such a wonderful day I can hardly imagine."

Still, although Zara's dream is hinged to her past, something has broken in her, she says, and she knows that Syria is not home anymore. I like to imagine Zara as she sees herself—*in nature, with lots of greenery, walking a straight path.* But in my mind, the green world she is traveling through is precisely *here,* along the Gulf Coast of Texas. Crimson salvia and bluestem grasses brush the hem of her abaya, while muscadine grapes and jasmine vines twine in the trees above as she brushes aside beautyberry and wax myrtle and lantana. In the purse on her shoulder is her wallet with the photo of Emmi. Everything she needs, Zara carries. She is moving with the current, not looking back, striding—prayer count 2,159—toward some distant sun, rising or receding, it's not quite clear which.

11 *Translations*

One of the oldest stories that humans tell to explain difference and division is the parable, in the Book of Genesis, of the Tower of Babel. Once, the story goes, the people all spoke a single language and lived together with a unity of purpose. They wanted to build a city, and a tower within that city that stretched up to the heavens. "Let us make a name," they said, already fearing the worst, "lest we be scattered abroad upon the face of the whole earth." God had created humans in his image, able to shape with their hands what they conceived with their minds—but like all authoritarians, he was unsettled to see that his creations had a mind of their own. He struck them down by confounding the language that had united them, so that they could no longer understand each other. And he scattered them—meaning us— abroad, refugees upon the face of the earth, divided from one another and from their homeland in Babylon, in present-day Iraq, the place where everyone had once all belonged.

There is no homeland we can all return to, no common language we will all ever speak again. But in the United States, there's English, and knowing it can make life here, if nothing else, more manageable— from trying to get your food stamps reinstated when you inevitably fail to follow the esoteric online re-enrollment procedures every six months, to being able to make a doctor's appointment within the public healthcare system, to being able to enroll in that system in the first place, to finding more dignified work, which might solve all of the above. Not to mention how knowing English might help you feel connected to others, and that you belong.

All of which is why some of the women of the Transformed Program have been enrolled in English classes in a nondescript office building on the far southwestern fringe of the city, near Sugarland, once a sugar plantation worked by slaves out here in the fertile floodplain of the Brazos River, now a suburb of Houston. Several days each week that fall of 2018, as the country hurtled toward the midterm elections, I sat in on classes with Mina and Mendy. Alia had asked Mina to drive Mendy because Mendy had no license and no car, and this nondescript building did not sit on any bus line. From the seventh-floor window, as the instructor, Marc, went over vocabulary, I would look out at the water towers blooming across the landscape like mushrooms, at the steel latticework of electrical pylons stretching to the horizon, at the gray clouds hanging above like insulation.

"Okay, let's see: *fortunate*," Marc is saying.

"*Unfortunately*?" Oktay, a Turkish man with thinning gray hair, dressed in a button-down shirt as if for work in a downtown high rise, tries to clarify.

"That is the *opposite*," says Marc.

"Opposite . . . yes," murmurs Mendy.

"So *un*fortunate means what?" Marc asks.

Mina suggests an Arabic word, but Marc, who, in addition to accented English, speaks Arabic thanks to his Moroccan mother and French because his father came from France, ignores her.

"Unlucky," answers Mendy.

"*Un*lucky is *un*fortunate. So what is *fortunate*?"

"*Mahthuth*," Mina offers, in Arabic.

"Lucky," says Mendy.

Besides Mendy and Mina and Oktay, the class consists of several Turkish women in long sweaters and light coats and headscarves; Nour, the wife of a diplomat from Saudi Arabia; and Habibilah, a college student from Turkmenistan.

"So, an example?" Marc presses, steering the class back to the word he is trying to get them to understand through context clues rather than through direct translation.

"I am not fortunate," Mina says flatly. And the others sit in the awkward silence until Marc jokes with her, "You are fortunate to have met me!"

And then Mina, her long hair free today, slowly breaks into a wide, wild smile as the meaning of his English words seep in. Her eyes catch fire and she laughs.

"Mina," Marc chides her, "I always say, *Think positively!*"

Now Mendy, her reading glasses a little lopsided because one of the arms has broken off, offers, "I am fortunate someone paid for this class."

And then the students are off. "I'm fortunate because I'm learning English from you," Oktay says haltingly. And Habibilah suggests, "I'm fortunate that I took a visa and came here." Oktay, more boldly now, confesses: "I'm fortunate because my daughter and son get a good education."

Picking up on the infectious positivity, Mina begins, "I'm frotunate . . ." And like chickens clucking and bustling around tossed seed, the students converge on Mina, trying to help her with the pronunciation. They sound it out again and again until she hears it at last. "For-chi-nit?" she asks. "Okay, I'm for-chi-nit because I live in the United States."

"Tell them that when you go for your citizenship interview!" Marc laughs, encouragingly.

"I'm fortunate," she goes on, "because I have a green card."

"True," nods Marc.

"I'm fortunate," Mina finishes, "because I have a daughter. She speaks and writes English and she will be something in the future."

Marc moves down the vocabulary list. Turning to Oktay, he offers a scenario: "If I ask you, 'How do your employees *refer* to your workplace?,' what would you say?" But before Oktay can answer this somewhat inscrutable question, Mina jumps in: "Sorry . . . what's your job here?" she asks Oktay. And Oktay explains that he *had* a company in Turkey that produced playgrounds for children, and that these playgrounds were shipped all over the world. "I send to Iraq. Libya. Egypt," he remembers. "Sixty-five different countries."

"I like Turkiyah," Mina says. "Why not go back?" she asks Oktay.

"I have prime minister dictator," he answers. "Bad people."

"Very bad," Mendy chimes in, tsk-tsking with her tongue.

"Dictator . . . yes," agrees Oktay.

Mendy understands dictators perfectly. But Mina seems oblivious to the mounting tension in Oktay's voice. "Me, I like Erdogan," she says.

"Erdogan is very bad people," Oktay repeats firmly. "A lot of woman in the jail. Seven thousand woman in the jail."

"No!" Mendy protests in solidarity.

"With children! Maybe one age, two age—a lot of children in the jail."

Now Aynur, one of the Turkish women, asks Marc to pull up the website of a hospital in Turkey on the classroom computer. Oktay does his best to translate for her. Erdogan had taken this hospital from her husband, she explains, who had been the director. And Marc says, "I have many students for two years now—lawyers, doctors, a lot of teachers—they lost everything in Turkey. They have a lot of friends, family members, in jail."

But Mina, who perhaps doesn't understand what is happening in English, goes on in Arabic, so Marc reluctantly translates to the class. "For her," he says of Mina, "living in Turkey, everything looked good because she came from Iraq, and in Iraq at that time, everything was gone." Mendy starts to tell the class how her family's rural land had been seized by the government in Khartoum. "Do you know what's happening in my country?" she asks. But no one answers.

. . .

"Everything changes," Alia was consoling me. "If you compare—I don't want to talk bad about our country, because I'm still Iraqi—but if you compare between our country and here, our country, they do not give citizenship to anyone. And they are racist. That's why we are moving down and America is moving up."

"Well, right now . . . ," I pointed out, doubtfully.

"That's temporary, believe me," Alia insisted.

This had been a week before the start of the semester. Alia was trying to convince Mina that this country wanted immigrants like her. But Mina was feeling hopeless. Her supervisors at the high-end hotel where she worked, cleaning fifteen, sixteen, sometimes eighteen or nineteen rooms in an eight-hour shift for $11.03 an hour, would not yield on her schedule so that she could take the intensive English classes in which she had been longing to enroll ever since she arrived as a refugee, but which had been impossible to take until now. She had received four months of assistance when she arrived, but that had gone by so quickly. And even though her resettlement agency had arranged testing with a local language school, which had given Mina the information on how to sign up for classes, they had also urged her to find work. Without a husband, without another soul to turn to in Houston, with a daughter to support, and rent and food expenses, Mina didn't feel she had ever had a real choice to take English classes. Until Amaanah stepped in and Alia enrolled her.

But Mina's supervisor, who spoke Spanish and English but not Arabic, would not allow Mina to work shorter shifts on the days she had class, though she did say Mina could start in the afternoon, after class was over, instead of in the morning as she usually did. Except this would mean Mina would not get home until nearly 11 p.m., leaving Tia, who was still just ten, alone after school and all evening. And when Mina called Alia from work and asked Alia to translate for her so they could try to negotiate, her supervisor refused to talk. "Don't worry," Alia told her, "You can ask HR. I'm with you. You are not alone here."

But that same day, her supervisor kept sending Mina back to the rooms Mina had already cleaned. "Do it again," she insisted. "Do it again." Mina was sure that she was being harassed because she had tried to insist on the change to her schedule. She suspected her supervisor was pushing her so that Mina would get frustrated and walk away. But without English, she could not be sure, nor could she make her own case.

And then Mina had to go to the hospital for a chemical burn to her hand that she got while cleaning a bathroom a second time. Mina could see that this unnerved her supervisor, who had called in security as she filled out Workers Comp documentation about the incident. Alia worried that this whole experience would infect Mina's view of America, and undermine the work that Alia had been doing to try to build Mina's resilience here.

Mina was feeling demoralized. "I'm alone," she complained to Alia. "Because I'm alone, I miss many things. I want to study. I want to work. I want to shop. I want to take care of my daughter. But I don't have enough time to do all of that."

"All your life it will not be like that," Alia reasoned with Mina. "It will change. You will learn English, and you will learn more about the system. Only give yourself time to get what you need. You should be more open to accept your life now, to keep moving. If you keep saying *I can't,* and *I have a hard life,* you will not move forward. I know you are tired, but believe me, you can. You *can.*"

When she received her green card, Mina admitted, she had definitely felt more stable. "This country *loves* people like Mina who have a goal and a plan for the future and who want to succeed in their life. It loves you," Alia said, and she believed it.

I, however, feel wary of this idea that only the "good immigrant" deserves this country's welcome. Whose definition of good? If we were all created equal, doesn't our intrinsic worth require this country to accept everyone? But Alia's larger point, which she came back to woman after woman, again and again, was *You belong.* Other than those indigenous first peoples who migrated here long ago—and even them, really—we all come from somewhere else.

"Even Trump," Alia went on to Mina, "if you go back to his grandfather, he was not American. And your daughter, in the future when she is married and has her baby here, that baby can be president!" Mina said something in Arabic to Alia and Alia laughed then replied, "She wants me to consider running for president. I wish! Open the border to all single moms in the world to come here!" Alia shouted this, as if into the whirlwind. "Because America is our place to live in freedom with a bright future for our kids. I wish," Alia said, more solemnly now. "If I could bring a few people like Mina, this country, it would be bright in the future."

In the end, the school changed its schedule to accommodate the work schedule of Mina and some of the other students. On the first day of class, Marc shared the story of his Moroccan mother, his French father, his own immigrant story of coming here. And when Mina talked about why she wanted to learn English, about her travails at work, Marc reminded her of an old Arabic aphorism: "The caravan passes and the dogs bark."

"We have this saying," Alia explained. "It is a very old Arabic saying. I remember my grandmom, she said that," Alia said as she and Mina tried to translate the phrase for me, to get at the meaning held within the literal words, like a flower within its seed. "It means, *Move forward*. Don't listen to stupid people who are like dogs around you. They are howling. Don't listen to them. Don't care."

Mina nods. "Don't care," she repeats.

"Move forward and don't listen to the dogs," Alia continues. "They want to confuse you. Move forward with the caravan to get to your goal."

.   •   .

"*My . . . favorite . . . childhood . . . memory . . . is . . .*" Marc is writing on the whiteboard with a marker. "You know what 'memory' is?" he interrupts himself to ask the class, his back turned to them as he writes. "*Thakira?*" Mina says in Arabic while other students nod their heads. Yes, they understand. "*Visiting . . . my . . . grandmother . . . in . . . her . . . town*. You understand?" he asks again. "Yes, yes, yes."

"It was a big place," Mendy suggests.

"*My favorite childhood memory,*" Marc writes as he speaks, "*is visiting my grandmother in her town. It was a big place.* Good! Continue." But the students are hesitant. "It doesn't have to be real!" Marc encourages. "Create something!"

So Mina, her hair pulled up today and piled on top of her head, earrings dangling, gives it a shot. "It was weather mild," she says, then doubts herself. "One second!" She scrambles through her textbook.

Marc tries to help her. "The weather was always . . ."

"Winter," says Oktay, in his plaid checked dress shirt and shiny black shoes. But Marc points out that this is supposed to be a story about a *favorite* childhood memory. And Oktay laughs, a little self-conscious now.

"How about, *The weather was always mild?*" Marc suggests.

Next up is Gity, from Afghanistan, another Amaanah Transformed mother and new to the class. I had once sat in her apartment and listened to the story of how her husband, here on a Special

Immigrant Visa for his work with American contractors in Kabul, had, inexplicably and without warning, taken their young children and returned to Afghanistan, leaving Gity alone with their baby. He had told her to prepare an elaborate feast for friends who, supposedly, he was picking up in Dallas. But as the evening turned to night and the food grew cold, and Gity made desperate phone calls to the friends in Dallas, she came to understand what had happened. Her husband had left her for a woman back home. "It was very beautiful," Gity added to the story on the whiteboard, and Marc took dictation. It will be one of the only classes Gity attends.

And so this kind of Ur-text, this primordial story connecting the students, builds.

"The neighbors were very friendly," Ayda from Turkey adds.

"My grandmother was very happy . . . when she sees me," says Mendy.

"Very good," encourages Marc. "I like that. My grandmother was very happy when she *saw* me—past tense."

Nostalgia, which means an ache for home—*nostos,* home, plus *algos,* pain—is not limited, of course, to refugees and immigrants. I, too, have a deep ache for the home of my grandmother, who spoke German as a child in her small immigrant hamlet along the Mississippi River south of St. Louis, among a cluster of villages all named, nostalgically, for the villages along the Rhine River in Baden, Germany, where they had come from. My grandmother dyed Easter eggs yellow with the skins of onions, and made peach jam, adding a final layer of melted paraffin wax to the canning jars to preserve it. She had a pink bathroom, and after my sister and I took our baths in the pink bathtub, she would stand us on the pink toilet and powder our tummies. On Christmas Eve, she would cook a huge Pyrex dish of mostaccioli, coffee burbling in the percolator on the Formica counter. All my family—aunts, uncles, cousins—were there. But now my grandmother and her pink bathroom are gone, and everything with them.

It is in no way the same as being forcibly displaced from a home for which I ache, but my nostalgia for this irretrievable past is one way I have to try to understand what that means.

. . .

I got in the habit, that fall, of picking up Mendy and driving her to English class on the days that I attended to observe. Although Alia had arranged for Mina to drive Mendy, it was out of the way for Mina, and I passed so close to Mendy's apartment anyway that it seemed silly not to offer. Mendy would open the car door and greet me with a huge smile. "Keeeeeeeem!" she said, as she folded her body into the seat beside me, wincing a little from the pain in her feet. Usually she wore a headscarf, tied stylishly to the side, her favorite perfume from her nephew in Jordan, Hashem, trailing her.

Mendy loved studying. For now, she had put aside the A+ Computer classes to try to learn more English, which would make the computer classes easier. As we drove, she showed me the writing she was doing, and picking passages from her textbook, she modeled her reading skills. When she reached a word she didn't understand, she highlighted it to look up later. Mendy kept running lists on notebook paper pleated into long, narrow accordion folds of the words she was trying to learn, which she would write over and over again. Her handwriting was a little clumsy and childlike—probably how my Arabic handwriting appeared to anyone fluent in that language. She had never taken an actual English class before. In high school, they taught some basic phrases and a little grammar. "But I try to collect," she told me. "I try, try, try to collect, collect, collect."

"To collect what?" I asked, not quite understanding.

"To collect new words."

Listening to Mendy, I thought about her father, the autodidact, who taught himself Arabic and English. About how he and his wife spoke their local language together, but required their children to speak Arabic, to try to give them a leg up in a country that discriminated against the indigenous people of the south—in Darfur and the Nuba Mountains. Her father was dead now, but Mendy, even from this great distance and with so little money herself, was keeping his spirit alive, sending money home for her younger sister so that she could finish her degree in Khartoum, encouraging her to go on for her master's. But how much good any of this would do seemed uncertain. Mendy's family was littered with people holding multiple degrees who could not find jobs, who ended up working in factories.

In order to be able to devote herself to the English classes for which Amaanah was paying, Mendy had cobbled together a little DIY financial aid package. She had grants in the form of the rental assistance from Amaanah, along with money she'd received from her tax return. And she had loans from a cousin—a couple hundred dollars, which she would repay. But Mendy had also stopped turning on lights and the television to save on electricity, and after running the A/C for an hour or so, she kept it turned off, though in Houston it could be stifling well into October. She would find a job again after the class was over.

She had always tried to work it so that she could be home with Shahad and Mohammed in the summer. "I like to stay with them, to know them," she told me once. "If I work all the time, I cannot see how they are thinking." But she had recently received a letter from the Department of Health and Human Services telling her that she needed to renew her food stamps, which she—like all recipients— was required to do every six months. Without food stamps, it would be impossible to feed her children. "But I am not working," she said as we sped down the highway to the nondescript building where classes took place. "They will ask me." She would need, she said, to have two pay stubs for proof that she had a job. And the clock was ticking. She had two weeks to renew.

Each day after that, as we drove back and forth to classes, I could see the restless unease in Mendy as she went over with me the places she was trying to find work: the hospital near the highway that was two bus rides away, where she could work in housekeeping; the grocery store near her apartment where she might be able to cashier, though she'd have to stand on her feet all day; a mail-sorting facility where one friend, who could give her a ride, worked an overnight shift; a fiber-optic manufacturer that, another friend told Mendy, was hiring. "I search every day, every night," she told me. "I think about everything: how I can work, how I can leave my kids."

Every possibility she heard about, Mendy would approach in person, trying to make a human connection. "If you know someone, you will love them," she said of her strategy to win over hearts and minds. But every time she did this, nevertheless, Mendy was told that she needed to apply online—a task not so easily accomplished with her unreliable service on her unreliable phone. Maybe she'd use the childcare certificate she had earned with the help of her resettlement agency when she first arrived to find a job at a daycare center, even though that work paid so little. Maybe she'd open up an unlicensed daycare in her apartment. Maybe she would just go back to the hotel near downtown where she had worked before the surgery on her feet. Though if she did that, with the hours she would be gone, including the bus ride there and back, it was unclear how she could continue her English classes, much less be home before her kids' school let out. She wanted to be there with them, to monitor them and develop them. "It is very difficult for me, the life here," she said.

She really had no one she could rely on to watch Mohammed and Shahad on any kind of regular basis. Though in a pinch, she could ask neighbors in her complex—an Iraqi woman who lived next door, a Burmese woman downstairs, her Syrian friend, Dahlia. When Shahad had caught a cold and had to stay home on a morning when Mendy had to get to class, Mendy called Hashem, way over in Jordan, to ask him to keep in touch with Shahad while she was gone. And then she'd prepared some food for Shahad to have if she got hungry. Finally, she'd told her neighbor from Burma where she was going, and the woman reassured Mendy, "Don't worry. If she needs anything, tell her to come down to me."

"You have friends from everywhere, Mendy," I said to her as we drove to class.

"What I can do, Kim? I try to collect my family here. If I have good relationships here, I will be good. I will not worry for anything."

But she was worried, for the moment, about finding a job, and each day she seemed to grow more desperate. One morning, Mendy told me that Nour, from class, had offered to hire Mendy to clean her house one morning a week. "You'll miss class?" I asked. "Yes, Kim. No money." When she told Marc that she had to take this work to cover her bills, he told her he would let her make up the assignments that she missed and would send her anything he handed out when she wasn't there. But she hadn't yet figured out how she would get to Nour's. So I told her that, at least that first day, I'd drop her off on my way to English class, and pick her up after it was over. It was just a little further for me. But we both knew this wasn't a real solution.

That afternoon, Mendy was waiting out on the curb in a black smock—a remnant of her uniform from her days working housekeeping at the hotel. I found this insistence on professionalism, on her own dignity, a little heartbreaking, all the more so when she told me about her morning cleaning Nour's two-story, four-bedroom, two-bath pale brick house in a development of houses that all looked the same, off a road that ran past other developments that all looked the same, punctuated by narrow swathes of as-yet undeveloped land—native prairie grasses bordered by stands of burr oak, chinquapin oak, and bald cypress. For her work, Mendy had been paid $60, though Nour had originally promised $80. Maybe Nour thought that the discarded rugs, the battered teapot, the handbags, and the tub of salsa she had given Mendy made up the other $20. "But what I can do?" Mendy said.

She was quiet on the drive home. "The embassy gives them money," she said at one point; then added, "This is like home—like Saudi Arabia." The exploitation, Mendy was saying. Later, she started to laugh her infectious laugh. "It is very funny," she said. "What's so funny?" I asked. "If you did not come to pick me up, I would give this for Uber," she replied, holding up the $60. Not funny, *ha ha*. Funny, *insane*.

Mendy had been missing phone calls from the companies to which she'd been applying because, to save money, she'd tried putting her SIM card from T-Mobile into a Cricket phone. She had figured out the problem and fixed it, but then a new crisis emerged: Mohammed had been diagnosed with a hernia, which needed surgery. Between her feet and his post-op care, she didn't know how she was going to make it alone, much less get a job in the meantime. She'd had to miss class for a few days running now. Alia called that morning when Mendy was at the surgeon's with Mohammed, to ask what was going on.

Mendy's eyes filled with tears. "Maybe I will move to Jordan," she said, as if this was an actual option. There at least, she reasoned, she would have people around her. Her nephew, Hashem, for example. "We were split in half, the family," she told me. "When I was in Jordan, I wasn't this tired." Hashem had helped her with the children, and they had been attached to him. With his upcoming surgery, Mohammed had been telling Mendy he didn't want to have an operation alone—he wanted Hashem there with him. Almost as if on cue, Mendy's phone lit up. She showed me the photo of the caller, and there was Hashem. But Mendy didn't answer. Maybe, since the UN didn't appear to be approving Hashem's application for permanent resettlement in the US, Mendy would move to Canada, she mused. Maybe the Canadians would give them refuge there, all together. But like moving back to Jordan, this was not a real alternative.

Later that week, Mendy managed to get to class. She brought Mohammed with her, and an administrator took pity on them and squirreled Mohammed away in an empty, windowless room, with a few piles of children's books and a plastic bin of toys, a space that they were hoping eventually to set up for childcare. After class, we walked over to collect him, and Mendy asked the woman—from Pakistan, I gathered as we spoke—about working in the daycare program once it opened. The woman smiled with such warmth, her eyes full of encouragement, and she said that they hoped to have it up and running soon. When she heard that Mendy was a refugee from Sudan, she said gently, "God has made a way for you. He polishes through suffering. You will be shining." It wasn't really a solution, but her words felt like a gift of some kind. And then she said—a woman after Mendy's own heart—"But education is a must!" As we walked to my car, Mendy said wearily, "I need to sleep without thinking."

. . .

By late October, although Mohammed's surgery has gone off without a hitch, Mendy still has not found work. In the lobby of the nondescript building in the far-off suburb that had once been a plantation, Halloween decorations plaster the walls. "Are your kids going to dress up?" I ask Mendy. She casts her eyes down and rubs her fingers together: *Too much money.*

Marc begins class by asking everyone what they had done over the weekend. "*On Saturday, I . . . ,*" he directs. "I went to Rice University Saturday evening," Oktay begins. A professor from Oxford had lectured on the Prophet Mohammed, he reported.

The weekend updates continue. One of the Turkish women says that she went to Costco to buy bread and meat and fruit. Another says that her children helped her with her homework.

"All right, Mendy, your turn," Marc says. Mendy is uncharacteristically unprepared. She seems not to have been following. "What did you do this weekend?" Marc repeats the question.

"Two days I sleep," answers Mendy.

"All weekend?" Marc teases her.

"Yeeees," Mendy replies, laughing a little now.

"Why?" Marc asks her.

"I am very tired. For that reason, I sleep," she says.

"Slept," Marc corrects.

"Teacher, please!" Mendy mock pleads for mercy.

Then Mina turns to Mendy and says, playfully, "You can talk about how you lost your cell phone!"

Mendy cuts her off. "Forget it! I will cry!" she says.

Later, during a break, Mendy draws near to me as I am looking out a window over this simulacrum of a landscape—manmade lakes gouged into cul-de-sac neighborhoods, a drainage ditch running parallel with the power lines as far as my eye can see. "I have to tell you something, Kim," she says. And then she tells me the story of Ashraf Obeida.

Back in June, the husband of Mendy's friend and neighbor Dahlia, the Syrian refugee, wanted to know how to become an Uber driver. Dahlia was the first Arab Mendy met in Houston. They had both arrived around the same time, and they grew close. Sometimes, Mendy would leave her kids with Dahlia, to play with Dahlia's daughter. Now, Dahlia's husband said he was interested in driving for Uber, so Mendy suggested that he invite a Chadian friend of hers, Ibrahim, who was an Uber driver, over to talk shop. When Ibrahim came over, Ashraf, an older Iraqi man, had been visiting Dahlia and her husband. Afterward, when Ibrahim mentioned on his way out that he was going to drop by Mendy's apartment, Ashraf invited himself along.

Mendy had still been recovering from the surgery on her feet, and Mohammed was, at the time, suffering from the effects of his hernia. Ashraf asked a lot of questions about their health. Then he said to Mendy, "I'm going to help." He told her not to let the doctors operate on Mohammed. Ashraf said he was going to get disability for him. Which made no sense, but how was Mendy supposed to know? Everything here was different, and she didn't have the language to navigate the system. Maybe Ashraf knew something she didn't. "Because you don't understand English," Ashraf told her, "whenever you need to go somewhere, just call me and I will take you." Ashraf told her to call him "Uncle."

Ashraf had also already been helping Dahlia's daughter get disability for burns on her back that she'd suffered in Syria. He told them, "Because you don't know English and I do, I am going to take you to the SSI office." He was at their house all the time, and Dahlia would even cook for him. They considered Ashraf family. But when their application succeeded and disability payments started coming through, Ashraf demanded $2,000. "I took you back and forth in my car. It cost me time. It cost me money. I want my fees for my services." But he had never explained this up front. If that was how he made money, he should have said so. Dahlia and her husband were scared that he might hurt them in some way. But they didn't have that kind of money to give him.

Early in October, Ashraf called Mendy and said, "I have a job for you. You are going to work as a home healthcare provider." Ashraf brought her to an agency, which acted as a middleman between clients and caregivers. There, Mendy met Saleh, an elderly gentleman, also from Iraq, an acquaintance of Ashraf's. Mendy would be hired to care for him and his wife, who herself had vision problems—four hours a day, four or five days a week, for $8 an hour. They were there to sign the contract.

Mendy and Saleh had already been in touch by phone, to get to know each other a little, to see if they each felt comfortable. Saleh appreciated that Mendy spoke Arabic. Other caregivers they had tried before had not. He was familiar with the Sudanese and felt comfortable with them. He liked Mendy and wanted her to work for them. Mendy had only one request: to begin their contract after Mohammed had surgery for his hernia—to which Saleh easily agreed. And, presciently, Saleh told her, "Ashraf talks a lot. Don't listen to him."

But after Mendy signed the contract, and as Ashraf drove her home, he announced, "Once you receive your paycheck, you are going to give me half of it." And he warned her not to tell the agency about this deal. His tone had changed entirely. He was no longer "Uncle."

Mendy, who had been tortured by thugs, probably from the military of her own government; Mendy, who had demanded that those thugs tell her why they had kidnapped her and what they wanted from her; Mendy, who had decided that if she was going to die at their hands, she wanted to die free, unburdened by a lie she told to satisfy them—this Mendy told Ashraf, "You are not getting anything from me! Why didn't you tell me that you want part of my income before I went through all of this? You used me!" Then she said she had recorded him telling her she had to pay him, even though she had done nothing of the sort. "And don't think that I'm afraid of you," Mendy told him, demanding that he drop her off at the pharmacy near her apartment.

But he was still waiting for her when she came out. "Give me a third of your pay," he tried to negotiate. Mendy refused to talk to him anymore. But now she was afraid. "You feel that he is dirty on the inside," she says to me, as Marc calls the class back together.

.   .   .

"But how do you do this there?" Mina is asking me, pointing to my legs.

"I shave," I say.

"With a machine?"

"No . . . with a razor," I tell her, wondering what kind of contraption she could possibly be thinking of.

"Oh, a razor. Look," Mina says, laughing and stretching out one of her legs, stippled with dark hair against her light skin. "I don't have time!"

Mina is lying on Mendy's couch in Lycra short shorts, sunglasses perched on top of her head. In class that morning, Marc had gone over the present perfect tense, used to express a link between past and present—which, true confession, I did not know. Examples: *I have never been to Sudan. I have never been to Iraq. I have lived here all my life. I have never seen sugar waxing.*

In Jordan, Mendy had a friend who worked in a high-end salon in Amman. She helped Mendy perfect the art of making sugar wax on her stove—sugar mixed with water and lemon juice and heated slowly until it turns to a warm, sticky paste—and then removing body hair by smearing the wax across the skin and quickly yanking. Though a common form of home hair removal for women throughout the Middle East, I had only heard of it recently when I watched the Lebanese movie *Caramel,* which takes place in a Beirut beauty parlor. Mendy worked in her friend's salon, taking the bus from Zarqa, where she lived below Aboud and his Palestinian wife and their children.

"So do all Arabic women do their arms also or just their legs?" I asked.

"All the body!" Mina replies.

"Everywhere?" I ask, naively, starting to get the gist.

"Yeeees," replies Mendy.

And nearly in unison, both women say, "Very important!"

"Why?" I ask them.

"If you are not clean, your husband cannot stay with you!" Mendy answers.

And Mina jokes knowingly, "Really, even though I have no husband—it's important!" And they laugh hysterically.

"In my country," Mendy goes on, "if you are not clean, your husband can go to another lady."

"The same in Iraq," says Mina.

"That's a lot of pressure," I say.

Mendy, wearing a long housecoat, white flowers on a black background, her head wrapped with a scarf tied to the side, has on her black-rimmed one-armed reading glasses. She sits on a plastic stool, scooping sugar wax from a plastic Tupperware container and working it with her fingers up Mina's leg, her movements graceful and mesmerizing, like ballet. Behind Mendy, *Veep* plays on the television, as Arabic subtitles unfurl along the bottom of the screen. On the dining table the parakeets in their cage are twittering madly. Mina, meanwhile, veers from laughing to screeching out in pain.

"Kim?" Mina asks. "In English, this . . . what's the name?" She's pointing to her—well, there are so many names. Which should I tell her?

"Well, *bottom* is more formal," I decide to go with, but is it really?

"Bottom?" Mina repeats.

"Or *butt* if you're with your friends." Confusion. "B-U-T-T," I spell out.

"And this?" she asks?

"Breast," I say.

"This? This thing?" Mina says, gesturing in circles.

"Bikini, bikini," Mendy jumps in with certainty.

"The bikini area," I nod. "Also vulva," I try to say, but my tongue gets twisted.

Just then, Mina's phone rings. She gets up from the couch and wanders around the room, talking, one leg still daubed in sugar wax.

When she hangs up a few minutes later, she's frazzled. "People in Iraq, they think when you live in America, you are rich," she says.

"Yes, and you have more money," Mendy agrees.

Mina tells us that her sister back home, who has a job and a husband, has been asking for money. "I gave to her! For three months!" Mina cries.

"Don't let them do as like this," Mendy says, tsking. "Say, *I have a daughter. I am alone.*"

Mendy has begun the dance of smearing and yanking again.

"What's this?" Mina asks, pointing under her arms.

"Armpits," I answer.

"Pits?" Mina confirms, then says, laughing, "I'm practicing English!"

.   .   .

In the end, the elderly Iraqi, Saleh, had tracked Mendy down through some people he knew in the Sudanese community in Houston. He told the home healthcare agency that Mendy was like his daughter. "This man Saleh is very good for my life," Mendy told me. "And his wife is very kind." Mendy was working for them a few days a week, cooking, cleaning, doing laundry and ironing. She could take a bus to their house—it wasn't too far. And they were flexible with her—they knew she had kids. The wife even suggested that Mendy do the laundry at her own apartment rather than waiting around their home for the wash and dry cycles to end. This way, Mendy could be with Mohammed and Shahad.

"I am free," Mendy told me. This was her perpetual struggle: to liberate herself as much as possible from the burden of low-wage work in order to carve out some small room of her own in her mind where she could focus on learning. "I try to study, Kim. I *need* to study," she told me again and again.

Mendy was feeling more hopeful now. In an act of manifestation, as she prepared herself for that day in the future when surely she would have a car, Mendy decided to take driving lessons. So one afternoon after English class, we stopped by The Alliance, a resettlement agency, to enroll her in their Driver's Education and Mobility Center, a social enterprise offering free driving classes for refugees.

And some kindness seemed recently to have awakened in Nour, Mendy's classmate from Saudi Arabia, which had buoyed Mendy further. One cool fall day, out of the blue, Nour and her daughter arrived at Mendy's apartment carrying plastic bags from Walmart filled with milk, fruit, vegetables, oil, sugar. Nour's husband, the diplomat, had told Nour, "Mendy is a good woman. Go to her."

When Mendy tells me this about Nour, I think about Mendy's optimism and her gratitude, the way she always takes the small offerings of others with grace. I say to her, "You send out good feelings into the universe, Mendy." And she says to me, "You know, I try to collect many people from many countries. My cousin, he tells me, Mendy, don't have relationships with people only from your country. No! Take a flower from each country. Learn about other cultures and how people from other cultures deal with life. Learn from them how they use their time, how they learn." When Mendy lived in Jordan, her neighbors would do whatever was necessary to get by. They even took Mendy to clean houses. In Sudan, this work was not respectable. You were the daughter of someone, so you didn't do those things. "I learned from Jordanians how to organize myself, how to spend my money," Mendy goes on. And here in the US, Mendy learned from the people she met that you must work and be independent. That you must use your time efficiently. "From this experience with different people," she concludes, "I learned how to live my life."

I asked her then, "When you think of America, what does it *mean*? What does it stand for? What is the central idea?"

"What I found in the US I did not find in my country," Mendy said, and she spoke about the discrimination she had experienced in Sudan in trying to get an education, and about the way she and her kids have healthcare here, while her sister died of cancer that had not been treated when she'd been a refugee in Jordan. "So you have opportunities here," Mendy went on. "If you study something, you will get employed using your education. You don't need to have your connections to get somewhere. The government here is on your side."

"Do you feel that America is home, or is it not yet?" I asked Mendy. As so often, we were conversing through a translator, and as the two of them conferred, an Arabic word she used caught my ear. It was the same word that Sara had used when she told me the story of leaving Syria, her *watan*—her country, her homeland. *Watan*—the word for the place where you belong.

Trying to be sure I heard correctly, I asked, "Did you use the word for your 'country' or your 'home'? Or maybe it's the same?"

And Mendy answered me in English: "The same. I used the word, the strongest word you could ever. *Watan*. This is my home."

12 *How to Build a Country*

When Elikya was drowning in the trauma following the assassination of her husband, the army colonel, beside her, and after years in hiding, on the run, she converted to Islam. By then she had made it to Burundi, and the camp where she'd been sent was majority Muslim. She was raised Catholic, an inheritance of the Belgian colonization of Congo, but she never felt committed to that religion. And in the camp, she didn't want to be alone. She converted, she says, to get through. When she was by herself, images would come back to her—how they killed her husband, how they tried to kill her, everything she'd gone through. Islam helped ease her pain. It told her how to pray. It kept her from being alone.

Later, in mourning for her daughter, Aline, who had died during the surgery on her goiter, leaving four young children behind, Elikya converted again. She had been watching her children and grandchildren playing outside—or bickering, really. But then Elikya saw a girl, maybe twelve years, telling the others that arguments come from the devil, that Jehovah doesn't like fighting. Elikya observed that the child brought light and comfort and peace. When Elikya spoke with her, the girl told her she had come to play with the others because she'd heard there was a loss in Elikya's family. Elikya asked to meet her parents, and when she told them how much she appreciated their daughter's character, how different she was from the other kids around, and how she longed for her own children and grandchildren to be like their girl, they told her they were Jehovah's Witnesses, and that this was the way.

Today, Elikya and her children and grandchildren attend church services in Swahili for immigrants from Congo, Rwanda, and Kenya at the Jehovah's Witness Kingdom Hall on Beechnut Street in Houston's Chinatown, where all of the signs are in English and Vietnamese. I went once to a Sunday service with them, and as we drove, Elikya's teenage daughter, Lydia, told me proudly how, all over the world, every Jehovah's Witness was reading the same passages that day, following along on printed booklets or electronic devices, working through the same lesson together whose answers to certain spiritual questions were neatly enumerated.

Lydia would sometimes tell me about things she remembered from Congo—her grandmother's farm, with mango trees and banana trees that she would climb, the cassava and other vegetables whose English names she doesn't know; how her grandmother would gather food she had grown and prepare it for the family; the way her grandmother stored water in clay pots that kept the water cool; how she would make Lydia work in the field with her, and how Lydia would try to escape.

The sanctuary of the Kingdom Hall, with its fake palm trees and lectern and padded metal chairs, felt to me like a hermetically sealed conference room. The music, though in Swahili, sounded joyless and sanitized. Maybe after such trauma and upheaval, though, what you want is order, clarity, a direct path toward salvation.

When they'd first arrived in late July 2015, Elikya's resettlement agency placed them in an apartment with four bedrooms, to accommodate Elikya and the eight kids. The pantry and refrigerator were full of food, and Elikya thought about how she had always had to make one sinewy chicken stretch for a couple of days with cassava leaves, pounded and cooked down. Or how she'd never even think about buying milk if she wanted her family to eat. But here in Houston, she could cook enough that they'd have leftovers. If the children threw food away, Elikya would scold them. "Don't do that!" she'd say. "There are places in Africa where there's nothing to eat!" There was so much food that she would sometimes take pictures and send them back home, and people would write back that life in America was incredible.

In the camp in Burundi, they had slept on mats laid over thin poles. Here, they had beds and mattresses. She took pictures of those, too. Once, she found a beautiful mattress near the dumpster, and she just couldn't leave it, so she carried it back to their apartment. Then she realized it was infested with bugs. Her caseworker told her, "Please don't do that again!"

Elikya laughs now at what she used to collect—the waste was everywhere—and says she doesn't hide what happened to her, how naïve she'd been. She would tell the kids to watch out for what others were throwing away and, if they found anything good, to bring it home. Her room looked like a depot store, she says. After the initial assistance from the resettlement program ended, they moved from that apartment to a smaller one because the rent, at $1,700 a month, had become far too expensive to maintain on her salary as a dishwasher at the downtown Hilton. Of the man who helped them move, Elikya says, "May God bless him," because it was trash that they carried. Elikya found it hard to part with what they had found for free. She even brought with them a broken television. The man made four trips back and forth. "Elikya," he joked, "you've only been in the United States one year. I've been here ten years. How do you have more stuff than I do?"

Despite the excess all around them, Elikya had quickly realized that here in America, the first rule was to work. When they had arrived, among the paperwork she remembers signing at the resettlement agency were documents attesting that she would become self-sufficient and support her family—that the government was not responsible to raise all those children or provide for them. If you say you have children, Elikya says, and you cross your arms and declare you won't work, the government will do the same—cross their arms and declare they won't work either. When the letters start coming in the mail for payment, the government won't be there.

The dishwashing job at the Hilton that Catholic Charities helped her get was far from where she lived. And the managers would change the schedule all the time. Sometimes, she would have to wake up at 4 a.m., shower, eat something so she could take her medications for diabetes and high blood pressure, then catch the bus to work. Other times, she would work late into the night. Often, by the time she had changed out of her uniform and started for the bus stop, if she didn't run she would find that the last bus had already passed by. When that happened, she ended up sleeping outside on the street. That's when she quit—just never went back to work. She didn't even tell the managers.

It was too much for her head, too stressful, and Elikya pleaded with her case manager, "How am I supposed to survive? You brought me here—do you want to get me thrown in jail?" She was worried about those papers she had signed where she had promised to become self-sufficient. "Before I get put in jail, just send me back to Africa, because I can't manage this situation," she said. That's when some people from the church had helped her apply for public housing near downtown. Eventually, when she and the kids got situated, Elikya tried to get her old job back at the Hilton, since it was so close to where she now lived and on the rail line that had a stop right outside her apartment. Four times she asked for work there, but they wouldn't give her a job because of the way she had left. So she learned her lesson. After that, she got the job cleaning offices in the high-rise buildings after hours.

It's a lot of work to live here, says Elikya, but it's better than what they had back home, because there, you tried to find work and you couldn't. As painful as work can be, with her body put through so much stress, when she walks in the door to her apartment she says, "Thank you God," and she showers, massages herself, takes her medicine, and the next day she goes back again. When the check comes in, she wipes her tears and forgets all her pain from the work for a little bit.

What you need to survive, Elikya knows from experience, are connections. You have to build friendships with the people around you, in your community. She left Africa and all her family, but now she's here, and if she has problems, she has learned how to reach out to people to ask for help. If you hear somebody speaking your language, you try to create a friendship. If you are struggling because you have little children and no childcare, go to that person and say, *Please, help me. I'm working and making this much. Can you help me watch my kids for a couple of hours? I'll give you a little money—just help me a little bit.* Elikya says that she has learned how to read people. When a person talks to you and they want to communicate and have a relationship with you, you have to put in the effort. But when a person wants distance, you maintain that distance. Everywhere you go, though, you can find someone who becomes your family.

That fall of 2018, Elikya had been struggling and in need of some connections who could help her. At one of the Amaanah home visits, she mentioned to Deeshawn, the case manager, that she wanted to leave her work cleaning offices at night and find a daytime job. She knew the kids were wandering around through the complex while she was away—misbehaving, she feared. They were probably slipping back in just before she came home. She wanted to be able to keep an eye on them.

I liked Elikya. I liked her style—the various wigs she wore, from cloche cut to blue neon braids; the way she moved easily between dresses sewn from psychedelic wax-cloth prints and dark-rinse skinny jeans that accentuated her voluptuous folds. She told me once that you must be chic or you will feel old before you should. Though we were roughly the same age, the years of her life, like the pleats of an accordion, seemed to have opened up and swallowed so much more than mine. She was big-hearted too, but she could also be pretty demanding. Sometimes I wondered about her relationship with the kids in her household, those she had kept safe and brought here with her. Elikya often complained about the older boys, who had jobs but didn't help her out with the rent.

Later, after it happened, I wondered if it was Elikya who had called in the women from the Jehovah's Witness Kingdom Hall that day, the summer before, to talk with Lydia about peer pressure and read biblical passages about the temptation of Jesus, praying over her, trying to save her from the danger they feared she was in—if that was Elikya's way of using her connections to help her daughter survive. "Heavenly Father," they entreated, "we want to say thanks for this time that we have spent discussing your word and helping Lydia to apply the scripture to her everyday life. We know how important it is to you that young people are obedient to their parents and choose their friends wisely because we want to do all things for your glory and to bring praise and honor to you." And I remembered, too, how Lydia had told me that she had no friends in this new school, near their new apartment, across the city from the apartment where they'd been resettled among all the other refugees, many of whom spoke her language. How she ate lunch alone and texted her friends at her old school.

So when I woke up one morning in late fall to a text from Elikya telling me that Lydia was pregnant, looking back, I felt that I should have seen it coming.

By then, Elikya had found a daytime job as a dishwasher at the University of Houston. She could take the light rail there early in the morning and be home before the kids got back from school. But even before she got the job, it was already too late. When Elikya called Amaanah to tell them about Lydia, Alia was put on the case. And so, one overcast day, Alia and I met up at the university and walked across campus, faces of the children and grandchildren and great-grandchildren of immigrants and refugees and the enslaved like a great tide eddying and pooling around us.

Elikya joined us outside the cafeteria during a break, and with Sonya, one of the women from her church, on speakerphone serving as a translator, Alia sussed out the situation. Which was that Lydia had stopped attending school—the smells in the hallways and at lunchtime made her nauseous. The administration had been trying to contact Elikya, but maybe she'd gotten a new phone, maybe she couldn't understand the messages left in English—at any rate, she hadn't responded. There seemed to be an option whereby Lydia could do her work from home and receive tutoring services. But Elikya wanted her in school. She didn't trust Lydia, in the apartment all day. She didn't think Lydia was responsible enough. She wasn't a self-starter, Sonya translated.

"What about Lydia?" Alia asked. "What does she want?" And after some back and forth, during which Elikya spoke with a fierceness that could have simply been pain, Sonya said, "Her daughter likes the idea of studying at home because she wants that freedom." But, Sonya repeated, Elikya was concerned that Lydia wasn't disciplined enough, and that she would use that freedom to run around. "And being that she's underage, it will come back upon the parent."

Alia was wearing a gauzy leopard-print shirt and an abstract-patterned headscarf in ivory, gray, brown. Peeking out from beneath the blocky black polo shirt of Elikya's uniform was also a leopard-print shirt. They had both once been wives of high-ranking military officials, and then those husbands had been murdered beside them. And now here they were, mirrors of each other.

"What I see from all this conversation between you and her and me," Alia was saying to Sonya on speaker—"the issue is between her and her daughter. Elikya has the key to fix this issue. She is smart and strong. She can fix it if she trusts her daughter and talks with her." Turning to Elikya, she said, "Be close with Lydia. Be a friend to her. Give her advice—she needs to continue with her studies because you love her, and because that is for her, not for Elikya." Again she addressed Sonya: "If she keeps going with Lydia in that way, Lydia will accept to go to school without being embarrassed and shy. It depends on Elikya's way with her daughter."

Alia, who was talking down into her phone, looked up toward Elikya. "I see Elikya. She has a full heart. And I understand. She loves her daughter. I'm sure she loves her. But Lydia's age, it makes her not want to listen to her mom." Again she focused on the phone. "Lydia knows she did something wrong. But we give her advice—that it happened, that no one can skip making mistakes, but that it's important to move forward in her life. So we need Elikya to change her way with her daughter."

"I've been trying to work with Elikya with how she deals with her children," Sonya acknowledged to Alia. "There's a dynamic of being an immigrant in the US, and you have certain norms in one country and certain norms here and I'm trying to help her appreciate the differences and adjustments you have to make. When she first told me about her daughter's pregnancy, one of the first things I said was she has to put her own feelings aside, focus on being loving, being a friend. She shouldn't do things that would push Lydia away because then she can't help her."

. . .

Alia believes in paying it forward. She believes in listening to the stories of the refugee women with whom she works, in treating them with dignity, in encouraging them, in making them feel that they belong. "The important thing," she says, "is to reach their heart." Because refugees need financial help. They need healthcare. They need English. They need a job. But they need kindness too. That kindness, she believes, buoys their spirits and makes the rest easier to attain. It also leaves what she once called "a fingerprint in their mind." Then, when they are able, they will pass their own rewards on within the community to which they have come. "Life, it is recycled," Alia says. "What you get, you give it back. I took this impression from Amaanah. That's why I give it to others." God had created human beings with two hands, Alia would tell me, again and again, so that when we receive something with one hand, we can give something else away with the other.

All this might sound a little woo-woo. But listening to Alia, watching her at work, I have become convinced that there's so much at stake in these simple acts of kindness that she advocates—namely, the fate of the country. "Because in the end," she had told me a few weeks before we met with Elikya, "if we help the single mom, if we give her a hand, she will give that to her kids, to respect this country. She will tell them, 'You see? These people helped me to succeed in my life. And this helped you to succeed in your life.' And she will give them advice: 'Please keep going to help people when they come here.'"

But if she is struggling and alone, said Alia, "She can't continue. Even if she continues, she will think: hard life, hard work, no one to help—*this* is America." And if that happens, if her children watch her, confused, exhausted, her struggles unseen, "in the end, they will not love this place. And if they don't love this place, they will not feel this is their home. And when they feel this is not their home, even though they take their citizenship, they will not give anything to this home." Alia paused for a moment, thinking, and then concluded: "If we don't build love inside them, they won't give love to this place."

Alia remembers when she took her citizenship test, back in 2013. The administrator of the test had Alia's file on the desk between them. The woman opened the file and Alia saw her own photograph that the UN had taken of her, back in Jordan. The woman was kind. She asked Alia questions about her story—her husband's death, the birth of the son with whom she'd been pregnant when her husband died, the work she now did with refugee women. Then, after a few questions about US history and government, she congratulated Alia and hugged her. "You are a strong woman," she told Alia. "Welcome to America!" That same year, after Alia was sworn in as a citizen, she decided to buy the brick house with the windows in the suburbs, because she loved this country, she says, and because she felt stable now, and she saw that this really was her home.

. . .

Winter, such as it is here, has arrived at last along the temperamental Gulf Coast, with cold fronts blowing in like waves. Sometimes, out walking or running errands, or on your way home from work, you'll feel the front hit. One minute, the air is still and muggy. Then the wind sweeps the torpor away and you are left shivering in the cool clearing. A few days later, the chill washes back out to sea and the temperatures rise, before the next cold front pushes through again.

One brisk morning Alia and I meet Mina and Mendy at the cafeteria during a break in their English class—a last official visit as the Transformed Program ends for the two of them. Alia is looking radiant in a lavender silk scarf, her nails freshly manicured in a pale nude. "I colored my hair," she tells us, pretend-preening. "My friend, she has a salon." Mina, laughing, asks Alia to give her the phone number, then exclaims, "The program is not finished . . . please!" First in Arabic to Alia, and then to me in English. Mendy, though, is already in tears. Which makes Alia's voice grow soft and her eyes fill, too. "We'll be friends!" she tells Mendy, pulling her close and speaking directly into her ear, insistently. "We are like sisters together, all the life. Okay? I'm with you all the time. If you could see your phone number in my phone . . . Look, I put *Sister Mendy, Sister Mina*. Because I don't have sisters. You are my sisters, okay? Come!" And we all slide into a cafeteria booth with our Styrofoam cups filled with weak Lipton tea.

Alia explains how Amaanah will pay another month's rent, and she gives them the date for the graduation ceremony, which will take place at a nearby Indian restaurant on Hillcroft in the Mahatma Gandhi District. But today is not really for business. Maybe to console Mendy, Alia tells both her and Mina, "I feel I'm strong because you are with me. Sometimes, I feel I need someone strong around me, like you ladies. So give me positive energy, to be strong, to continue in the life. Okay?"

"We will promise you to do that," Mendy says, earnestly and insistently. "We cannot stop in the positions that you put us. We promise you to update ourselves."

"I am sure of that . . . ," Alia says, and before she can go on, Mendy adds, "And one day we will visit you and show you!" Then she breaks into her infectious laugh, and Alia laughs with her.

"And I'm sure in the future you will help other ladies who come here as single moms," Alia encourages them. "They will need ladies who succeed in life, same as you."

"Yesssss," Mendy nods.

"Please promise me!" Alia presses.

"Yes, I promise," Mendy affirms.

"Because some people are not as lucky as you. They did not find people to give them a hand to continue in their new home. So please, don't forget! Give them your hand to help them." And then Alia repeats her mantra: "God, he gave humans two hands. When we get something in one hand, we need to give to people from the other hand. So that's why I like to continue with this program—to give to you. And I'm waiting for you ladies to give to other ladies with your other hand."

"Yes. I will promise," Mendy repeats. "Anytime you need us to show the ladies how we did it in our lives when we came to this country, call us. And I promise, I will come. I will come and tell them, *Nothing is too difficult. Not anything is too difficult for the single mom.*"

During this exchange, Mina has grown quiet. And now tears are running down her cheeks. She speaks in Arabic. "Your word, it affects me a lot," Alia translates. Mina says something else. "You give me hope," Alia translates. And then she turns to Mendy and Mina. "Because you know why?" she asks them. "I'm the same as you ladies. I came here, the same as you. I'm a single mom. I have many issues behind me . . ."

"Right, right!" Mina interrupts her. "You are the same. But a lot of women are the same"—a lot of women, she means, have lost their husbands and their homes to war, have carried their children across borders to safety, have flown across oceans to land in cramped apartments in foreign cities, have had to begin again. "But you are different," Mina insists.

"That's why I'm thankful to God, that he brought me here. Because I was, in my country, *nothing*," says Alia, the woman who had been born into the Baghdad cultural elite, who had married into a military family in Saddam Hussein's Iraq. "I'm something here. So really, I pray daily, thankful to God that he brought me here . . ."

"Yes, also me," Mendy interjects.

". . . to do something for other people"—Alia nods at Mendy and keeps going—"because before I was a person who got help from others. I never gave anything to other people. But here I started to give something to other people. So I'm lucky, the same as you. Because I'm here." By now Mina and Mendy are weeping together. "We should not cry!" Alia cajoles them, crying herself and wiping away her tears with her manicured nails. "We need to laugh, okay? It is the end of the program, but we will continue with the life here in the USA, like friends and sisters."

Did I make a mistake in coming here? That's what Alia had asked herself all those years ago as she sat on the floor of her empty living room, her children leaning against her that first night they came to this country. I think about what Alia told me, remembering the kindness she received when she had grown most desperate and alone in those early days: *Life, it is recycled. What you get, you give it back.* And she did. And I think about all the women whose lives she's made better, and about the good they now want to do to welcome others because of the sisterhood they have made together. And I think about what Alia believes: that *this* is how you build a country. *Did I make a mistake in coming here?* Alia's life itself has become an answer to the question that she asked herself when she was first a stranger here.

Coda

The Transformed Program ended for Mina, Mendy, and the others, the old year turned toward the new, but the stories, because they were lives, kept unfolding.

In Sudan in the early days of 2019, protesters rallied in the streets, calling for the resignation of President Omar al-Bashir, whose government was the reason Mendy was here now. She would forward me shaky videos from her family and friends back home—of men and women and children walking en masse and chanting, of soldiers menacing the emptied streets with machine guns, of the injured being carried on stretchers—while on the BBC Radio Hour, I listened to Sudanese government officials suggesting that reports of unrest were fake news. Mendy worried for those she loved, but life here continued, oblivious to the suffering.

One afternoon when I visited Mendy, she and a friend were hauling a bunk bed frame that someone had given her up to her second-floor apartment. If she could fit the bunks in the bedroom, she would no longer have to sleep on the floor. "Now I can dream," she told me. Soon, she would get a car and a job at a nearby apartment complex minding the children of other refugee women so they could learn English. President al-Bashir would be overthrown in a coup d'état. And in a possibly related metaphor, the parakeets that Mendy kept in a cage, like a human heart beating within curved ribs of bone, would escape one day soon, out the front door that Mendy had accidentally left open.

In March, Elikya's grandson was born—the first American citizen in her family. Back in Congo, President Joseph Kabila, who had lost reelection in December, finally agreed to leave office, and when the new president, Felix Tshisekedi, was inaugurated just after her grandson's birth, it was the first peaceful transfer of power since Congo's independence from Belgium sixty years before. But Elikya, knitting an outfit for the baby from red and yellow yarn, seemed disconnected from the politicians in her homeland. "None of them are going to feed my children," she observed. "Congo is not a place, not a country," she said, recalling atrocities that she witnessed there. "Even if whoever is in power brings peace to Congo, I don't care. I only care about what's happening here."

Mina found a new apartment further west, beyond Gulfton's crowded complexes and the cement that covers everything. She left her job in housekeeping for a position as a cashier at Walmart. "I want to be better," she told me. And Sara completed a certificate program that trains people to analyze EKGs, and began working from home, reading heartbeats on her computer.

Meanwhile, in Iraq, demonstrations protesting corruption emanated from the southern city of Basra and spread throughout the country. And in Syria, the government, backed by an alliance with Russia and using internationally banned weapons, continued to recapture regions of the country that had been held for the last few years by anti-government forces. With the growing repressive calm, Syrian refugees displaced to neighboring host countries—Turkey, Lebanon, Jordan—faced increasing pressure to return home.

Though her scattered family remains in Jordan and Turkey, in France and Germany, and in Syria, Zara feels she is safe because she is here. And one afternoon, as winter was turning to spring, I drove her to the airport to pick up Emmi, who was coming with Wisam, her youngest son, to visit. That's what Emmi's husband had been forced to promise when he was trying to get her to come home, when he beat her so badly she said she would never return. On the drive, Zara was giggly and anxious. Before we left her apartment, she had prepared some of Emmi's favorite dishes—stuffed grape leaves, freekeh, shakriyeh, and molokhia.

At the terminal for international arrivals—where every one of these refugee women once arrived, clutching their white plastic International Office of Migration bags and holding the hands of their children—we inched through the crowd closer and closer to the automatic glass doors, beyond which lay passport control and baggage claim. The doors parted and travelers from a flight from Panama flowed through. Then the doors closed again. Zara paced nervously, clicking the prayer counter strapped to her index finger. She wandered over to talk to the drivers who spoke Arabic and were holding placards with names, to see if she could get any inside information. After a while, the glass doors opened again and the Emirates passengers, with cellophane-wrapped baggage and Gucci purses, began arriving. Women in black abayas and headscarves. An older man in a pale green turban. Younger men in skullcaps and jeans. Women wearing bindis.

And then, at last, there was Emmi in her mauve headscarf. Zara had not seen her since they'd held each other in the hallway between their apartments in Jordan, just before she departed for America. Zara ran toward Emmi and Emmi ran toward Zara and they held each other again at last, held each other for so long that the other travelers had to part around them like a river around two stones. Wisam, born in the days just before Zara left, was a physical manifestation of the years the women had been separated. Now he was wheeling a hot pink suitcase in circles around them. The suitcase was about as big as him, and it kept tipping over. He would right it, and turn in another circle. And still Zara and Emmi held on to each other.

. • .

In the fall of 2019, the ancient pecan tree that had always shaded our back yard died, and when it was removed, we saw that the sky had opened up and sun was pouring in and we could finally have a garden. My husband dug out the threadbare grass where our daughters had run barefoot when they were young and built a series of raised beds where the tree had stood. Constant, the Congolese farmer with Plant It Forward whom I'd written about and had once visited with Elikya and Lydia, showed us how to lay down cardboard inside the beds to keep the weeds from invading, and brought us a truckload of mushroom compost and helped us shovel it on top of the cardboard. I read obsessively about growing vegetables in our Houston microclimate, then planted a winter garden—lettuces and snow peas, kale, chard, mustard greens, carrots, some broccoli that never really took off, mounds of parsley and cilantro, green onions. It was a miracle, all of it, grown from seeds to become food that we loved and that we didn't have to pay for.

Months later—the week the pandemic shut the city down, coincidentally—I had just purchased two nucleus hives of local bees, to be delivered to my house in May, by which time, of course, the US borders had been closed, refugee resettlement had halted, everyone in Brooklyn was baking sourdough bread, and the nation had become, impossible though it seemed, even more deeply divided. But as the insatiable virus spread and the catastrophe of the pandemic deepened, my garden's own urgent hunger to produce, which was really its hunger to reproduce, both consoled and overwhelmed me. Sometimes I would take a break from writing to pick tomatoes or to try to beat back the squash vines from colonizing the bean trellises. Then I would lean against the fence and allow myself to become hypnotized by the bees, endlessly sifting down onto the entrances of their hives, the pollen they carried on their hind legs making them look as if they were wearing Victorian bloomers.

With the exception of a few male drones, all the tens of thousands of bees in a colony are females—daughters of the solitary queen, whose only job is to lay eggs, which are like the cells in the body of this superorganism. The bees, therefore, are all sisters. And that pollen I would watch them carrying in from the flowers in my garden is what the youngest nurse bees feed the larvae that hatch from the eggs, which, when they pupate and chew their way out from the cells capped with wax, will join the sisterhood. Everything was connected and, like the virus, wanted to live.

The fall before the pandemic, I had learned about several Women's Empowerment Groups (WEG) for refugees in Houston, and I'd been attending their weekly meetings, intending to write a story about them. The first had been an Arabic-speaking women's group, which had started as a coffee social several years before, with the influx of Syrians, but had evolved to include swim lessons and a car maintenance workshop and plans for a cookbook, among other activities. Another group for Afghan women had just begun that winter. Women, children in tow, would bring food to share, and, after a weekly discussion about resources in Houston, they could practice their English with volunteers. Both groups were run by Interfaith Ministries, a large resettlement organization. A third group had been started by FAM Houston, a small nonprofit that worked, post-resettlement, largely with refugee women from Congo, Rwanda, and Burundi. Elikya had been attending those meetings. I can't really explain how it happened, but as the city shut down and the in-person meetings halted, I started volunteering with FAM.

Actually, I can explain it. Or I can explain why. In those early days of the pandemic, as I was writing her story, Alia's words kept coming back to me. *If we don't build love inside them,* she said of refugees, *they won't give love to this place.* I was thinking of the life cycle of kindness she talked about—how you receive with one hand and give away with the other, and how, like the microorganisms in my garden soil that nourish the vegetables and flowers growing in it, kindness gives those newcomers a reason to root themselves where rough winds have blown them. And I was thinking, too, of the sisterhood of bees, evolved to work cooperatively for the survival of their young. I was sick at heart over the politics of division and the injustice all around me. I needed to be part of something life-giving and grounded in connection.

At first, I volunteered with Anne, originally from France, to drive our cars—which, unlike the refugee women, we possessed—to various schools around the city that were partnering with the Houston Food Bank. We waited in lines that stretched for blocks to pick up loads of food, which we'd then deliver to the Congolese women and their families, many of whom, including Elikya, were no longer working and, unable to read and write even in their own languages, had been bewildered by the online process of trying to claim unemployment. Their babies were in danger of going hungry, and they didn't know how to navigate the system.

As restaurants shut down in this city that loves to eat, and in the days before we knew that the farmers markets would stay open to become a crucial lifeline, I had worried about the Congolese farmers I knew from Plant It Forward, like Constant, who sold to chefs and at the Saturday markets. Some of the women in the FAM Women's Empowerment Group were also Plant It Forward farmers. So Hannah Terry, the executive director of FAM Houston, quickly raised emergency funds to purchase weekly CSA (Community Supported Agriculture) farm shares from Plant It Forward, which were then donated to the families of the Women's Empowerment Group, along with cleaning supplies and staples—flour, beans, rice, tea, sugar.

But in the end, these stopgap measures for feeding families proved unsustainable.

I remembered the gardens and farms in their homelands that the refugee women described. The fruit trees in Hama, Syria, under which Zara's family would gather in the afternoons for tea. The Sudanese fields in which Mendy's father labored, and from which her sister and her nephews had been forcibly removed. All the cultivated land that Elikya had left behind in Congo and Burundi, and that little patch of earth in front of her public housing unit where she grew roselle, amaranth, okra, cassava. I thought about my friend Judy, who left Vietnam with her mother on a boat when she was a tiny child, and whose job it was at their apartment in southwest Houston to weed the patch of herbs they grew in a sunny spot outside. I thought about all of the concrete in that part of the city where most refugees are housed. And I thought about my own garden now, which fed me and my husband, our daughters when they stopped by, occasionally our parents and siblings and friends—how empowering it was to grow food to nourish those I love, and how lucky we were to own land that we could grow it on.

Just about all of the Congolese women had practiced subsistence farming in Africa. With a little land, they told me, you could feed yourself and your children. You could be self-sufficient. But here in America, there was no possibility of owning land on which to grow food, even though, as a refugee, you were supposed to achieve self-sufficiency within a few months of arriving. So you worked at low-wage jobs, which didn't pay enough to live, but which made you eligible for food stamps, which, because of your low-wage job, you needed in order to feed your family. Maybe you were self-sufficient by some technical measure, but it wasn't a dignified life of human flourishing, and the work was stultifying and isolating. And in any event, with the pandemic in full swing, much of that work had ended or grown even more tenuous than ever.

What FAM Houston's WEG women needed was open land on which to grow food, but which could also be, in those days of isolation, a site of safe connection. So, with Hannah Terry's blessing, a growing band of women—including Elikya, some of the Plant It Forward farmers, an immigrant from Sierra Leone, and another naturalized Houstonian like myself—set out to look for space on which to build a small community garden. In my mind, this meant a place for the twenty or thirty women in the Women's Empowerment Group to each have a raised bed or two in which to grow food for their families, maybe four feet by twenty feet, like those my husband had built in our backyard.

We investigated the open land on easements beneath electrical transformers controlled by power companies. We reached out to area churches, which sat on the little green space that seemed to exist in Gulfton. We sought out public officials to inquire about public parks. We visited community gardens and urban farms to ask advice. But despite our relentless efforts: no dice.

Then one day in July 2020 I got an email from Liz Vallette, president of Plant It Forward. They had been looking for land for their farmers, too, and had been offered a parcel in Alief, not too far from Gulfton, owned by the local ISD (independent school district), in a part of town that reflects the diversity of the city as a whole (and now perhaps more widely known through the Netflix show *Mo*, featuring the comedian Mo Amer, who grew up there). The International Management District that managed the land on behalf of Alief ISD had actually been looking for people to farm it, to help alleviate food insecurity in the neighborhood. They were even offering to put in an irrigation line and pay for city water to irrigate. But the land sat in the hundred-year flood plain, and Plant It Forward had decided they couldn't take the risk of losing a season's worth of crops in the event of a flood. Would we be interested?

Masked up, our leadership team went out to look. It was an entire undeveloped city block, largely abandoned to invasive grasses that had made it look like a peaceful meadow, bordered by trees. A few days before Thanksgiving 2020, we gathered to break ground. Women walked the perimeter of the field, singing a song of blessing over this land that we had decided to call Shamba Ya Amani, Swahili for the Farm of Peace.

In the early spring, not long after the January 6 insurrection at the US Capitol, Larry Frank, an old white farmer who had helped Plant It Forward through the years, arrived with his tractor. When he was a young man, he had been sent to fight in Vietnam. But, swords into plowshares, he helped us now to break open the hard clay soil, buried beneath which were tires, rebar, and chunks of concrete. As we pulled out what the tractor hauled up, Larry made pass after pass, mixing in compost and expanded shale to aerate the clay, then shaping rows in the community field, as we were now calling the quarter-acre we had decided to start with. In this field, we would grow food for the collective, which meant food from home, which meant vegetables I had seen in Elikya's tiny garden: okra, roselle, molokhia, cassava, amaranth, taro. On another quarter-acre, we built a series of raised beds, four feet by twenty,, for women to grow whatever they wanted for their own families' particular desires. At first we had twenty beds. Then we added some for women with disabilities. Then we added twenty more. We now have nearly sixty.

That first growing season during the summer of 2021, Elikya, still out of work, took the bus to the farm a couple of days a week—over an hour each way—to keep the field watered and weeded. She was also procuring seeds for the farm from Africa, sent to her by her brother in Kinshasa. Though at first she did all that work of her own volition, FAM soon enough received funding to hire her. On Saturdays, the larger community would come to help and to tend their family beds. We grew everything organically, and divided up what we grew, and everyone took home a share of the bounty.

Sometimes, working the field, I would listen to the women gabbing and laughing together as they shaped rows with these massive hoes they use called jembes, purchased at a store on Harwin Drive, which I'd driven down with Alia the first day of our home visits together a few years before. Many of the women who farm at Shamba Ya Amani are older, even elderly. A few come with babies strapped to their backs. Almost all are illiterate in their mother tongues. Almost none speak English. But often as we worked, the women would break into song, a solitary voice throwing out a line that was then picked up by the others and carried all together. I didn't need our translator to explain what was happening: the farm was becoming a place where, in this brave new world, they could feel like they belonged. *Dada,* they called each other, and me, too: *sister.*

We needed bees, a pollinating sisterhood. An organization in Austin called Bee Mindful, whose founders I had heard on a beekeeping podcast, offered, when I wrote to tell them about our farm, to mentor us in the building and keeping of bees in Top-Bar Hives, which, unlike the conventional hives in my backyard that are both expensive and precise in their construction, we could make ourselves. One of the founders of Bee Mindful, Nathalie Biggie, originally from France, had been hired by the Republic of the Congo to design and lead a beekeeping training program for their network of farming trade schools. The other, Les Crowder, author of *Top-Bar Beekeeping: Organic Practices for Honeybee Health,* has been keeping bees for nearly forty years, first in New Mexico, then around the world, and now in Texas. After our first season at Shamba Ya Amani, we were asked by the Houston Botanic Garden to build and manage Top-Bar

Hives throughout their site as well. They are paying beekeeping apprentices from the refugee community, whom I, along with other local beekeepers, are mentoring. These beekeepers will mentor more apprentices. And so on.

In our second season, we began selling produce to small local markets in southwest Houston that cater to various immigrant communities, providing them with fresh, organic, and nourishing foods that their customers remember from home. By the third season, we were selling to the Houston Food Bank, which had provided boxes of donated food to the women in the early days of the pandemic. In addition to Elikya, FAM now pays three other farm stewards to work the field during the week. And they pay me to coordinate all the moving parts.

Saturdays are still communal workdays, except that the community has expanded to include volunteers from all over the city who hear about Shamba Ya Amani and want to participate. Often these volunteers are the children and grandchildren of immigrants and refugees. They tell me about the gardens of their grandmothers back in Pakistan and India and Vietnam, or about the okra and eggs their mothers made for breakfast in El Salvador, or about the winged beans grown by a Filipino father, or about the bitter greens whose seeds a sister sent to them from Nigeria. Sometimes, the origins of the family have been lost, but they remember the farms of relatives in East Texas or Oklahoma. Sometimes, as in my case, the links have all been broken, and they just come, in this era of disconnection and despair, when our democracy and the earth's climate hang in the balance, to dig in the soil and to feel connected to other human beings within the abundance of creation.

Early on, Elikya proposed what has become the motto and rallying cry of Shamba Ya Amani: *Umoja ni nguvu!* Together we are strong!

·   ·   ·

I did not set out to write triumphal immigrant narratives. Yet although no one is saying their lives are easy, in working with Elikya nearly every day, and in speaking still with the other Transformed women I followed, I sense that they see their own stories in that vein.

In 2019, Alia left Amaanah for a newly formed Houston non-profit, whose focus is to provide case management, mental health counseling, educational outreach, and financial assistance through a culturally conscious lens for Houston's diverse Muslim community. She still works primarily with single mother refugees. On Thursdays, she hosts Tea Time on Zoom. The women—from Syria, Iraq, Afghanistan, Palestine, Jordan, Yemen, Sudan—bring their steaming cups and process their experiences with each other. Having a space to share their burdens, Alia observes, keeps them from sinking into isolated despair.

Before, Alia carried the stories of the women with whom she worked within her. And because their histories were in a sense her history, she could never escape her memory—memory that brought pain to her heart. She began to see how, all those years, while she had buoyed other women and helped them to move forward, she, in some ways, had stayed behind. When this understanding came to her, like a reflection in a mirror, she knew that she, too, needed to move on. Around this time, her husband, Osama, came to her in a dream. His face was joyful, and he gave to her the ring on his finger. Alia took all of this as a sign. She told herself, of her past, "All of that is only memory. It is not your life now. It is time to start a new chapter." Soon after that, she remarried—an Iraqi immigrant, an engineer and writer. Her children, too, are marrying and having children—and that is a whole new American story.

Mina recently became a citizen. Citizenship had been her dream. When she received her passport, she touched its cover and cried. Everywhere, life is hard, she says, but she wants to make something out of her life here—to use it responsibly. During the pandemic, her job at Walmart shifted and she began filling online orders for pickup. But then she heard about a pharmacy technician program that Walmart would pay for, and she enrolled. Now Mina is making her way through the exams and practicums. She sent me links to the YouTube videos she had to post as part of the program. Wearing turquoise scrubs, nitrile gloves, and a gold necklace in the shape of Iraq, she demonstrates the skills that she is learning, all in English.

Zara is now the head chef at another Mediterranean restaurant called Fairouz, after the Lebanese singer who is like Celine Dion. Zara created the menu. She works full time, preparing falafel, fatoush, hummus, babaganoush, kofte kebab, kanafeh. There's even a special named for her: Chef Zara's Sajiyeh, tender pieces of lamb cooked in the iron skillet that gives the dish its name. Zara, too, recently became a citizen, and along with her, her children. She has changed her social media name to "mysoulusa."

"My soul USA?" I ask, to be sure.

"Yes," says Zara. "She gave me everything," she goes on, speaking of America. "She gave me freedom. She gave me a job. She gave me my children . . ." Zara trails off. "That's why I love this country." Then she points to her wrist, her pulsing veins. "She's here. She's in my blood," she says. She talks to Emmi every day. Now that Zara has her citizenship, she will try to visit Emmi in Jordan.

Mendy recently received her citizenship as well, she tells me, as a parrot named Farujah sits on her shoulder, reaching over from time to time to peck Mendy on the cheek. Back in 2020, for Shahad's birthday, her daughter had told Mendy, "My mom, I need a dog." But they lived in a small apartment, so she'd bought a parrot instead. It was so tiny and young that Mendy had to feed it with her finger.

Mendy is still watching over the children of refugee and immigrant women who come to learn English at a nearby apartment complex. She is still working on her certification courses so that she can turn to IT work. "You know, Kim, why I am focusing on my studies?"

Mendy asks me. She and Farujah both look at me searchingly. "Because I want my kids to follow me. When they see their mom going to school, I'm sure they will love school, too. They will put it in their minds: my mom attended school, she was working, she was taking care of us." And then, like Mendy, who watched her father teaching himself Arabic and English after long days in the cotton fields on the tractor, they will want to be like her.

When civil war broke out again in Sudan in 2023, Mendy was fielding texts from relatives all over the country, whenever they had electricity to write her. She sent her entire tax return to try to help some of them move to safer cities, only to find, days later, that those cities, too, had descended into anarchy and bloodshed. Whole families were being slaughtered for nothing. In her apartment complex, Mendy was reaching out to neighbors from Chad, Burkina Faso, Cameroon, in some desperate hope that, if she could get her relatives out of Sudan—which was basically impossible—and if she could get them to another country where they could register as refugees, perhaps someday, somehow, eventually she could get them here. Alia has invited Mendy to speak at an upcoming gala at the organization where Alia works, because she sees Mendy as such an inspiration.

Sara became a citizen at the start of 2023. She has begun working to bring her parents, who are in Syria, to America too. Maybe she'll buy a house someday. She already has the sense that she is fulfilling her dreams, and she's doing it on her own. She's not finished yet. "I have a lot of dreams, you know!" Sara says. "When I was young, people told me I was smart, and I tried to study. But after I got married and had kids, I didn't do all that I dreamed to do. But in this country, I am doing it, because I want to do it. For me, I am always looking for another thing: the better, the better." (At this point, perhaps doubting her English, Sara has asked her son, Adam, something in Arabic, and he replies. Then Sara turns back to me and says, "My son is telling me, 'You're doing good!'")

Recently, Sara's daughter, Jojo, who is now in fifth grade, had to do a report on someone famous. Jojo wanted to write about Sara. When Sara asked her what she would say, Jojo told her, "I will say you were married young, and you had two kids, and you came here from another country, alone, and you worked and you studied." And Sara had thought, "Oh my god, my kids *do* know what I have done!" Jojo told Sara, "I want to do my report on you because you are a strong woman—nobody does what you are doing!" But in the end, her teacher wouldn't let Jojo write about her mother, because her mother wasn't famous. She picked Elon Musk instead. He made the Tesla, so there was a lot to write about. But, Jojo says, Sara is way more interesting. She's basically a hero, she says.

· · ·

The generosity and common sense of the 1980 Refugee Act, though diminished over the years and nearly destroyed under President Trump, is still within our grasp. And there is real reason to feel hope that we might be slowly returning to something closer to those earlier objectives. For one thing, under the Biden Administration, refugee resettlement has begun again in earnest. In September 2021, just after the disastrous US withdrawal from Afghanistan, President Biden raised the admissions ceiling to 125,000 refugees for the following year. That was before Russia invaded Ukraine in February 2022, setting off the largest refugee crisis in Europe since the Second World War. After the invasion, Biden announced the US would be accepting up to 100,000 Ukrainians for permanent resettlement.

Then on March 31, 2022, Cindy Huang, director of the Office of Refugee Resettlement, announced that the eligibility period for Refugee Cash Assistance and Refugee Medical Assistance, programs outlined in the Refugee Act, would expand from eight months to a full year. "Most of the refugee populations ORR serves are fleeing from an unsafe or traumatic experience in their home countries. That trauma, coupled with making a new home in an unfamiliar place, can be a difficult transition," she stated. "This extra cushion of time will alleviate a little of the burden as new arrivals find a job to support their families, learn a new language, and acclimate to a new culture."

In early 2023, the State Department launched a new program, inspired in part by a highly successful Canadian model, in which private citizens, banding together into groups of five or more, can apply to sponsor refugees to resettle in the United States. This Welcome Corps (a variation on a much smaller effort begun in October 2021 that allowed Americans to sponsor Afghans and Ukrainians) would be responsible for raising money to help refugees during their first ninety days in the country: $2,275 per refugee. Vetted, certified, trained, and monitored by a consortium of nonprofits with an expertise in refugee resettlement, these private sponsors will use the funding they raise to provide the services traditionally supported by resettlement agencies: securing and preparing housing, enrolling children in school, helping adults find employment, linking families to healthcare and social support services. Although the obligation is only three months, and although a couple of thousand dollars doesn't go very far, perhaps the bonds that form between sponsors and refugees will ease the trauma of resettlement and will be more lasting and more sustainable. For Americans overwhelmed by the incomprehensible scale of the global refugee crisis, the Welcome Corps might offer a concrete path for being part of a more sustainable solution. I'm also reminded of the words of Geleta Mekonnen, who works in refugee resettlement, when he advised Mendy to do whatever small and seemingly futile acts she could to help her nephew, a Sudanese refugee stuck in Jordan. "Really, we help ourselves," he told her. "We don't really solve anything. There's not really a solution. The solution is: Do something. When you do something, you are hoping that one day some good with that will come."

Other ideas have been floated for reimaging the entire refugee resettlement system and providing transformational support to refugees. Let me focus specifically, though, on single mother refugees, whose stories shape this book, and on the solutions for helping them that are coming out of Houston.

"Refugee Realities: Between National Challenges and Local Responsibilities in Houston, TX," a report written by Yan Digilov and Yehuda Sharim and put out by Rice University's Kinder Institute for Urban Research in 2018, draws on research conducted within the Houston refugee community. Digilov and Sharim advise, for example, resettlement "tracks," which could be implemented at the federal, state, or local level and would take long-term responsibility, rather than offering only short-term assistance, according to each group's specific needs. "Creating an option for single parents, and particularly single mothers, is first on the list of necessary alternative tracks," they argue—in addition to a track for large families, another for those who arrive without education, and one for those who come with degrees and other certifications.

But regarding those single mothers, they go on:

> These families require an upfront investment that ensures the single provider is able to speak English, receive the emotional support of local community institutions, and make long term plans to care for the family. Financial assistance may be required for 10-12 months while those investments are made. In addition, arrangements must be made for children of single refugee parents to be placed into free childcare or afterschool care facilities.

These ideas alone would solve so many of the problems I saw the women in this book encountering.

And Digilov and Sharim have other inventive solutions as well for the resettlement program as a whole: convening formal public dialogues between resettlement agencies and refugees themselves so that refugees can voice their needs and forge alliances with one another; engaging a more diverse group of businesses to hire refugees and to seek refugees as patrons and clients; offering intensive ESL classes in camps abroad so that refugees don't struggle so much to learn English here; investing housing funds into apartment units that would be owned by the resettlement agencies or by local nonprofit service providers to deal with the problem of affordable housing; offering free public transportation during the resettlement period and free loans to assist in any recertification processes; more personalized mentoring from members of the community at large.

I also admire the various Women's Empowerment Groups, which resettlement agencies and post-resettlement organizations have begun in Houston and which I had been following pre-Covid, and out of which grew the farm we formed. Women's Empowerment Groups are easily scalable within this city and beyond, and they are infinitely malleable, given the particular needs and ethos of any given community. These groups bring together formerly isolated women into a sisterhood with a shared background, where they can hear about local resources, engage with organizations whose services they can use, meet local Houston women, and just be with one another. I know refugees for whom those couple of hours each week are the ones where they feel most alive and hopeful, most resilient, most integrated.

To integrate single mother refugees into this country by fostering a sense of connection and belonging has been Alia's work all along. The sisterhood I watched her create is not the antithesis of self-sufficiency, but rather the foundation upon which it is built. At this historical inflection point, as we reimagine other systems of injustice, let's redefine what refugee self-sufficiency means, too. Bringing people here who have lost everything, forcing them into work so they can just barely get by, or worse, allowing them to fall through the cracks, is a stingy vision for America. All that waste of human potential makes this country poorer. Conversely, to do this work of truly welcoming those who need refuge, and to do so while recognizing that we are all caught in Martin Luther King Jr.'s "inescapable web of mutuality," is to be striving toward that more perfect union which is the real American Dream.

In 1630, John Winthrop, governor of the Massachusetts Bay Colony, preached a sermon to those onboard the *Arbella* as they sailed across the Atlantic, part of the Great Migration of Puritans out of England. In this sermon, Winthrop laid down the central principle to which the community should commit itself. "For this end, we must be knit together, in this work, as one man," he exhorted. "We must entertain each other in brotherly affection." The mythology of the lone frontiersman, sufficient unto himself, had not yet taken hold. For those early refugees, it was love for one another that would save them. "For we must consider that we will be as a city upon a hill," Winthrop reminded them. "The eyes of all people are upon us."

For four hundred years, the patriarchy that unspooled from those early settlements on the eastern seaboard of this continent, built on the land of indigenous people, who already well understood what it meant to be knit together, to work with the forces that shaped them, has strayed and returned and strayed again from Winthrop's radical vision of community, his "city upon a hill," grounded in love for one another. Alia and these women, single mother refugees, know what it means to be knit together in affection. They know, like Elikya, what it takes to regenerate a wasteland. If we want to achieve that city upon a hill, we should listen to the sisters.

Portrait of Alia. *Photo by Meridith Kohut.*

Alia in her childhood home in Baghdad in December 1988, before her marriage to Osama the following spring. *Family photo.*

Alia and Osama as newlyweds at a friend's home in Baghdad, summer 1989. *Family photo.*

Alia and her daughter, Haneen, in Osama's family home, late summer 1990.
Family photo.

Osama with Haneen at home in Baghdad while on leave from his post in Tikrit, late summer 1990. *Family photo.*

Osama and Haneen at their house on the military base in Tikrit, 1990. *Family photo.*

Alia and her children in their second apartment in Houston, 2009. *Family photo.*

Portrait of Mina. *Photo by Meridith Kohut.*

Portrait of Mendy. *Photo by Meridith Kohut.*

Portrait of Sara. *Photo by Meridith Kohut.*

Portrait of Elikya. *Photo by Meridith Kohut.*

Elikya (back row, center) with her siblings and their mother, circa 1974. *Family photo.*

Elikya and her husband, Lieutenant Colonel Sebastian Abangya, in Goma, 2002. Later he rose to the rank of colonel. *Family photo.*

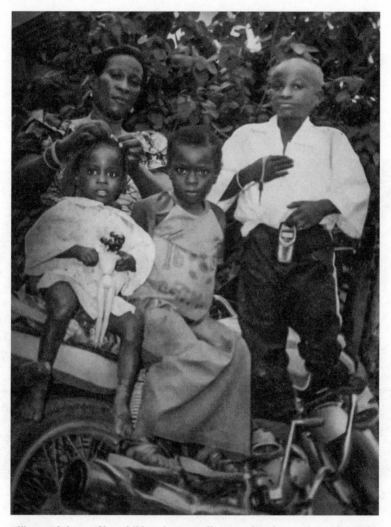

Elikya and three of her children in Burundi, soon after they registered as refugees. *Family photo.*

Portrait of Zara. *Photo by Meridith Kohut.*

Gratitude

My deepest thanks to all of the women who have shared their stories and their lives with such openness, depth, and insight. Many appear in this book, but some do not. And most especially I owe thanks to Alia Altikrity—*my sister:* your relentless generosity of spirit made our book possible.

Gratitude also to the all-woman, all-immigrant team of interpreters, beyond Alia, who sat for hours upon hours and, with sensitivity and grace, helped me to hear the stories of these and other women, and to understand the cultural contexts in which their stories took place: Luwam Hagos, Nour Haikal, Fayda Karaman, Ndjabuka Francine Murhebwa, Katia Sabsabi, and Pierrine Spitaleri.

To the University of Houston students who transcribed the hundreds of hours of tape recorded over a year of conversations—your work was invaluable and I thank you all: Hannah Ajrami, Sherin Johnson, Kiran Keneally, Maureen Lax, Saul Martin, Sabine Meyer Hill, Austin Mitchell, Ammara Mukhi, Anni Schwans, and Nimra Zubair.

The interpreters and the transcribers were funded by a generous grant from the Houston Arts Alliance. A writing fellowship at the MacDowell Colony gave me the space to begin mapping out the stories of the individual women and the larger story of the book itself.

Wendy Sherman, my agent, is the best matchmaker I could ever have hoped for, and the warmth and encouragement of my editor, Naomi Schneider, throughout the writing of this book buoyed me. Her clear-eyed and intelligent work made the writing so much better. Meridith Kohut's accompanying photographs have opened up other visions of these women and their stories. It was a profound honor to collaborate with her on this project.

Many thanks as well to Elizabeth Gregory, Oleg Jolic, Chloe Krane, and Jessica Wilbanks for reading early drafts of this manuscript and providing crucial feedback.

Finally, to my husband, Terry, and to our three daughters and their partners, to my grandchildren, to my parents, to all of my dear family: thank you for understanding why this work has been so necessary for me to do, even when, at times, it took me far away.

Note on Sources

This book is, at heart, a work of narrative oral history, based almost entirely on the remembered stories of the women who appear in it and on the translation of those stories by interpreters, who often helped me understand the nuances of particular words and phrases as well as the larger cultural contexts and deep histories in which these stories took place. In doing this documentary work, I was profoundly inspired by Svetlana Alexievich's *Voices From Chernobyl: The Oral History of a Nuclear Disaster* (Dalkey Archive Press, 2005), both in its methodology and in its form. For this and other of her works, Alexievich spends time with hundreds of subjects, everyday people living everyday lives when disaster strikes or war intrudes. With her, they remember what they could not comprehend as it was happening, and the details they recall contain unbearable truths. In a deeply democratic practice, Alexievich listens carefully and trusts in her subjects; she records what they say, then gathers their stories together into this polyphonic tragic chorus—"a kind of temple made of human lives and human voices," as she told the *Los Angeles Review of Books*. "It's a novel of voices."

At times and regarding certain types of information, I needed to move beyond the work of oral history, however. The following are some of the sources I relied on.

To understand the history of refugee resettlement in the United States leading up to the Refugee Act of 1980, I turned to *Americans at the Gate: The United States and Refugees during the Cold War* (Princeton University Press, 2008). For more specific information on the legislative history of the Refugee Act of 1980 and the goals Congress hoped to achieve through its passage, I found the *International Migration Review* article "Refugee Act of 1980, by Senator Edward Kennedy, one of the sponsors of the act, helpful and hopeful in its documenting of the bipartisan support for this legislation, though hinting at the division to come on the topic of immigration more broadly speaking. And "Unfulfilled Promises, Future Possibilities: The Refugee Resettlement System in the United States," a 2014 report by Anastasia Brown and Todd Scribner in the *Journal on Migration and Human Security,* helped distill some of the shortcomings of the programs put in place by the Refugee Act.

For up-to-date data on forced displacement worldwide, the website for the United Nations High Commissioner for Refugees has been an invaluable resource. The UNHCR tracks numbers of internally displaced persons, asylum seekers, and refugees as well as their demographics, the countries that refugees come from, the host countries that take them in. I also turned to UNHCR's Refworld—which contains a vast collection of reports regarding countries of origin, as well as policy documents and documents relating to legislation and jurisprudence connected to refugee law—to try to understand certain stories that the women of *Accidental Sisters* told me about the upheaval in their home countries that preceded their leaving.

Beyond the many background interviews I conducted with people working in refugee resettlement in Houston in order to understand how resettlement operates at both the national level and the local level, the website for the Office of Refugee Resettlement served as another rich source of information. Collected there are the ORR's annual reports to Congress, a repository of policy letters, admissions and arrivals numbers, and fact sheets on the various services and programs overseen by the ORR.

To understand immigration, including refugee resettlement, to Houston, I turned to immigration research data collected by the Houston Immigration Legal Services Collaborative. The collaborative commissioned reports by the Migration Policy Institute, including "A Profile of Immigrants in Houston, the Nation's Most Diverse Metropolitan Area," (2015) and "A Profile of Houston's Diverse Immigrant Population in a Rapidly Changing Policy Landscape" (2018). The collaborative has also collected a trove of other specific data on the impact of immigration on the city and the state as a whole, including the economic benefits that immigrants bring.

For many years, I have been following the work of Dr. Stephen Klineberg, the founding director of the Kinder Institute for Urban Research at Rice University, which has been charting Houston's profound transformation since 1982. His *Prophetic City: Houston on the Cusp of a Changing America* (Avid Reader Press, 2020) has helped me contextualize the evolving role of immigrants in Houston, as well as Houston's place at the vanguard of changes happening across the country. Another work to come out of the Kinder Institute has been "Refugee Realities: Between National Challenges and Local Responsibilities in Houston, TX," a report researched and written by Yan Digilov and Yehuda Sharim and published in 2018. Their findings affirm much of what I was learning anecdotally about the challenges of resettlement as I visited with refugee women and families beginning in 2016. Their recommendations for solutions, drawn from the deep listening they did to refugees themselves, seem wise and necessary to me.

Finally, although *Accidental Sisters* is grounded in the entirely specific experiences of particular human beings who live in my city, in this country, now, I also see their stories as new variations on an ancient theme, one that begins in the Western world with Homer's *Iliad* and *Odyssey*, works that I taught for many years and that influenced the way I have come to understand the wages of war endured by women, including those I write about. These may be epic poems of men in battle and of men trying to return home after destroying a city and its people, but threaded through them are the women's stories, too, told with a deep empathy for their suffering. Women like Penelope, queen to Odysseus, left alone to raise a child and craftily defend the household she and her husband shared as its wealth is slowly consumed, not knowing if Odysseus, twenty years away at war, will ever return. Or Andromache, a refugee herself whose family had all been killed by the Greek warrior Achilles. Now the wife of Hector, the great, doomed son of King Priam of Troy, Andromache knows that if Hector dies in the fighting outside the walls of their city, her infant son will be thrown from the ramparts before her eyes, and she will be led off into slavery in a distant land, to work the loom of another man and haul water for the Greeks, their enemies.

The *Iliad* concludes before the fall of the city of Troy, before Odysseus has tricked the Trojans with his hollow horse filled with warriors, who pour out to slaughter the populace after they've been let inside the gates. By then, Hector, the city's defender, has, as Andromache feared, been killed by Achilles, and Hector's father has traveled across enemy lines to recover his son's mutilated body. A ceasefire is in place to allow time for Hector's funeral. This poem of war, then, ends in mourning, and with the lamentations of three women—Andromache, Hector's wife; Hecuba, mother of Hector; and Helen, wife of Hector's brother. They mourn his loss, and the way that loss dooms them as well. It is a sisterhood of grief.

It was all there already, thousands of years ago: women whose husbands left home and never returned, women whose husbands died violently in war, women displaced by war, women who have lost everything, women who want only to protect their children. But the sisterhood is there, too, telling their stories. Homer doesn't say, but I like to imagine that the mourning of those three women gathered them to one another, and that their shared song of lamentation was, as all art is, a resistance to their coming annihilation.

Index

Abu Bedawi, 216
Abu Ghraib, 1, 31, 32, 41
Abu Suleiman, 169–170, 171–173
al-Assad, Bashar, 77, 127
al-Assad, Hafez, 127
al-Assad, Maher, 128
al-Bashir, Omar, 21, 49, 50, 261
Alexievich, Svetlana, 23
Alia: Amaanah Refugee Services'
   Transformed Program, 11–12, 21,
   30, 44, 87, 89–90, 157, 214; and
   brothers and sisters-in-law,
   196–197; and children, 81–82,
   86–87, 125, 199; citizenship, 256;
   and Elikya, 253–254; entering
   America, 24–26; escaping Baghdad,
   1–4; and father, 65, 66; Houston, 11,
   29, 46, 81, 91, 157; and husband
   Osama, 33–36, 57–59, 65–67,
   194–195, 272, 281*fig.*; interviews
   with, 22–23; and Mendy, 44–47, 51,
   56–57, 157, 256–258, 274; and Mina,
   30–31, 37–40, 42, 193–194, 200,
   228–231, 256–258; and mother, 65,
   66; philosophy, 255, 259; photographs, 280*fig.*–282*fig.*, 284*fig.*;
   privilege, 91, 195; refugee journey,
   20–21; and Sara, 61–64, 67–68,
   73–76, 88, 167, 180–184, 189–190;
   self-sufficiency, 83–85, 278;
   sisterhood, 18, 19, 278; and
   students, 85–87; Sunni Islam, 2; Tea
   Time, 272; time in Jordan, 12, 20,
   158, 198–199, 215; translation
   services, 89–90, 126, 140, 193–194,
   258; and Zara, 210–212, 213, 221–222
Al Qaeda, 2
Al Sudani, Ali, 181–182
Amaanah Refugee Services: Alia, 12,
   90, 91, 157, 214, 255; case manager,
   95, 251, 253; founding of, 86;
   Ghulam Kehar, 86, 89; Gity, 231;
   graduation ceremony, 11, 257;
   Mendy, 234; Mina, 228; post-resettlement organization, 11; single
   mothers, 30
American Dream, 19–20, 88, 159, 279
Amer, Mo, 268
Amman: Alia's escape to, 4; Alia's
   time in, 59, 198; Alia's visits to, 95,
   215; author's time in, 131–132;
   driving services, 171; Mendy, 150,
   153–154, 242; Sara, 63, 77, 174, 177,
   179–180, 186

Arendt, Hannah, 220
asylum: applying for, 37, 150; cases, 85, 170–171; claiming, 13, 14, 111–112, 115–116; granted, 153, 206; process, 198; seekers, 8–9, 12

Baghdad: Alia, 281*fig.*; cultural elite, 26, 258; curfew, 74; danger, 196; houses, 25; Mina, 31, 32–33, 36, 191; Osama, 283*fig.*; people from, 21, 90; safety, 34; society, 196; streets of, 1; university, 65
beehives, 264–265, 270–271
Brown, Anastasia, 15

Clinton, Hillary, 10

Danius, Sara, 23
Deeshown, 95–96
Democratic Republic of the Congo (DRC), 4, 97, 110–111, 115–117, 121–122, 262. *See also* Zaire
Digilov, Yan, 15, 277
Displaced Persons Act, 13

Elikya: author's cooking lesson, 117–118; and children, 113–116, 121–122, 248, 252–254; collecting belongings, 249; employment, 250–251, 252–253; English class, 106–108; farming, 118–119; garden, 95–96, 122–123; and grandchildren, 262; growing up, 97–99; healthcare application, 108–110; and husband, 99–101, 102, 103, 104; leaving Congo, 111–112; Mama Turkey, 117, 120; photographs, 288*fig.*, 289*fig.*, 290*fig.*, 291*fig.*; religious conversion, 247–248
English classes, 40, 166–167, 207–208, 219–220, 224–228, 233–236

Eritrea, 88
Ethiopia, 88

Fallujah, 1
FAM Houston (nonprofit), 265, 266, 268, 270, 271
fear: of abandonment, 60; of accepting financial assistance, 163; Alia, 1–3, 33, 197; Alia's clients, 44; of deportation, 87; Elikya, 251, 252; of human rights violations, 8; for one's life, 133; of persecution, 13; Zara, 128, 131
Frank, Larry, 269
Free Syrian Army: arranging apartments, 168; controlling El Taebah, 78; controlling hospitals, 75; in Hama, 128; stronghold, 73; taking down Bashar al-Assad, 73

Gaddafi, Muammar, 165
gardening, 95, 96, 110, 117–119, 125, 212, 264–269
Gulfton, 87–88, 91, 157, 211, 262, 268

Habib, 26, 33, 86
Hama Massacre, 127
Haneen: age, 13, 33; poor health in US, 81–82, 86; struggling, 199
Holman, Elizabeth, 14
hope: for Alia, 58; of Arab Spring, 61; for author, 164, 168, 275; Elikya's name, 123; for Emmi, 136; false, 164; in grassroots work, 11; between hopelessness and hope, 153; lack of, 216; for Mendy, 245, 274; for Mina, 258; for refugees, 19, 278; for Zara, 140, 212, 219
hopelessness: of American Dream, 20; of Mina, 193, 194, 228; of Sara, 176, 179

Houston: airport, 205; Alia, 11, 29, 46, 81, 91, 157; author in, 41, 165; community, 222; during the 2016 presidential campaign, 22, 155; Elikya, 21, 106, 122, 249; Gulfton neighborhood, 87; Mendy, 21, 49, 51, 56, 160, 234; microclimate, 264; Mina, 192–193, 199, 228; minority majority, 6–7; public housing, 95; refugee experience, 23, 86, 265; refugee resettlement, 4, 6, 8–10, 17–18, 95, 278; refugee women, 96, 277; Sara, 180; soil, 124; southwest, 109, 132, 211, 267, 271; streets of, 90; Syrians arriving in, 206, 216; teaching English to refugees, 107; Zara, 131

Houston Community College, 57, 158

Huang, Cindy, 275–276

Hussein, Saddam, 32, 33, 65, 66, 92

Iran: Iraqi invasion of, 32; war with Iraq, 33, 58, 65, 66

Iran-Iraq War, 33, 35, 58, 65, 66, 173–174

Iraq: Alia, 20, 24, 26, 83–85, 91, 197–198; army, 67; demonstrations, 262; invasion of Iran, 32, 58, 65; invasion of Kuwait, 33; Mina, 31–32, 36, 41, 42, 193–194, 228; refugees from, 4, 8–9, 12, 46, 86, 181; Saam, 173, 185, 189; Saddam Hussein, 66, 92, 258; shelling and bombing in, 82; US declares war on, 41, 62

Jordan: Alia's entry, 2; Alia's exit to America, 85, 90; Alia's time in, 12, 20, 158, 198–199, 215; Amman, 63, 77; author's time in, 12, 131, 157, 164, 172; border with Syria, 78, 134, 219; capital, 5; humanitarian action

in, 131; Mendy, 150–156, 159–161, 237, 242, 245–246, 276; refugee resettlement, 4, 21, 92, 132–133, 137; research, 5; Sara, 167–168, 170–171, 173, 175, 189; Shari'a marriages, 139; Syrian border, 77–78; traveling back to, 214–215; Zara in, 134–139, 142–143, 145, 147–148, 207, 219

Kabila, Joseph, 262

Kehar, Ghulam, 86, 89

Kennedy, Edward, 14

King, Martin Luther, Jr., 279

Klineberg, Stephen, 6, 7

LGBTQ refugees, 16

Mekonnen, Geleta, 161–164, 276

Mendy: abduction, 51–53; and Alia, 44–47, 51, 56–57, 157, 256–258, 274; and children, 149–152, 158–161, 237–238, 273–274; citizenship, 273; diverse friends, 245; employment, 236, 244, 273–274; fleeing Kadugli, 54–56; growing up, 47–49; helping refugees, 274; and husband, 47, 59; learning English, 225–228, 233–236; and nephew Hashem, 153–159, 161–163, 237; parakeets, 43, 47, 261–262; photograph, 286fig.; studying, 149–150; surgery, 43, 45, 56

Meza, Andrea, 19–20

Mina: and Alia, 30–31, 37–40, 42, 193–194, 200, 228–231, 256–258; America, 37–38, 39; citizenship, 272; and daughter Tia, 30–31, 37–38, 192–193, 199–200, 229; employment, 262, 273; and husband, 36–37; Iraqi widows, 193–194; learning English, 40, 225–228; and Maha,

sugar waxing, 242–244
Suleiman (author's Arabic teacher), 165
Syria: border with Jordan, 78, 134, 219; peaceful protests in, 61; refugees from, 4, 5, 6, 10, 133, 205; Sara, 68, 77, 80, 166–169, 173–174, 182; Syrians in Houston, 206, 216, 265; Zara, 124–126, 135–136, 142, 147, 208, 212

Tikrit, 65
Trump, Donald, 5–6, 10, 12, 20, 40, 275
Trump, Melania, 164
Trump administration, 5, 18, 20–21, 22, 106, 163
Tshisekedi, Felix, 262

United Nations, 25
United Nations High Commissioner for Refugees (UNHCR), 13–14, 97, 150, 162, 198
University of Houston, 23, 85, 252

Vallette, Liz, 268
violence, 8, 18, 146

war: Afghanistan and Soviet Union, 64; Alia's clients, 40; chaos of, 63; civil war, 21, 61, 131, 274; in Congo, 97; effect on families, 61; Gulf War, 33, 67; *Iliad*, 58; Iran-Iraq War, 33,

35, 58, 65, 66, 173–174; in Iraq, 32, 193, 195, 198, 199; Iraqi invasions, 32–33; losing homes and husbands, 258; refugee status, 8, 30; in Syria, 126, 142, 143, 147, 184, 186; trauma, 11; US war on Iraq, 41; war story, 73, 74; war zone, 77; widows, 13, 105; WWII, 13, 275; Yom Kippur War, 65
Welcome Corps, 276
Winthrop, John, 279
Women's Empowerment Groups (WEG), 265, 266–267, 268, 278

Zaire, 97, 103. *See also* Democratic Republic of the Congo (DRC)
Zara: abuse from husband, 207–209; and Alia, 210–212, 213, 221–222; and children, 124, 143–144; citizenship, 273; cooking, 124–125, 127, 140; divorce, 210; dream of restaurant, 222; and Emmi, 135–139, 145–148, 217–218, 221, 223, 263–264, 273; employment, 218–219; and Firaq, 143; head chef, 273; home in Syria, 212–213; and husband, 140–141, 207, 213–214; learning English, 207–208, 219, 220; leaving Jordan, 205–206; leaving Syria, 130–131; photograph, 292*fig.*; pop-up shop, 142–143; stay at women's shelter, 209–210; Syria, 124–126, 135–136, 142, 147, 208, 212
Zarqa, 131, 134, 150, 151, 155, 158

Founded in 1893,
UNIVERSITY OF CALIFORNIA PRESS
publishes bold, progressive books and journals
on topics in the arts, humanities, social sciences,
and natural sciences—with a focus on social
justice issues—that inspire thought and action
among readers worldwide.

The UC PRESS FOUNDATION
raises funds to uphold the press's vital role
as an independent, nonprofit publisher, and
receives philanthropic support from a wide
range of individuals and institutions—and from
committed readers like you. To learn more, visit
ucpress.edu/supportus.